The Desires of Mo
to Please Others in Letters

The Desires of Mothers
to Please Others in Letters

BERNADETTE MAYER

SplitLevel Texts   Nightboat Books
Washington, DC   New York

ISBN: 978-1-937658-67-0

Cover design by Kevin Woodland
Design and typesetting by Karla Kelsey
Text set in Kis Antiqua Now and Adobe Caslon

Cover: "Starr Cinema" by Max Warsh, 2015

The Desires of Mothers to Please Others in Letters was first published
by Hard Press in 1994.

Cataloging-in-publication data is available from the Library of Congress

Distributed by the University Press of New England
One Court Street
Lebanon, NH 03766
www.upne.com

SplitLevel Texts
Washington, DC
www.splitleveltexts.com

Nightboat Books
New York
www.nightboat.org

Table of Contents

Introduction by Laynie Browne 9

Plural Dream of Social Life 17
Public Lice 21
A Bean of Mine 24
Horror Story (A Reminder) 29
Cista Mistica 32
Kempf's Delicatessen on Forest & Putnam 35
Designing Disruptive Concealment 40
The Fly Has Married the Bumble Bee 45
Gardening in Containers 50
To the Tune of "Red Embroidered Shoes" 54
Under My Green Jacket 56
Dear Alive 60
The Well of Loneliness 62
Two Known Lilies 67
Eine Kleine Nacht Musik 69
The Prostitutes at the Eldorado Club 73
Worse Than the Noon Whistle 76
The Slicing Machine I Seen Through the Door of the Eldorado
  Club in the Dale 81
Dear Only 86
Pursued as She Stumbled about You It Could Signify Nothing 88
Dear Ed 94
A Proem Added 96
The Day Thurman Munson Died 98
Dear Peggy 102
Dear Rosemary 105
Dear Grace 107
Lady Mary Wortley-Montagu's Letter to Her Sister 108
Niagaraphobia 110
Anacolutha 115

Jobless Petty Criminal in 20s　　　　　　　　　　　　120
Don't Film　　　　　　　　　　　　　　　　　　　130
Grace Drives a Twenty-Two-Foot Truck　　　　　　　134
Pregnancy Mask　　　　　　　　　　　　　　　　139
The Notch at the Flume of the Gorge　　　　　　　　145
The Great Stone Face, The First Frost　　　　　　　　150
The Red Paint People　　　　　　　　　　　　　　154
The Vanity of Mount Hunger　　　　　　　　　　　158
The Men's Men at Women's Words　　　　　　　　　163
Gargling with Marbles　　　　　　　　　　　　　　168
Pear Pie　　　　　　　　　　　　　　　　　　　172
Lighthouse　　　　　　　　　　　　　　　　　　175
Lewis Stapling Books and Watching the Series (Pittsburgh-
　　　Baltimore)　　　　　　　　　　　　　　　　179
Dear Alive　　　　　　　　　　　　　　　　　　181
Days, Stamps, Stamp Packs, Ties, Socks, Note Pads, etc.　184
A Falling Together: To Make Strong Again as in, etc.　　190
Equinoctial Tears　　　　　　　　　　　　　　　　195
Brilliant Bravado October 20 Night　　　　　　　　　198
To Live Above (Survive)　　　　　　　　　　　　　200
Different Prescriptive Tedemones　　　　　　　　　　203
"Warnings Out of Town"　　　　　　　　　　　　　207
Look Out for a Second　　　　　　　　　　　　　　211
Eating a Wasp　　　　　　　　　　　　　　　　　214
November Jack　　　　　　　　　　　　　　　　　217
To View Bacon Lift Flap　　　　　　　　　　　　　221
Assworks　　　　　　　　　　　　　　　　　　　227
The Black Velvet Midgets　　　　　　　　　　　　　231
Visions or Desolation　　　　　　　　　　　　　　236
,.;:?.(-")!　　　　　　　　　　　　　　　　　　　240
Hand-Shaped Poems Like Snow-Making Machines　　243
Dear David　　　　　　　　　　　　　　　　　　247
I'll Drown My Book　　　　　　　　　　　　　　　249
Portrait of a Man Holding a Glove　　　　　　　　　251
Molson Golden, Golden Lights　　　　　　　　　　255

The White Squirrel Again 259
What Went Wrong 261
List the Kinds of Poetry 266
Accidental On 270
Female Poets of America 276
January 2, Full Moon, No Snow, Thin Ice 281
The Physiology of Taste 284
The Marbles of Arp 290
Two Days After Joanna Had Two Stitches 294
An Inch of Free Snow January 22 297
Almost at the Second Predicted Time for the Third Baby 301
Place All the Time 305
A Few Days Later It's with Pleasure I Write 317

Introduction

AS A DEVOTED READER OF BERNADETTE MAYER'S WORK, I must resist the love letter I wish could stand for a rational prelude to her text and confess that like so many of her admirers, I have been intoxicated by her writing for decades. I first encountered the original Hard Press edition (published in 1994) in my early twenties. Her letters evoked a complexity I associated with real persons. They moved with a liberating momentum, indefatigably resonant while eluding convention. Reading them again as a young mother the book behaved differently. Encoded passages provided necessary accompaniment and spilled invaluable counsel. Now this book is better than ever: urgent, consoling, intimate, and wise. *The Desires of Mothers to Please Others in Letters* is one of those books you may return to at different times to find that it opens an entirely new creature: spell book, source of solid advice, feminist discourse on writing and mothering, body of mysterious trysts, meditations on the quotidian, literature, and the obligatory politics of survival.

Traversing boundaries between poetry and prose her letters are like rooms inexplicably expanding to accommodate guests. Mayer extends hospitable language in which the opaque is made personal and astonishingly original. As a woman, a writer, a mother, and a publisher operating with little means, she confronts issues of gender, class, economy, and place. She makes legible a politically engaged poetics for generations to come, not as a "project" but because these concerns are interwoven in her work and life. While this text is always socially engaged, it never professes omniscience, or stumbles in the wake of gravity. While I would not call Mayer's letters autobiographical, they are not separate from life. Her daughters Marie and Sophia appear often, as does her partner at the time of composition, poet Lewis Warsh. The text is literally pregnant. Her third child, Max, whose artwork is featured on the cover of this new edition, is the baby she carries as she writes. She begins writing in the summer of 1979 and finishes in February of 1980. Correspondents include a constellation of friends, notably Peggy, Margaret, and Grace, and poets such as Bill Berkson, Ted Berrigan, Clark Coolidge, Fanny Howe, and Alice Notley, among others.

In Mayer's hands the letter is the form that includes everything. Just as the individual letter, or character, is the substance with which all thought is constructed, letters may include: micro and macro lists, history lessons, arguments, asides, dramatic interludes, found dialogue, revelatory commentary, and astute observations. The letter may be the most personal and the most cloaked of forms. In Mayer's magnificent epistolary text a reader will readily note the innovation of titles in place of salutations. "You" becomes plural, hypothetical, a placeholder for individuals occasionally named and the process of divulgence which opens an endless stream of permissions and possibilities.

Like many of Mayer's texts, *The Desires of Mothers to Please Others in Letters* is also a time-based experiment. A gestational process, the letters were written over the nine months of a pregnancy. Read it and re-birth your assumptions on the nature of love, reproduction, and hybrid poetic forms. One conversation rushes urgently into the next, creating sublime collisions, and often it is impossible to separate one thought from another. Mayer's written connective tissue is vast, like a series of fine capillaries which branch everywhere, each letter discrete, yet interacting and accumulating to form an organism of prose that is both incremental or durational and also somehow outside of time. Speech is combined with text, apostrophe and soliloquy with borrowed language. The personal is polyvocal as the mumbled and murmured marry the loudly elocuted or proclaimed. The reader encounters voluminous insight, light on the eyes. One sentence clings to another. The entire book is alive.

Reinvention of poetic forms is one of Mayer's great contributions to poetry. By her imaginative example I find myself asking, how is the letter—object, bird, pigeon, dove, flapping, running, small, clasped in hand yet large as heavenly bodies—carried close at all times? When does a letter become apparel, wrapped about the neck, a draped cape or shawl? How is a letter a shoe? Letters move locations, are all about locomotion. A letter creates a dwelling in the words of others. In the letter titled "A Bean of Mine" she writes: "I've got to tell you I often talk as if you were both me you and a third person, another person too. I do this to subsume my desires to tell everything in confusion, but as if it were public" (26). From this sentence we are given permission to write a letter in which you are not limited to "you" as speaker or writer. You could be anyone.

A particular letter may have been written with one person in mind but is finally written to the reader. Mayer addresses: "a you who is not you, a you who is nothing, an identity not to be found" (206). Clark Coolidge writes of this book: "And so at last these once secret letters are addressed to everyone." Universal address is present in titles such as "Plural Dream of Social Life" and in statements such as "There is a way of observing everything like Hawthorne like an innocent with no point of view" (209). In Mayer's loquacious sentence is an implicit acceptance of that which perturbs, and an attempt to amplify as well as to capture not a positive or negative but a vivid reciprocity of poetry.

This book is also that confidential friend who offers: "An esoteric history of the poetry of the world, we have so many bills to pay" (150), "it just does rain along with the alphabet" (213), "THE SECRET SEX POEMS" (182), and "Gargling with Marbles" (168). In other words, nothing is deliberately left out. Expansiveness is actual, the equivalent of a household in which everything is recycled, composted, or upcycled including texts, conversation, bodies, weather, questions, and the composition of the music of daily life which is akin to John Cage's notion of silence. Music or poetry is in everything. We don't have to look beyond the edges of our own reluctant or reversible features to find this "everything." And yet Mayer also transmits abundance and humor even when documenting economic uncertainty, fragility, or fear. She writes: "A ROOM OF ONES OWN...is an odd book to read when you're broke and worried about your female sexual organs" (23).

Call it an unwillingness to shy away, Mayer's candor in regards to love, sex, pregnancy, birth, and childrearing is rare. In a time when the pressures upon women as providers and creators is increasingly fraught, this welcome book reads less like performance or persuasion or didacticism or prevarication—and more like an intimate attempt to proclaim, to celebrate, to rant and lament, yet never to romanticize. Regarding childbirth she writes of "the feeling of the baby leaving, aside from being slithery, resistant and natural, is as if it were an adornment to one's entire life so far and one wonders then why one isn't or hasn't been doing this activity all the time..." (287). And she also writes: "...the thing I resent most is when someone says you won't have time to write if you have a family. All the men for all time, this silly time we know about, had wives and children without anybody saying anything about it" (64).

When I say the form contains everything I am also thinking that hers is a text that leads to many other texts. The letters, for instance, of Lady Mary Wortley Montague, of Madame Sevigne, Elizabeth Bishop's "Equinoctial Tears" (195), Donne's "Devotions Upon Emergent Occasions" (310), "Life is too fucked up for words. Homer could not have said that too busy visualizing battles and who was who" (122). A text that leads to food becomes economic commentary: "don't laugh at me, often my own writing seems to me to be having too many cheap ingredients like poor people's food however at least I've never written a salmon mousse" (36). A text that leads to dream becomes a gathering of artists: "I think I already mentioned about the dream of Lou Reed, Alice and Ron where Reed kept offering everyone a communal bath and then the old woman said, 'Do you do crewel work?' Call me Ishmael!" (41). A text in which we find the question: "Why doesn't anybody pay me for my work?" (54) is an apt examination of inequity and women's expected roles. She writes: "it seems like you are not supposed to act like a person or a mother when you're a teacher, you're supposed to be sophisticated, not hungry or lonely, and to beat about the bush" (195).

I call this an alchemical text and a holistic text and a comprehensive text, an integrated assembly of "he and I and all these people I've begun or tried to love, absent spirits who cannot fly like moths, met at the four corners of the world again" (66). Mayer's work equates an unspeakable intimacy with poetry, a form of love insisting upon collective address. She writes: "…it was exactly like love, that exuberance which saves or salvages both the place and moment or time, or whatever it became is not something that's there anywhere but in poems"(91).

Every reader is a mother of something. Mayer's writing allows us to revisit the urgency of birth, the necessity of constancy and the potential neurosis of any devotion. Dare to separate one sentence from another and you will find yourself trying to pry apart beloved bodies. Mayer's writing reminds us that love is a living body of letters, an indivisible form.

Laynie Browne, 2016

The Desires of Mothers
to Please Others in Letters

Plural Dream of Social Life

THROW STUFF AWAY, I've got an apartment above you in the city like food, I think it's #12A too, a small fast clock. Bigger than I thought with a lot of corners and you bought an extra table for me you left downstairs in the restaurant, you live just down the street in zoology but when I went upstairs I saw there was already a nice one in the fast clock and it was even marble. I wondered if I was going to be able to keep it. Pointless and from all the windows you can see trees and out one that's broken it's balloons and a zoo like pointing to a town in northern Colorado or gossip about that, even a misplaced vehemence like you saw on the face of that guy who came in when you did. Archaic, it wasn't the balloons that were broken or otherwise how could I have seen them, it sure seemed like a good place to live because even though you could have described it accurately as small there was something about it, I could only say it was full of surprises and some of them were rooms you could fit beds in though if you were rich or something you might call them closets, anyway a lot of us could sleep there. Impassivity, I was surprised and things were better for a minute than I thought they would be. That was the dream, did I mention you lived down the street but not printing?

In panicles, now what's his name's been here, Yellowstone National Park, and in some involuntary and faithless way he wound up insulting us, it was as if he didn't notice or know any better though, not consolidated. Women in the armed forces, well there was something about divisiveness as if to achieve the gathered material like a rose or pleat among the senses of power, cactus, even the prickly pear type but I've no sense of what it was but I've had it with the Nobel Prizes and Virgin Mary being a bad friend, any of a number of related trees and hideous acquaintances like Antoine de Cadillac and the aforementioned Mary making me nervous for no real reason for centuries, after all cement fastens things together, it's a smooth-skinned fruit like the way so-and-so played ball, great with great spirit, so did she and she did too and she also did in a circle like a Congreve match or else it was pointless. Gulf of Mexico, family life is so crowded in exile, we're broke too and every day is a fast clock but no news of the time or even of small size manages to come except archaic, I've gotta get back to normal thinking so I can do some probability toward the exile like a cactus to plan ahead or write but I can't till I find out where to throw out a fly like in fishing or being stung on the head by a bee in dreaming, certainly not no more teaching, I'm hoping there's nothing to teach, pointless printing of a small size like a clock that's fast or the old-fashioned Congreve match, I hope I'm not pregnant again. I'm sure all the gathered material and money will be in the mail tomorrow like you-know-who's anguish and I don't blame him I know exactly what he means except that his feelings somehow seem more genuine in panicles like the wheat or oat plant than mine which don't do that, gone fishing but I'll know tomorrow though I feel more than of a small size and love to work out like an atomic clock at softball or something but there's no use doing anything else till I find out I guess.

You always say something all of a sudden I didn't know you'd noticed since there are so many ways in which I feel I know you better than I really do know you like that guy quoting that thing he quoted by guess who about sex. I mean about coming I was thinking of writing first what I was talking about when I said that was Marie's teeth and the way you described them. Like taking the sense out of normal talking but it too is worn down or worn out so everything that's left is new like the idea of moving to New Orleans near the Gulf of Mexico like an exile just for fun though and the plural impassivity of seeing all new things but racism, you say maybe that's a superficial archaic printing do you think

I mean the town might be as justly quaint like the craving for a smooth-skinned fruit as this place is or someplace even worse than this maybe, it's taking a pitted chance, I forgot to say it also has a smooth pit too. A lot of them never do anything at all so why do we have them? I mean are we attracted to the exile of love and from even motion? Then with the gathered material using a lot of run-on dependent clauses in the archaic cities and not printing the towns like they do, we will go except I can't make them up they have to just happen because I can't get to remember what they even are, do you know what I mean, but if you point one out to me, and this is like the zoo, then I'll be able to name it instantly, is it Fool's Parsley or Poison Hemlock or just a wild carrot, commonly called Queen Anne's Lace? Nobody seemed to even want to think about it, then I thought vinegar, remember we mentioned it instead of using expensive lemons, still no money had come don't forget, I could do a book that could have that kind of friction Congreve invented in it, it would be designed with a structure the way I heard somebody talking about a Lincoln Continental but this would just be for mimeographing and rather than being related to money in any way it would be like the way she said that they were the kinds of things people said after they saw them, I'm astonished, I'm a changed person, it's amazing, you see it was a ritual kept secretly and only shown or open to I don't know who. But I think I mentioned those Eleusinian mysteries before didn't I? It wasn't the same Congreve by the way who wrote comedies of manners who did the match but they did have the same name, William, and the inventor did a rocket too. I won't mention that I wanted to mention, and not to one Congreve or which one, the idea of forgetting the loss of beauty without anger just to have some fun and not be so moralistic about it but it didn't matter anyway because I know you can guess who had this to say which is sort of why bother.

Then after I thought of the dream and I saw the older unexpected rooms in it more like instinct or the bee sting thing to be like a penis and so on, this pipe got too hot, it was the small one and I couldn't even finish the normal pipeful, it's like remembering a story I was telling "him" while we were walking across the grass, remember that day we had all played ball for a while, remember we found some kind of kitchen knife in the grass, I can't remember what the story was though, it had something to do with evil, oh it was about t.v. and shooting up heroine & about a brand new car, then it seemed like there would have to be some explaining to do because of my funny manner because I shouted and sounded all of a sudden like I was talking but still on the streets of Brooklyn and then I remember this story about "her" and it was she bought her father a new car, something really fancy, but then who said she wasn't going to or what was to stop her, or, what do they say, who ever thought otherwise?

In the sweet grass of the fast night's clock which I know is still there like a craving to get as high as some other time you can't even be sure you didn't remember wrong, when I think that I always think it's exactly like childhood, this was some experiment to see what would happen to the words, it's all so fucking ephemeral or streams or smokes in some way or else what I mean is sensational in the sensational sense except you can't help seeing I won't say it's all just talk. 1979-80.

And I didn't want to say either or nor did I want to mention by way of introduction that those words just walked or sauntered in, worse chance than having a guest who perhaps drinks all the beer very fast and then puts the wine you've been saving for dinner on the table for everyone to share on Sunday when you can't get any more. It's terrible to be broke and have no words from the beer and to run around as fast as you can and find the words that happened to come in have only introduced you back into exile from which you write letters harping about the truth having learned to speak at all from elucidating the mess of a certain house by mail to the landlady, and from describing babies, I don't know if you know what I'm talking about, I just think it was because one of us didn't have it in him or her just that afternoon, see you soon.

Public Lice

SO EXCEPT FOR THE WEATHER which is as lush as murky as you could ever want it to be things have been going horribly, let me just begin by telling you we've been getting hate mail—three letters of this sort, all from poets, in the last week, since we got back. The people who wrote them are lunatics I think, they can't seem to keep quiet, and some who had manuscripts rejected but they weren't solicited ones, you see I even have to defend myself against this corny lot. You wouldn't say I thought I liked bankers or bakers like you might say I don't like poets, I've heard people say that, but when what's-his-name asked me to be in that magazine and didn't ask Lewis it seemed like it was all more trouble than the rag would ever be worth, strictly New Grub Street: I know there's always that question of his right to do this to allied people but I say if you're gonna be friends you have to forfeit a few of your rights to this nitwitted honesty which is so defiantly stupid and based on some peculiar personal sensationalism, I mean it wasn't my writing that was at stakes or the stakes, the man had struck a bargain with himself. But this is all too boring and everyone is awful except you know who and a few others and a million ones. Boy the trees are beautiful, Lewis's parents are gonna come and stay at the Garden Gables which is daring of them, right up next to all the isolating trees a few hundred feet off Main Street, they said, "Will we have to cross the highway?" "Will Lewis walk us home at night?" "Will they lock us out like they did from the Village Inn last year?" I guess they will be complaining but it is so hard for them to agree to do something and the place has a swimming pool surrounded by fancy trees and bushes like a mountain stream. Anyway as far as I know I'm not pregnant as I wrote you but I still don't know why, if you know what I mean and now I'm wondering why I'm not and what ever else is wrong with me if that is so. So one could think about this all day long. I've even already had fantasies of having to go to the hospital, missing my children and so on, then I read this poem today by Fairfield Porter's wife Anne Porter which was called "In a Country Hospital" and ended with a shocking line about them bringing the "blessed Eucharist" in. The real elaboration of my anguish don't laugh has to do with a series of moods so fluctuating as to drive anybody crazy, I think I do belong in a hospital where they'd take care of me—and what about Lewis? I'm wearing Sophia's pregnancy dress with the dancing Indians with jugs on their heads, you remember, and they are dresses so unlike this town where everyone stares, now that we are all half-undressed, with eyes still full of winter, and I go around pretending I'm on an African plain, I'm sorry I can't seem to express myself. I keep feeling if I were pregnant again everybody would feel impatient with me as if I had finally gone too far again. Summer said when she read some poem of mine it made her love me, then I felt maybe she was on to me, at the same time I love to walk around in my circumscribed penal-colony-yard area here in shorn starched Lenox and so the idea of moving to New Orleans seems like meddling though I'd still like to do it though I guess we're too old and it's too hot though I don't feel afraid to do it, I have some idea I might get to be how I used to be as if the past really makes it, I'm drinking some awful cheap beer called Red White & Blue made by Pabst (remember Beverly Pabst?), $1.50 a sixpack, it's better than Falstaff Light, we're being what they call thrifty until we see if any money's going to come because if it doesn't that's kind of it, we won't die yet I guess but July will come and we won't be able to pay the rent at all, we even used all the Master Charge money up by paying the rent and bills with the silly secret checks they give you, $1300 dollars! Today we got $19 dollars in the mail, part of it from a painter named Rackstraw Downes who is a fan of

Lewis's work. I don't mean to rub it in with all this grubby talk of money, I just wanted to say to you how the idea of being pregnant makes you feel you could be exempt from society for at least nine months again, an orphan again, a ward of the state, but then all of a sudden you bring another person into the community. Marie's been wearing her dress and looks like a button, is that what they say, and Sophia too, happy as a lark, a big fat girl getting six teeth simultaneously nor does she give a shit. She won't sit in the highchair anymore & must have a real chair at table with us. And she is so beautiful! I only worry all the time, I worry about my cervix, I worry about my uterus, my ovaries, my pleasant vagina and that reading too many books by women about things will turn me into an even more unbearable crank than the cranky poets who write hate letters. I had a dream last night that two men I know in New York City wanted to put a piece of what you strike matches on, you know what I mean (not strike anywheres), on my ass so they could light matches, strike matches on me, this from reading A ROOM OF ONE'S OWN which is an odd book to read when you're broke and worried about your female sexual organs, I kept being distracted, the book didn't distract me, she is not of my class. I catalogue all the women I know and wonder how they would feel, each of them, if she and they were pregnant. One of the worst things that happened at Family Planning where I went for the test was I had to listen to another lecture on the necessity of what they call "checking one's breasts given your history," I must admit the next time this happens to me I'm going to freak out, now I wait till I get home to freak out, and make a big scene about how I'm a living person and I don't need to hear about how soon I probably will have to suffer and die! I can't stand it! Anyway before I found out I wasn't pregnant theoretically and scientifically provably though of course I still might be, I had a series of the famous bee-sting dreams. I've had them every time I was pregnant and never when I was not & just fearing it, this time I got stung on the head! Adrienne Rich was "allergic to pregnancy" as she describes it. I crave something that isn't there but if it was there maybe I wouldn't crave it so I don't know. I'll tell you what I would like is a great dinner, I am so hungry, with fish and sauces and wines and then pasta and then meat, all given to me. And then see how I feel. Much love.

A Bean of Mine

I HAD BEEN THINKING for a long time I was supposed to write you something that would be telling all kinds of awful secrets, like the kinds of things about men, women and children you cannot even write or publish not because they are so awful but because if you wrote them then you would no longer be able to associate at all with any human beings, you would be shamed, oh I guess I could still hang around with my children they wouldn't know about it. Remember you said don't tell me your dream it makes me forget mine? Like the way Virginia Woolf talks about Shakespeare and his writing independent of gender, it's sort of an old-fashioned idea, as are most of hers, thus since she can write sentences, to read her today is good escapism, however it doesn't work for me. Also then now I don't know too many writers who have the independent income but if you are to be a great writer anyway I guess maybe it could make you greater; surely it's or it could be more fun. Remember Ted gulping the cough medicine with codeine down and something else, I keep forgetting my every next thought and word because it is so hot. Lewis said nobody writes articles about us or any poetry, she was expecting to be able to maintain perfection, that's like being high or something—so people write fiction to say things like that, to write poetry is the least normal I guess, everything is said and then there is an accident, much like pressing for an elevator which immediately comes. But women can still wind up writing some unheard of things don't you think, I mean things that have never been written yet, not like the glow you see on the inside of the beautiful wood of the pipe when you hold a match to it with your slender fingers. Fucking pipe image, the pipe's too slow, you need to have a least two pipes or three and they get too hot, too funny. So she couldn't hack anything less than perfect or intense, so you get nervous. You get nervous when it's dull or normal in order to make it more interesting or fascinating and to take up the time, to put a match to it. I wish I had a dream disease, I mean dread disease so I could do a lot of dreadful things without being afraid. I don't mean I do, I mean of course this fictional person I am writing this prose of yes of course. There was another woman who had been so frequently accused of lying she said nobody would talk to her anymore, I said maybe that was good just as you never get to feel good which they describe as some queer satisfaction about giving up a pleasure or even abjuring it for later. I wonder why what's his name never likes any women. And you-know-who too, he just ignores them. Some of the women never take any chances as if chances were men, I wonder why that is. I mean they never behave like fools, nor do they shake, remember I'm this Eleusinian fiction. You are a poet but you don't know it but your feet show it because they're Long-fellows. You see the dictionary is resting on my sex. I had shaved my legs and cut the hair under my arms in a summer ceremony intended to render me less hairy so I could wear shorts and abbreviated shirts in Lenox, you see I can't say it, I wear a bra when we play softball or basketball, it seems athletic always to be a mother, I would like to be a mother's brother like my uncle, what would that feel like? What does anybody know about anything if you'll forgive me, I remember so many people's opinions and of course their opinions of me, even of my hair. To be an actor like Shakespeare would be to forget this dross, this variety of a sibling's fraternity, the one thing we can always all do until we get too old is sit tailor-fashion; Lewis had said about sitting (meditation): I've done a lot of babysitting. When you invite a babysitter, especially in the country, you often say: Will you be able to sit? I always think somebody will buy us a bottle of whiskey but they never do. It's so hard to get a hit or a buzz or whatever you call it today, I mean doesn't everyone go around thinking they'd be a total lunatic if anyone else had to be them? Love tunes are o.k., sense of decorum, why would anybody go to an orthodontist because they had a protruding chin and they were afraid their teeth would grind each other down wrong, I read that. Then again it's trivial to tell everything when you're told nothing yet, you see it's just because I know nothing again and I feel like I never wrote a poem and I know I don't know how to write one and it will probably take fifteen years again to find out how and I don't think I could get away with not practicing at all in the meantime which will make me ashamed like a shy girl working in the 5 & 10. Lewis told me today about Wallace Stevens' fascism and racism. Nevertheless we can't say we never knew the guy worked for an insurance company and it was stupid to think he worked there more like Kafka. I wish we could walk but everytime we try Marie says her feet are stuck to the ground or else she makes takes the tiniest steps so we keep having to say c'mon Marie so many times even Sophia can say it but that doesn't matter, I haven't gotten to the bad stories which would give me the certificate of authenticity, I don't mean that giving up a pleasure was ever good, I meant that feeling good about it was all wrong and not human though you might have to give it up anyway or think you do for some reason. I wish I could be high as a kite, does everyone else have all this all figured out? I wish you were here to inspire me further and to share the unlimited supplies of wine you seem to have with me, well I hope we can at least straighten this out because you know for me lately the words I can retrieve at all from some pretty chaos of not belonging there anyway, when I see them finally on a page of something I cannot for the life of me assess their meaning, perhaps occasionally I can stare down along the page's lines and see a structure but there is no coherence left as if from lack of memory though the words themselves might be only that, if you know what I mean. I've got to tell you I often talk as if you were both me and you and a third person, another person too. I do this to subsume my desire to tell everything in confusion but as if it were public. Then maybe I feel I can learn to forget to be talking and writing as if it had something to do with my father's way of smelling especially at night. But this clinical moon of June has already attracted too much attention and I didn't tell the horror stories I'd planned to tell, I promise I will next time. Maybe there is a way to write myself back to a revealing lack of syntax, do you think so? I believe it might be compared to trying to lose weight. Many people say it is impossible and I empathize most with the people who have to bear the weight but I can't stop believing that anything is possible, you see I have gotten myself back into that old thing about the perfection of states. Well last week on the same day family life was crumbling and the weather was making our heads and limbs hang heavily, I see that my eyes reflect the light with too much time included like the curvature of the lens, I can't speak about the value of seeing this, I'm bug-eyed, beady-eyed, I'd give anything to be lyrical and to have good teeth, those eyes are accused of something, it's being annihilated by circumstances so we tell everything in the hope of returning like I'm having the chance to do I think, if only I had some cocaine or something like the guy's supposed to have all those people said I looked like. I do have an eye, I mean my eye is palpable, not like June or July, do I have to make rules for myself or others, against my own feelings that barely even time exists and a picture of a poet needs to have some interesting light. The next time I shoot you remind me to pretend you are myself in this way. I'm never Shakespeare or anyone like that, Cecil Beaton whom I saw once at a concert of The Fugs. Being beautiful in any acceptable way is so specialized, I never understood if I had any beautiful qualities until after they had been confused, for example to seduce, I was too forgetful of being a woman or a girl, which was lucky, except of course when I was at my job. I don't mean writing but the job I had typing for a company for $65 dollars a week in 1965 but I hate it when anyone mentions that year especially anybody who says in '65 I blah blah blah and then I met Olson and so on. I mean I am just talking here about my job as a typist at Barnes & Noble, I hope you'll ennoble me by forgiving me for remembering. It was better than being a floorwalker which I feel like tonight like if you wanted to be scared enough to please me as I'm scared enough to want to please you all the time, then you might, what, take me to New Orleans but don't introduce me to Wallace Stevens down there and tell me traditional beauty is just this world and then forgive me my trespasses, not for thine is the kingdom and the power and the glory and so on for I wasn't brought up a Protestant, I

can't remember the right end, it's in the liturgy, this is the people's work,
I'm trying to do something specific here. Did you ever eat social teas?
But deliver us from evil, may it be so.

Horror Story (A Reminder)

LIKE THE DREAM I was a bus driver but the bus was cramped and the clutch was the far-right pedal but I did o.k. anyway and then the real driver, another woman, took over, she'd been waiting standing in front of the bus in her uniform, I don't know how I came to drive that bus at all but I was not sorry. Oh beginning and end I owe everything and everyone, I don't want anyone to teach me anything, but the poppies so bright and paperlike and the families of peonies like false love are in bloom, an abdication. I need the old bread and butter routine, he was in the shower he was showering. I'm always hungry, I'm hungry as hell, smoking's no good at all, I just set my leg on fire with a bad match Bill gave me, real flames on my real leg, whaddayou think about that, Dash? Gimme yours, get the whiskey, let's go to the diner. I am just this greed of speaking outloud all the time, she has nothing to speak of to eat, you know what? Swearing like the so-called Sunday traffic all either totally lonely or completely misanthropic and that means you too, I can't figure if like a figure I feel the greed freely from losing all the time what I keep rephrasing as the last past I had, it's even been repeated to ask will I get the bread and butter now. Sweet routine, what fluid are you talking about, there's some fluid you say we can't run out of or else everything including our own minds will go haywire because I'm not consuming all the sustenance I take to write so I began to get fat but before that I ceased to be a human woman and I got worried I wouldn't ever get to be one again, it was not communicable. Dash lonely smoking or sucking, I had an inkling it might come back but it wasn't courage it was those poppies, could they have been real, what a weird noise. Sophia says a tissue is a nose but that's kid stuff. The lost routine of the sweetest stuff is this regenerated turkey trot I kid myself into re-incriminating today like a recidivist adolescent who finally murdered that man and then cursed his only survivor, remember you mentioned it? There was a long song missing which was too far to do, is there a danger like smoke of being out of practice, shall we drill? I had a feeling it didn't matter what evening we came to as long as if it got recorded it could transmit a little of how it really was, it had been. That that communication would have to be our bread and butter in the sense of we had nothing else we could live on. This life reduced was once getting fat again that was when we began mentioning it looked a lot like we could almost use some lean times, but the funny thing was we had always been so much leaner than everybody else so when our vanity's compared us, well for me the thing was I hadn't read enough books and I knew if I did or if I would, those books'd make me just a bit less fat because of what I did say about the consumption of ghosts and weevils, ladybugs and anything I see while I'm writing and I don't spew out because the harmful if swalloweds don't work that way, it only says that. I'm not a bird or I'd be sleeping standing up right now and not awake at all, giraffes do too, it's such a small thing, we could have a muffin but it's wonder bread, that was all they had, how come I didn't call it "mommie dearest," and then like these shadows of the four empty black nails on the windows where no plants dare hang, nothing. Silly game like the dumbest watch, fucking Roman numerals doesn't that beat all, not like the picture of the real shirt you know. And the great one of the Renaissance characters before the field of perhaps Eleusis is who knows. It was you know who and one of her sons, so beautiful they looked like the field did. They were almost speaking, they were turning, I was so amazed to see it. To hear from you today would have been so welcome and sweet, peonies, poppies, magic white shoots like a bamboo from a frothy green plant it looked like an ordinary tree, the breeding gingkoes, the time of day with Ella Lerner, with Yamato's proprietress, pregnant.

The park is so succinct, I memorize the act of profligate whiskey-buying I'd do if I heard that it would rain hotdogs and papers, no, but I'd take that at this point wouldn't you? Even just the rain like a dim-witted friend you can never get close to, who cares, I'm getting used to this peculiar haze, it's o.k., don't worry about it, it's just not cheap enough, and so when you can't afford food anymore then you move out on into the street to live so all the rent money can go for food, is that right? We still lives like kingses and queenses all de time, I mean we gots plenny of bisgetty stored way fer memory, I'm sorry even Virginia Woolf began to get cynical about some question of the vote for women, then again love is like a letter or a letter is love and that is all above your knowing what my state is, like there's no use my telling you like some odd friend of mine suggested every time I get mad at the children, who would want to hear about it? Sweet diseases of the flowers and life, "Shane" is on. Will poetry as its sees me atrophy as I desert my Main Street window now or will I even gain or regain the sweet blatant love of some man who looks like Lewis if I poverty prove I can distract him from the harlequin cowboys on the broken screen because actually even Brandon de Wilde already died, and so did you. And sorry, we came to sing this song to the village of Bensons. So so long.

Cista Mistica

IT'S FROM THE LITTLE BASKET into the big basket and then back into the little basket again. This morning those papers arrived edited by it won't take you long to guess who full of errors and we wonder why we have to be these poor _____ living our _____ life today for the sake of this art of a perfection we never see, I don't exactly mean this less than you but I don't see the errors once I've left the room, this drink has enormous significance they would wind up saying, all by itself it could've induced the hallucinations of the visions. Then the water seems to talk and I am Joan of Arc or Jean Arthur hearing voices, I am neither a woman nor a man but an ethereal person leading two horses in another world; where my sex is there is something I can't recognize, the face of a mandrill, a kind of football, the drama of the wind blowing cold gray clouds past the sightless moon, you only see this figure on a screen from the room of the other dream I would have told you like prayers if the rain hadn't made me so pale and winter was my only memory, besides every-time I say I dreamed the phone rings and the kind young man replaces the window and seals up the hole above the heaters, it's Triptolemus, pour holy water on his head this morning. Morte D'Arthur, now a long delay becomes a threat, Freud's cigars. Just say so I said to her, but we ourselves are falling apart. It's this fire retardant crepe paper we write on and if we can't go to the playground after supper, I saw that the woman had volunteered to bake pies for us every day to make us feel better, before that there had been money for only the stingiest kind of meal except once in a while a windfall of sweet fruit or someone would come up with sweets from the bakery like butter and salt together in one main food, that was meat. Now it's like a hurricane coming or the missing boy not even as long-awaited as the cycle that distinguishes or does not distinguish women from men, it hasn't come yet. So that protuberance was my fantasy of turning into a monkey, then you could write about anything, this wind's not cold but we've been searching doubtfully for a friend, I think I'd take almost anyone but you are much more careful so we never see you. Then again at home all the time we miss fame and you can't really do anything when the place is always so deserted, I mean you still wind up wandering around with your thoughts instead of forgetting them at home where we always are anyway, I take that back. Demeter and Persephone were the same person. I'm gonna split, Persephone said, because she loved flowers. Greek Gregory Italian Roman Corso like a Manhattan restaurant or heritage. Demeter later invented beer. I guess she was a good mother, I'll find out later. We do see somebody occasionally and then too the dream or vision of perfection like romances of families, fails you. Remember to call Clark about the fluid. But that perfection is like imagining living in someone else's house and being them. I cannot even smoke it is so strong and what's the use, I wouldn't mind flying even on the mystical cracking plane, I'm sure I already have. Did you see that Laker had to fold? Really my daily thoughts are as passing and severe as what they call these items but anyway I'm supposed to crack them up into the looser mystical spheres or onto that other orb of perfection where though nothing new is happening there the difference is made and then I'm supposed to do that without even being reimbursed for my initial outlays for expenses for going with fear down the road when I see you played at it and now we are both wondering what sex I am. She had said oh you inane mortals you are always fucking things up by not knowing whether what's happening is good or bad. That was when she threw the baby in the fire. Worse luck might be one's intensity inadvertently turning into comedy because of being lonely. But we all know she would've turned him into an immortal being, the child had been growing without any food. I just do this till I can't anymore, the old mystery and the romantics they involved real diseases but the suffering like of people who decide to be Buddhists continues to go on anyway. I prefer to feel perfect that's why I might be called a lunatic and I said the new windows would look horrible all of a sudden because I couldn't see through them, then that young man, mother of the boys who whistled at me walking with my daughter from the car while my son Lewis was across the street watching me, thought I was crazy, just another dizzy dame or weird broad, an odd mother, a dippy damsel, an incipient gypsy or junkie. Everything you think is a reference to something, yes I often feel that just as everyone comes to see us on the same day but it's not a lyric, it's just that the bottom of my left thumb is numb from too much catching with a Ken Boyers mitt which I think is too old and dear mother the church is cold and no one goes to the country but people take pride in their clothes. You said you didn't know if Dash would even want the shirts but I kept feeling certain they would be of some use, you see experiments must've taught me to accept an orphaned gift though I'm still a fool like a mortal with wine or enough poppy juice to make it worth your while, what, to see that in the future when you die you are with me beyond word and image and we are happy on dope to see this and so it holds the world together instead of the leather that it broke on your old glove so now my fingers fly apart from the seams. See you soon.

Kempf's Delicatessen on Forest & Putnam

IT WAS SUCH A GREAT SURPRISE to be talking to you last week that even though I can remember everything you said I can hardly bring to mind anything I might have mentioned to you except that we were happy we will not be you know where this summer. Talking to you was such a pleasure I can't remember what I said, only what you said, except I know I said I'm glad we don't have to go to _____ this year. Now I'm biting my fingernails, I can't seem to keep a handle on it if that's the way they say it, I keep trying to find out if I'm pregnant or not, I feel pushed around, you know what I mean. All these men and women, it's angry and intricate like a color movie in a time like the time when people said if you dream in color it means you're crazy like trying to meet, then one person says what the other one intended or you can say what you're meaning to say but just to the person who happens to be there, you never waited for the person you were thinking about. Now with all these you's I still don't mean you you know. The person I'm thinking about never appears or if she does or he does we stand behind the door whispering without answering. You see we don't have time, we don't have a minute, besides everybody has so much money, we can't stand to see them, they don't remember us they just look blank. John Ashbery even bought a house in Hudson, that's right near here sort of, it's the town where you can catch the nearest train to New York, still it's an hour away.

Too bad the trains are being phased out, we are still working on the same issue of the magazine because of having no money. I like the idea that the entire corpus of a poet's writing will wind up looking all alike, like calling it almost all the plays, it being plays, I saw today the poetry of the so-called Dark Lady. Even the work of you know who is pretty consistent looking or is it? Maybe it's just because of Yale or the Plain Editions or because it's all printed willy-nilly. I had been writing so much both in letters and on paper it was getting me into trouble, there are experiments to see how many words can be gotten on the paper but only a lunatic would do them, like writing everything what they call tongue in cheek, I guess some people have done that. I'm so tired of poetry because I don't want to talk about it, also we're having so much trouble with the fucking mimeograph machine to get the ink to wash over every word of my poem, it has too many words for it. So I said to revolve the drum without running paper through, then the stencil ripped at Marie's name and we saw we would have to write it in on every page like an obsessive craving for sex and booze I was reading or to create one I've got a vodka and tonic now, Peggy got it for us. Sometimes all we say all day long is hurry, even Sophia can say hotdog. About food and money the family is one body which we seem to nourish as a whole or as a single one, not mystical though. What I mean is I eat the rest of your lunch and the water from your vegetables goes into our soup. We'd been thinking we ought to throw it all up and start a German Jewish delicatessen in Lenox. I think the machine needs a new screen but now it's too frightening to try to change it because it is so full of ink we'll have to wait till it settles. Now a rustling of papers is on top of my ear. There's no doubt about it poetry is different than prose I guess, I just showed Lewis how to tighten the screw we hope will make a greater tension on the machine's screen on the left side so...I couldn't write a poem now anyway my intentions are less than pure, don't laugh at me, often my own writing seems to me to be having too many cheap ingredients like poor people's food however at least I've never written a salmon mousse. I mean it's like the meats at the delicatessen counter, those awful rolls of chicken and ugly meatloafs, with pimientos in them or onion-flavored American cheese, luncheon meats, full of salt and pepper. And, thinking about food and money I get all the more confused, not like Basho's Travel Sketches. Peggy and I got some peonies the other night from in front of the abandoned hotel; at this time of year Lenox has a big night life at least it's big compared with life, a lot of people going to restaurants in suits imprisoned by the food but I didn't want to mention that, it's just an example of my intentions or the lunch meats. I'm the executor like reading a story that has a description of torture in it or about diseases, one who executes it. I don't mean the will is what I mean. A will, a William Shakespeare and the theories about his affairs, you see the woman was said to have been married off to someone she hated because she got pregnant and when Shakespeare sent the Earl of Southampton to tell her he had fallen in love with her she seduced him too, her poems all addressed to other women, some are religious and she tells her opinion about the Fall, not to blame Eve. We saw the hotdog man for the first time today, they're 60¢ but 70¢ if you want sauerkraut. There's been some trouble buying onions, they've gotten expensive too, one would think roots were the one thing that wouldn't cost a lot. When the leaves of the carrot plant are big, the root is still too small to eat. Special things like drinks, sweets, lavish foods in abundance, I can't figure out if the days are long or short because they never begin and everything is in abeyance, I am beginning to think everyone is equally happy or not because of that theory about feeding families, on the other hand I feel that everyone has forgotten about me & I think how easy it might be to write a sort of novel in which the main character would...Nicholas Ray died. Is sex one of those things, I forgot about it. To put something in one's mouth is not always the same, isn't anyone discovering anything, I don't want to hear about Dash again. All the writings are anyway like drops of a rain beginning you can only see if you look up against the building or some trees but it still becomes a whole work or life, I don't know how. The answer is to have another profession like prostitution but then you can't have any children and you can't write at night. I was reading this hateful thing written about someone famous, a couple of them, and it made you believe to be driven was like smoke filling the air everywhere without beauty of which we are all envious, still knowing nothing even of being human of all the various minds, maybe at once. The women were stunned to be included like the sauerkraut, if only it were free and you would just ask for it. No mustard on it either. I'm not saying I bought one. But it was the only joke that got made and the smiling about the way I was throwing and catching the ball, it got cold but we still had our shorts on. You could play ball morning noon and night, we all know that could be a profession. Also by the time writing prose seems to begin it seems to have already ended, someone said to me I wanted to write without writing anything so it was just an idea, it was someone who can't stand to sit still for it, as if it were all some medical operation, the violence of an abortion. But nobody said that, like the commercial owl on that drugstore folder. I can see past the drink to where the nail was ripped a little from my forefinger catching the ball, that could be construed as torture too but it wasn't. Attention to detail like making covers for the books of poems and I forgot pills. Losing an obsession might make the bus trip seem boring. The rhythm of the words gets too repetitious, the prose lets you study it I guess, the sentence goes up and down just like they said it would in rhetoric and then you let it end or vary the whole with shorter ones. Just like she did. When Marie and Sophia want to stay up later they start hugging and kissing and being clever about what they're reading, Sophia will repeat after you every word you say for half an hour before going to sleep, even hamburger and since Marie says everything Sophia says, and does an imitation of her saying it, all it needs is for me and Lewis to begin saying those same things too and then you can be sure it's like Willie Nelson singing "Summertime" if you will. First you go to school and then you do something, a friend of mine told me another friend we went to high school with seems much more mature than the rest of us, what happens to you when you write poetry. I was thinking and then I said I thought writing it ended when it was written and it didn't matter what happened after that but no one agreed with me. This more mature friend has a real estate business in California, Rosemary has a new type-writer. If it's fiction it's no good and it can't be imaginary, it's partly the desire to change things. Everybody makes it so you can't do anything without money, now nobody can hope to ride the train. Our mental activities generate hostile letters. Like the finite fuels, not wondering about my daughters again. You wouldn't believe how lush it is here, everything grows till it falls, nothing is trimmed or pruned, it's extravagant, there's always the smell of skunk or garbage or dead birds I can't envision, remember when we were smoking "Twenty Turks" and the cop said they smelled like a D.O.A.? The yellow lilies are so sweet they're putrid, then maybe they're jonquils, light bulbs exploding, damaged books exceeding the boxes' resistance bursting tests, we're covered with bites, everything grows fast and then it has to stop for a while, even the farmer said that, the prices of the fish are sky high, and like I said before every day is too long unless I'm wrong about that. When I finish this mystery I'll let you know what I was initiated into, being careful not to lose my life.

Designing Disruptive Concealment

SHORTLY AFTER PEARL HARBOR, it's either Rosemary or Alice. It's too hot to sit in the sun that other people know what you mean but then she said they don't even know if it's cold or hot and besides there's so much else to think about as women we can't be free of it or we are torn. They always say something because they try to say something like hey were you out rolling in the hay or else it's taking advantage of the sun, eh, while I'm trying to write. It started out I was telling you I had been meditating so much on the existence of flowers I didn't know what to say but now all I can think of is all about the doctor's children. There is a drawing in my book of many harpoons which do not communicate, you know I am always in a hurry but this is more for butterflies than thee. You see Lizzie was frightened by a moth and she cried but I had no fear walking up and down that street, even away from the house like slowly growing out of infancy. Rhythmic regularity of the pattern is another attention-getter, you see nature avoids regular repetition. So I know the fear can return to be attacked because it has the regular pattern of human activity like a hobby or profession or job that you can not only go back to at the same time every day, or else it's only for women, but also you can get what they call regular income from it like the doctor much from his treating people, this book but not the doctor is saying nature avoids being human just as it is unexpected of me to ask you to give me your shirt because I've been admiring it, but there are always stories about the man or woman who will give you the shirt off his back so you have to be careful of that because it might be embarrassing. I think I already mentioned about the dream of Lou Reed, Alice and Ron where Reed kept offering everyone a communal bath and then the old woman said, "Do you do crewel work?" Call me Ishmael! Lizzie said she could not sleep in the tent because it was so dark, it's great you found the lost postcards, who's that on the phone? Bill? What was David's girlfriend like?...Now Bill's been on the phone for a long time and I keep wondering if I'm pregnant or not, I've noticed lately that I can't seem to think of time as passing just the way it does and so I always think more time's passed than has and so I can't remember whether I told you about the doctor tearing up the bill because he didn't do anything but talk to me, I mean if I were a doctor I might be so preoccupied as to forget to do that and then he called to make sure I'd bring Marie over to play with Lizzie. His parents are old, I don't complain to him, I was just going crazy and thought he could solve something, when you're pregnant your cervix is supposed to be blue but I think that's something new, no one ever told me that before, in fact I never knew till Shelley told me you were supposed to mimic your cervix when you put the diaphragm in, I do find it and cover it like a water tower, plant trees to disrupt the shadow of it, it means neck, the bladder has a cervix too, but doctors say something about the tip of the nose to describe one, that's as it's reputed to feel, cartilaginous I guess. Straight information about the shadow problem is one of the greatest difficulties we have as women. As a rough rule of thumb I could say I am frightened of not being an Indian. At the same time anger is unlike Claire. Secretly I don't want to have anything. Except this knowledge to translate the golden shadow you can't see into that cast by a known but otherwise concealed target. Like deciding you are gonna both stay up late and get up early, boy Bill was voluble. So it was great to talk to him like athletes divide their knowledge or a drink or two or how the people in Southampton drink a lot. Like to protect yourself from a harsh whiskey you might hide the bottle, then I had a dream Lewis's mother like one of those silverfish that glide along the paper had sour cream with her and was demanding a peach but when I went out to get it even though I walked all the way from 96th to 89th and I wasn't even sure I wasn't going backwards I could barely walk it because my legs would give way like a prostitute made of lead. The best solution would be to eliminate the chimney or man entirely. You read about the intoxicated writers of China all the time but still you wonder if one can write while drunk, are you gonna share those cigarettes, you know there's always the question of feeling too good, that's a lot like the writing too long one. Or telling dreams, who needs it, I'm not dirty. Our life is pretty dull and what'll we do if we're pregnant, not only that we don't have any money, not even enough to make us feel good, I mean to do things to make us feel good and Lewis doesn't. He wants to go to the ocean, he hasn't seen it in five years, he's landlocked, there is disruption of outline, it is conspicuous. I try to tell him it is just as bad as no disruption and the business of disrupting this outline is then of great importance but the shapes are too definite and worthy of attack, he says, I see four years or maybe five more of infancy, pins, strollers, backpacks, outbursts if we have to have another baby, that takes up too much lack of harmony because we learn that the baby cries if we live like nature, that is in the disorder in which we love. But using lines <u>not</u> in harmony with the shape we disrupt our shape better. It's not natural it's raining, men do. A woman smoking a pipe isn't like a man doing that, Mrs. Andrew Jackson and still the existence of flowers. You could write simple songs using phrases quoted in the newspapers like, I don't know what the hell's going on anymore, and, I'd pay anything for gas. We know these lines of language are still a camouflage and we will only define and accentuate just what we want to hide! Half-close your eyes and you will see it. I'm sorry but I can only love you in this disruptive pattern, why I don't know. I seem to have learned it somehow, it's like saying if you will only change your coat I too will be able to see all the excitement of moving, you see we are trying to get this disharmony to hide the airplane of our love. I take this example of war to place this town easier here, or this crazy need to hide, I'll half-close your eyes for you with my fingers of tile false factory, false windows and lights, smoke effects so that the factory looks like a church and I am devoted to you though you are deceived, the road is hidden and the church is now a dummy and the highway it's on is too difficult to hide in anyway, love is simple to conceal. The town can be hidden but the river cannot. We know about smoke, now I have to get down to it, another man or woman like the man who was pretending to be a child to give us pleasure or the woman on the phone who knows nothing about us but the etiquette of some kind of love will say what makes us dream that we are close nevertheless, I keep thinking some fast food restaurant would figure in some poem. To feel great moonlight or some starlight could be enough if we weren't such a body, but I for one as they say always think that if the next were death then we must mention it or be up close all the time which fucks things up because you can't be caught napping then or wake up in the morning surrounded casually by all your books and poems but you get deliberately old like a blessing working all the time on the runways, glass windows, river and lakes to be covered, even in Manhattan you do. The town and the city are usually near the river or the ocean. So what if the sun heats the room and that in turn makes the window warm, can you tell? You just have to cover love if you love behind the windows with wire with laced cloth strips, the protective blanket is expensive and the whole war was dangerous. I wanted to tell you when Marie saw the other children she ran up to them to say, do you too have toys? Then what's the use of photographing the bottle of aggression like sandbags filled with cheap sweet bourbon when the barricades of love are so overwhelming you can't get in or out. I'd rather you know I had a fringed edge and could be like you, you seem to have a lot of trouble knowing we are the same, do you think I'm also not a fool? Even the industrialist and the tall trees like poplars know enough to hide things. We often read each other's writing without ever knowing that this is a way of talking like the idea of being someplace beautiful. If I were to drape light rope or net with rags hanging from it over the tall trees, soft cloths to allow for wind action, I could even conceal you in the future, no one would know you. Now how shadows envelop that shrubbery, we're so inspired to stay up late and see. For once the sharp shadow distorts our fear of lack of love and where is the moon mostly. The only trouble is we're beginning to be aware that most of what goes on is almost over and we'd better hurry up unless by chance we live to be old, too bad, then we have a lot of dignity's or despair's time. So should I write this over and take out all the most important parts and try to include them all in some smaller part so they can be apprehended like landmarks, Niagara Falls, New York Harbor and the Mississippi River or, fast becoming lost in a maze of gas tanks, power plants, garbage dumps and industrial disposal areas anyway, here is fertile field for the lost and most devoted lover when war ends and the scheme of grass, wild grass, is seeded into factory of love where it will grow fast and love the dust and heat we know and then it will all become a mess and everyone's a passenger then and grass is ideal to smoke but cocaine was mentioned, pilots and lovers are less obvious than people who drink all the time and the wheels make marks and yes, if given half a chance, nature is the master of the opposite of love.

The Fly Has Married the Bumble Bee

THERE'S ALWAYS SOMETHING to be said for some kind of nothing like having nothing on the other side though it might not be economic, there are millions of things you and I don't know about, did one or the other of the ones who wrote what has not been written for us to read think that. Something about the sun being so hot it hurts your face but then you say to me you are being so sensitive you cannot even eat for fear your desk is on fire at home but it's cold at night like it's supposed to be but never is. Why waste it on something that doesn't make any money she said but I had hardly ever thought that way, you are brooding. Your vacation sounded good even with the car. This painting of a woman is overwhelming and romantic, it confuses me like these alternating moods. Friendly enemies have been struggling to get watchdogs and money which they call the long green. It's amazing that the sun went down then as if we had even come close to uniform identification like sisters, yes or no. And then somebody had the nerve to say hang on as if each paragraph was about a different subject. He's the kind of person who makes jokes about my name that remind me of someone devoted to Max Beerbohm, or anybody's name for that matter. It must seem weird to other people for us to do anything the way we do it like the ocean is stormy whether it is or not. She told me she liked babies but the rest of the kinds of people were all fucked up but she didn't say fucked up, she said something else that was rather more architectonic and textile than musical. In high school when we learned new big words we took them one at a time and were supposed to use them in conversation three times so we wouldn't forget what they meant. I feel so crazy, someone said the good weather was making us all sleepy, someone else said maybe it's because you're pregnant but then it could be promise and just laws. One girl is "it," she is given both ropes. It said you capitalist company will make money if you are honest and patient. I can't forget the girl with the candy pacifier who hooted at the boy in the see-through shirt by our house or the shell-shocked veteran who dressed up as a policeman with a policeman's hat and a shirt that said "Security Officer." Like these moods I can't figure out if I want to be bordered with remembering. He said you couldn't write criticism anymore because no one was objective, I can't remember why but it made sense at the time, now it sounds like nothing. The night passes but there's still a little light in the sky, certainly he would never dream of writing novels. I gave the impression of being strong but I will tell you about the picus-nicus, that was how they began to try to teach me Latin, I'll never forget it. I couldn't figure out if anything should be done but I couldn't do nothing as if someone was ordering me to furnish the room, find the possum know your town, pass the fox. I was at the Greek Olympic Ball when I saw I would have to focus more on one thing, I am a tree. Those blue clouds will soon be black for hunger and the earth is pink for fun. The foodstamp people wouldn't be too happy if there were beer stains on the rent egret, I think marriage is designed to make you detailed enough for love but that love is different. She told me about the young woman whose hair turned white because of her ovaries, it reminded me of the pregnant woman who didn't see the doctor at all as I'd planned not to but then suddenly she found out she had a dread disease anyway. I won't tell you what it was, you see I could never say this in poetry, there is a difference to be told. Did I just want to take it easy like spin the bottle or the wit and wisdom of good Pope John or was I hoping to make something of my summer vacation yet I can't go home after that or it might be the frightening idea of having to tell my autobiography with all the steps between absorption and reaction as if life was an allergy. I had formed the first sentence in my sleep until I remembered hearing someone saying she was reading the novels of George Sand and they were wonderful. As every poem had become the same length so every sentence was beginning to end the same like taxicab. She told me why she was unhappy, shall I now tell you? So far we know a number of people who live around here who have to have two cars, that seems inedible to me, the other car would be strawberries, crabmeat, wine, not to speak of all the idiotic delicacies you can read about in the papers. The main car, it's the big one, it's the man's car sometimes, the first car, it's meat. Hideous meat with all its sluggish qualities, dead meat unlike the pleasures of squalid sex or a woman listening to somebody saying it's nine months of pain, one moment of pleasure (Simone de Beauvoir) or the cultivation of sadism for an art we all know about, I know the existence of another person has little to do with jogging in the sense that the women who love babies without realism foster the idealism of the absence of meat in our lives. So I have to say I wish I was twenty again because of the accuracy then of knowing what to do next whereas now I'm put in the place of the woman who looks like me who has to say I think I know more than you do, Doctor, but I am frightened and I too have presented a false picture, so I understand you. As we lose our beauty do you speak from memory or must I pretend to be as young but old as all the time that's seemed to pass would make me which I am. Do you know this flower, why can't I consult you, I was wondering if it was hemlock and what kind? Rosemary picked the bladder campions I had called St. Johnswort. Boy it is impossible to tell most of them one from the other but for the bean sprouts when they look like Indian Pipe and the pretty Swamp Saxifrage. How come I don't have nobody to tell me it's Featherbells or not, we belong in this word puzzle. This guy or that, our ideal men, never got us out of it, I don't mean nothing against men by that, I don't not mean it. I just meant this particular writer, a you know who, without any meaning, you get my message he was more than clear about everything. More than Roger Tory Peterson or someone. You see there are families of flowers and despite my own dispute with them I find what you are saying about families being all wrong all wrong, you say the family is a star or a commonplace bill; to be sure it is that general shape or structure with distinctions between the species. I am keyed to see the absoluteness of the will in brief and nontechnical descriptions of all families. Yet it's true, unlike conventional arrangements, you can view the whole by flipping the pages as of a book, you get a visual impression including color. Who will identify this system? Is a man or woman to be predictable yet again even while the nitwitted churchbells are still ringing where you or I am? The bells are not women, they are not built or woven, heavy metal things hanging there, nowadays recorded, not even rung by the rope like a poem still read without a lyric instruction. Numbers cultivate the extremities of will until I die because I wore my hair like a curtain and you saw nothing at all. They said she had no curtains but hung cases of showy flowers and frightening herbs in her windows, she took deadly poisons into her house because they grew omnivorously, her sister said she'd learned to expect to study them and take them in like beggars, no one could visit anyway because they had no money. She was the ultimate doctor's daughter, the landlord was afraid to breathe in her presence. I know chicory is blue and alien like the white wild chamomile. I would hope to be able to pay your bill soon if I were tall as this year's goldenrod. I cannot have another, I am a heart passed. Miss Daisy Fleabane with her white teeth will be whorled before us for love. How the ram's head lady's slipper got along with the male sleepy catchfly when they were in bed too is beyond us. Each smooth phlox like the wild sweet william is like I could rather say who each flower was like, I'll be then the pearly everlasting fool's parsley and you can be the wild cucumber they call a balsam apple but that it makes us not a family, my yellow vetchling. We had a list of names and names of automatic plays of flowers to stay our later love, you mentioned you had walked in this chaotic absent space that's covered here and I couldn't help but do what you were doing. In order to tell you I will rearrange the house but it's not a house. Left alone it's just an ousted flower I have to iron like a long poem written by Philip Whalen in script that could then be rolled up and placed in a tube. Or if it wasn't a tube what could it be? We aren't even sure we want all this continuing on with all there is to notice. So I'm afraid that is just how I'm feeling, like a zigzag relay, tomorrow I'll have another pregnancy test too and it's to be given in the King's English so that How To Write will become a Modern Herbal and if the book I write in becomes a dictionary I'll be embarrassed to have said that I had seen myself this way, like the young woman in the picture, the huge spider with eight legs and two small forelegs who is sitting on this page with the tenacity of a love I cannot stop watching for fear it will fall on my leg.

Gardening in Containers

YOU LOVE TO DRINK TEA, the dark sky is dark blue. I can't believe it is so strenuous to be pregnant again yet I don't feel a thing. Some people fear the lack of space but then they have a great gaiety about going on with it anyway as if our lives as poems were blessed, which I think they are in one way, and, not deprived of so many useless objects, I go to sleep fast at night. It is strong tea but just Tetley's and not coffee. Nearly every minute Lewis is thinking about being somewhere else. I mean strenuous in the sense of feeling one way and then right away having the opposite thing happen like the rain, it's supposed to be this way all week but you get to know what time of day to expect the storms that always threaten, that the grass and crops need so much and that ruin the afternoon concerts for the few tourists who can still get to them, the grass is all parched. I always need to talk about it and we use big words without reserve together, I hadn't realized till our conversation about sex when the actual storm began how pervasive and still new to me the situation of being a mother is, I guess now I ought to call it a condition, since I spent so many years not being one and not thinking about it yet being a woman and learning about sex in that exclusive way which is the way mostly everyone I know knows it and so we all continuously think like what they call young people for an overlapping time. I wonder if men would be making anything of this and what we said, I mean men who are younger than, say, Paul or even Ted or Bill, but they don't like gradations or statements of conditions like that about dead-serious sex, it seems like it's only women. I wonder if women will always be saying things about men. I had a few cigarettes, it's hard not to smoke them when I see them but I'm looking forward to spending a few months in the bathtub. Sex and being a tailor, I mean a mother is sometimes like two things, the androgynous exhaustion of the limbs isn't needed and every already learned pleasure and its moment is changed and set at a time when there has been no time of emptiness before it. I told you she said oh no, you are going to become exhausted again because that is what she fears and so she fears it for me. If I had a thicker skin I wouldn't even mention to you as if I could forget it like they say oh forget it, that when he got on the phone just for a minute he only said how're you gonna support yourselves and then hung up and they still treat me as a stranger so I am always posing. Then she said we'd both or either have to get ourselves altered like iced fruits coated with sugar so we would stop breeding like the thunder. There is nothing simple, there is no pleasure in it, I'm supposed to be able to feel both ways about everything, not only that it really is all a contradiction and there is no sheltering it. It was as if she was concealing everything she really thought except her voice was like weeping or distress and I was tempted to say why can't there be a joy in anything, I hate you and I don't love you. So even if it's just out of contrariness, I like the idea of this new baby. If we are going to get ourselves into a lot of trouble we'd better move back to New York but I can't see how we could ever get there, what could change it and make this environment less an orphanage for us, you see I still can't even figure out like Orpheus what the writing might go beyond even though I have a few clues like forgetting certain things, no one asks me questions so I might wind up orchestrating the whole set-up even to the fragments of food left from a meal or painting the kitchen, encouraging some air without lightning to pass through the imaginary dividing up of space the windows make. I was reminded of the smell of death so many times, could they say I had lost the ability to say anything like designing a vision for the mysteries, who did that? We don't ever go and look for anything we need, we just forget about it, you can need something more all the time so easily, it's too tiring to assume the self is not particular, transparent and beyond at least half of it. That seems like what forgetting might be, I don't mean food. We knew perfection was a murder from beforehand but I can not imagine a man I know as if he were a woman and something enables us to picture that woman as a man, even if she just dresses up that way. I needed this time to not have to think of every word in a smaller kind of structure, it's queer to be studying though. Like the books like romantic women I might accumulate images of while I'm pregnant to accommodate a form for these daughters that will permit me to be smart about it. I had learned that sex had been driven to be, and this is just me, a reassurance of survival in the recognizing face with love and the body overwhelmed together practicing with another person as a presence and as what we know so that it was easy to say after that it's a relief to go on, I don't mean you'd be glad it's over but that you didn't have to be concerned with ending then and you were sure you existed, a hangover. But not death either. Then with children, which is probably why they say you can't really have them anymore for fear of losing something, your looks maybe, or your talent or even your genius, they do take away that fear of there being no knowledge, nothing, never again and so on, the blatant stack of emptiness we had all met. Of course there's also the fear that you would always be pregnant all the time and the alteration of your sense of time like the habit of timing the space between lightning and thunder and so you are always waiting while opposite sits like Persephone's rape and Demeter's consequent invention of beer, the face of nothing between two windows, fear of every dimension. I'd better stop this. We can share a lot of the same things going on whether you are pregnant too or not, that sounded like a tree, but you will be so busy this summer. I love telling about the form of things, now people are running, it's impossible not to feel the rain even if you were blind but in a town you have to assume the whole burden of all the close people, are you scared yet, instead of practically owning the trees and squirrels that light up your room like private property if we were in the woods together. Now the air slowly offers a picture from the smell of it and the boys turn their radios up high to fight off what might be the drama of the storm, I don't think it's silly. We have SOMEBODY'S DARLING from the library and it's due back in seven days so I have to go read it, people seem to wind up calling and they find out we're pregnant but it's not really any fun telling them except for Peggy because, like having friends who think your poetry is silly, nobody can really see any good or joy in it, just problems. That one was like a flashbulb, it must be great to watch this from Clark's house. In the morning at breakfast, Marie and Sophia talk about the different bugs on the window. Sophia can almost speak clearly now because she finally has teeth, she is both conspicuous and recalcitrant in her grace. What else? Marie ate the bean pods from some celandine poppy flowers today and screamed at the taste of the hideous orange juices, actually she just got the stuff on her fingers and then put them in her mouth. Do you have a house yet?

To the Tune of "Red Embroidered Shoes"

IT'S A RARE WINDY DAY where the sun never goes away, some new weather must be moving toward us very fast as they say, you always say I notice the weather too much, that most people don't know if it's hot or cold, I find it hard to remember I'm not supposed to have to include it all. I think to myself I've gotta say that to you and then when I forget it it's lost. To celebrate without a plan—will he buy her an ice cream on the way home? I had one and then I had another, I stole one—was it ripe? I had been thinking of writing him another letter but I can't tell him we're to have another baby, a third one, just like he did. I think of suicide she said. Why doesn't anybody pay me for my work? I bake bread and even cakes, wrap packages, make cole slaw, wash clothing, clean up crumbs, make phone calls, write, and it's me you owe a letter to. I kidnapped the boy. Everything is equal remember? Each of the ballplayers holds his book of poems in his hands; one tells me he loves me. You see I can't tell whether one thing or another is fitting in or not belonging because I think I have a fantasy it would be great to write without concentrating at all, just let the impishness of the sounds of the forms of the letters propel themselves, then afterwards at the picnic each of them can write how he wrote those poems without the fanciful blowing of the leaves on the trees a day like today, words aren't swept or compared like a mirror next to a picture of a woman, and he was dispiriting when we told him and as for her, she, I was tempted to say doesn't have to fucking have the baby, it's I who will. While we were talking I remembered the dream of Harris and Ted driving a truck into a piano we were hiding behind while I go to get Marie a wading pool Bob and Shelley are bringing up and walk back across a field where Hannah and a bird are flying around in the door of a church, it was snowing besides. I've been baking things ever since I knew this and when she was born it was an extensive birth, people are sometimes so false and only say what they do from a determinist misfiring of the desire to please, she thought nothing of space when she was born. Raise anger tomorrow or the next day to read it. Between two days there were thirty dollars made but no hamburgers. The thirty was mainly spent for less expensive stuff, not like the flashing blue lights of the town police policing the distinct or discreet boy-men near the new trash can. I think I'll go do the carrots so I won't be discovered writing this or even die like a phallic chin. I knew there was a discrepancy when I asked if she thought it would be interesting if she didn't know me, no one knows because like parents the writing is of another generation, and though it's already written it hasn't been conceived. That's why we can't look out for it or look for it or cease. Others will say there's a discrepancy in this, just tell them to clean out the fish tank; in the living of it it is so small. Like listening to anybody's footsteps or seeing them, careless, obsessive, nothing. You did it wrong. Are you mad at me?

Under My Green Jacket

IN SOME FUNNY WAY it's a beautiful night and if I'm lucky I'll be able to remember everything. They just left this afternoon so I feel like it's been weeks since I've remembered anything and I can't say, like I usually do, nothing really happened, or, I can't remember. Now before I can even do what you call collecting yourself, Marie comes running in saying she wants the other baby that's on my desk. I have two signs of being pregnant at last, I want to eat everything (like reading) and I have a backache (like pretending). I guess it was just a day or two before they came I was offered the job and it wasn't long before that we became certain no other money was going to appear & we'd have to either move, which we couldn't do, or find some kind of job around here like typing or selling shoes, remember that? And how come something like teaching in a college which is the very thing I never wanted to do returns to be what happens, we didn't talk about that but we figured out just about everything else uselessly in advance like waiting for poems. We even got the atlas out of Sophia's room while she was sleeping and found Concord on the map with the population. It has the reputation for being the most conservative place and I read it described as the second-fastest growing state after Florida yet it is 80% forests, all this in an article about a famous anti-communist newspaper from there, do you think we'll have to live in a condominium, maybe at least life will be cheap. It seems far away, Rosemary even thought it was going to be next to Canada, I mean how much colder can it get, Harris will never come there though he does go to Boston. When Kenneth asked me if I had any real books published I only thought he meant another book and then he said that those three books published in one year wouldn't seem like real books and that we'd better not mention any prose ones. I just talked to Dash on the phone but the conversation was shortened by too much to tell and even when what's his name asked about the job I needed to see what the rest of the world still looked like or how I figured in it like a plain dolphin almost completely surrounded by water before I could see what I would say. It's something like anger where you cannot have it alone. Or like the requirement of newborn babies that they be surrounded with their mothers and also other relations, it seems natural. It's because one person can't sustain a new baby alone and you need what they call help for that to be realized or seen in the air from object to life, or even if you will, love object to life's love. Before I forget about everything else I want to remember this thunderstorm, I guess it was after we found out there wouldn't be any more money and before the idea of the job, it was right on top of the house or the town, right next to us, right up our alley, all the lightning could be seen and before you could hear the thunder you could already hear the babies crying out and us saying it's only this. Thunder was anger to them too and it makes awake babies electric; I read lightning won't come through a window if it's closed, why did I have to learn that? Two whole families in one house is always weird and there was even a lot of bickering within each one before the other. Now I think it's raining and it reminds me of the strange red-headed boy who's been hanging around in our backyard and by the house, Lewis thought the boy threw a stone up at him or at the window tonight. The other day he walked around our yard jerking his head about a hundred times like a sex experiment, tonight I saw him playing an imaginary harmonica. It's rare here to feel threatened at all, he had tried to follow us into the house, why model a fictional character on him, Marie has to go to school tomorrow anyway, you see she doesn't have to do anything like that but she likes to, it's not an order but she likes to have some order. False wisdom is also like Claire's picnic which was full of strangers and food, even raspberries and chocolate cream pies and beer and ice cream and even a swimming pool for the kids because as soon as we heard about the job we got invited to come to parties and picnics and drink free wine on the grass next to the beautiful willows and watch sunsets and be asked questions, I even met the woman from Family Planning who had told me I was pregnant, she turned out to be Jo's neighbor and to live with a Chaucer scholar and together they also lived with a man who played an instrument. That day we had borrowed Jo's car, the car that used to be William Shirer's, to take everybody to Interlaken for another picnic, I don't know if anybody liked it, it was too cold to walk up the stream into the woods. Now you called and we talked a long time, you kept making fun of me for wanting to write something, I never mentioned what it was, you kept implying to have a baby could be the only thing, I forgot to tell you the way I knew I was pregnant was it wasn't fun to get drunk anymore, I couldn't get high, and also about the self-serving babies, this look you see on the faces of the ones you don't know at all, they are almost arrogant, they have everything right at the moment. Bob made chili and Shelley made a beet greens salad to eat with it. You're practically the only person I'll have a long conversation with during the time I have to work so in a way you compete with that, I haven't done anything in a week or more, since I got the call about the job. I've been on the phone a lot, it's like an epic, do you think I'll have to jettison the vegetables, did those plants I gave you take root in a garden, when other people call they don't seem so far away, it's a reverse discrimination or backlash. Everybody keeps saying the name of the communist paper when they mean the anti-communist one, even you. You used to say you were a conservative, remember? Once for a long time someone you know said he wanted to study constitutional law but now I wonder if you didn't say that too, so much writing about things isn't worth reading because as a poet there is always the distance of it and the fragility of that relation, this is something I can't ask you to understand, I can't request it. Since I am a woman I got accustomed to the other part of life too as if there were two parts, I don't forget I am a poet but I forget to be being one except for the writing or I even pretend love is the same and all the rest, that's why I might take such a chance, that's why I say it's a piece of cake, that's why I'm redundant and exaggerating, afraid to lose you and not only you, but are you another? I've never had a pseudonym, I often need to recover from having had this or that, I think I may have sounded like a fool; loving to talk and having learned it, I might get in trouble but only I know about it because I'm slightly wrong and thus it isn't knowledge. The thought was sent, it was as if an intimation, it was even bickered about, an intrusion, a member of a family doing something one way, idiosyncratic, foolish, out of context. Families are so seriously whole, worked at not like poems, not gotten from the air, still the spirit in the moth attracted not to the light but to the hands to speak harmlessly, if I don't see it, scares me. Mayakovsky's death or the death of another or the dead body of another may have expressed this fragility as if it could be a sentence, but Mayakovsky was a man. The rest of the whole thing is like daring the vegetables to die anyway, being careless about them, without experience for them, refusing to use certain words. I learned too much this week, I can't remember what it was, it was an unexpressed rehearsal for some poem, it was never words though except to think about being on a ship or in a balloon and jettisoning something, some stuff, objects. The whole idea of taking such extreme care as if anyone knew what anything was is a trick like what Bob said was the manipulation of the news, Skylab falling or something. There's a number you can call to find out the latest version or report. I will call and they'll say it will not fall nor will the poem ever be completed and a baby is not to be born says this moth because your mother only had two, another absence of knowledge. Sweet curses filled out see that the lepidopterous thing rests on the window frame as if dead or sleeping this night full moon. Now it flew away to all those places like rhyme. The director said to do it more slowly, to pretend to be a picture of an edible seed on the skin of the person portrayed like an unexpected freckle which might, but doesn't, portend some awful news or disease. You are too sentimental, it makes you reject the dreadful. The king is dead, long live the king and so on.

Dear Alive

I WAS TRYING TO THINK who would like to hear this dream I had and then I remembered Bob & Shelley told me you had written a poem about your period which was something we talked about a year ago while we were sitting in Edith Wharton's mother-in-law's house, remember, the bar we walked home from in the fog in Lenox, and I want to see the poem. In exchange I'm sending you a 15th-century Chinese poem about _____ and my gossipy dream which goes: Gary Lenhart was living with Simone Lazzeri in a store called "The O" where they sold o-shaped things. She was crippled so he had to carry her everywhere like Elizabeth Browning. You see we got lost walking in New York and wound up in the worst neighborhood I've ever seen where we saw a man in coat of lights near Essex & Delancey Streets. Then "The O," which the kids liked. Joe Brainard was with us and he told me if we ever had the chance to sleep together he would never stop fucking me. There was a type composer everybody, especially Ed Bowes, kept misusing by putting menus with tassels on them into it and then a relief map of a city in Australia would rise up out of the composer so that when you hit the keys explosions would go off and destroy the buildings. If you really knew how to use the machine, other cities could be destroyed and you could see all past wars. Ed sneered at me for correcting him & said he, unlike me, would never hesitate to get on a plane without a ticket, even to Iran.

Then I read Clark some poems he had written and when I woke up I was reading him this line:

And I

To a man deadpan as myself

Now my dream is ended. And we may be moving. And I may have to be a teacher while I am trying to give birth to Peggy or Max Theodore. Let there be no mystery about it, I send love & the poem of Huang O:

If you don't know how, why pretend?
Maybe you can fool some girls,
But you can't fool Heaven.
I dreamed you'd play with the
Locust blossom under my green jacket,
Like a eunuch with a courtesan.
But lo & behold
All you can do is mumble.
You've made me all wet & slippery,
But no matter how hard you try
Nothing happens. So stop.
Go and make somebody else
Unsatisfied.

The Well of Loneliness

THE LAPIS LAZULI BEADS got unstrung and scattered all over the floor, we never see Tim anymore, it's crazy to move and have to write so many more letters, to have to think all the time of so many more people, Marie's little, there's skywriting at sunset, Lewis is afraid she'll catch him watching the broken t.v. like smoking cigarettes, it's become the hottest night, a pink line. By the time we get old we may have lived everywhere though we've lived nowhere being unlike anyone. The novel is a rigid form, it's not like life like they say it is and it makes money. The new mother automatically protects and praises her young (ones) no matter what she thinks. I'm not saying I'm leaving out the murderous anger and fear of hostile retaliations, they are like dialogue part of the form. The aggression necessary for self-preservation has a peculiar expression in capitalism. Frogs leap, this dishtowel would be filthy if we had a dishtowel, once again the women were not represented at all, some say there just aren't any great women writers but I know there is at least Huang O. She met a fellow she detested with whom she did not discuss anything. I asked the man what Red Sox game he had seen, he was such a smart ass, it was only Toronto. Heat rises and the heat of summer can't be stored up for winter, a cave is always the same temperature. Elizabeth said she went to a party but the caviar wasn't for her. The sake too was just for the saint. Oh Susan, I guess by now you've heard from your sister what our plans are. Tell me about her, I have a sister too. On her way to L.A., Peggy sent a picture of a spear fisherman from Brazil. Susan has a little orange desk to work at and a job selling cookies and ice cream in a movie theater, wait till she hears the news. Helen likes Alice's poems and says she knows a man named Cave or Caves. Rita moved, she grew up in New Hampshire. John got involved in something about an unnoticed swastika and he lost his job. It's so hot here I wonder why when everyone else is doing the opposite of the very things that women have always detested and abhorred and run away from, especially women poets, I have to be stubbornly doing them. But I am not just a woman, are you always a man, I knew I'd have to be remembering all this sometimes without any minimalism or philosophy, it just came to me. It's impossible not to think of one's mother, transgressing her example now in detail: having come close to being her after not being her, my imitation of her becomes today flawed. I know some women I admire, especially one whose mother's name is Beulah, who don't seem to have to think like this, who can cultivate plants without it, who have a life of events not rigorously connected but each thing that happens stands up or stands around so that these women seem to me like saints without pasts like the way my own criminality might be said to have been caused by something, caviar to some. What great women they are to know. Sometimes men seem like that too but it's a less great achievement for them because you can't tell if it's real. Grace said she didn't want to talk about social work with me, she wanted to go horseback riding. This moth is tickling me, it's shaped like a skate, I'm as hot as the light. I mean the fish not the kind of skate I feel like when I don't vary this. The person regarded with contempt by all. I know a woman who wants to keep everything having a pleasant surface that is plastic like the novel. I guess it's impossible if you have all the children you could have or would have for it not to be a chaotic invasion like the colors on the beautiful shelf that will have to come down and then we'll have to remember it, the day we moved, how dull and awful it was. Something prevents me from thinking it will be awful now. Remember the Night Owl on First Avenue, that was awful but I remember it with happiness. Before my relationship with Lenox dies, I'd like to go to the Price Chopper at dawn. I don't think Beverly was ever a hippie though I'm not sure. Did your mother ever say anything like we have enough food to feed an army? What is the difference between the sublime? What is the purpose of the idea of discipline in writing? It's shit, throw it out, the hard work is the dross, the thing I resent most is when someone says you won't have time to write if you have a family. All the men for all time, this silly time we know about, had wives and children without anybody saying anything about it. I mean those men must have had to do something that took time to take care of those children too, like get a job even. Even Freud at least at last dallied with his. And now everybody acts as if, well if you can do it that's fine, you're extraordinary, if you're a woman doing it, that is having a man living with you and having children and, they say, still writing. So finally they've convinced me it can't be done, I'm going to give my children to the Museum Anti-Trust Home for Bigamous Mothers and Lewis will have to go too, to be cast back on the world where he isn't living now. When you have children, besides all the sympathy you get for it, you get the children. Remember that woman I told you about who came to take a picture of Lewis and he said I was a poet too, and she looked at me and Sophia and Marie carefully crawling on me and she said, oh really and when do you get to write? There's no use ever actually saying you're a poet, it's a disservice to yourself except for the wonder you can sustain among the moths, but you'd better say it anyway. The first time I ever saw a June bug was in New York City and we were so scared of it we put it in a box and took it outside to be released. Even among the poets no one wants to read anything of any great length, except some people will like taking a pill. I wonder what it is we're doing being these pretentious cupbearers in this whole life of nothing but writing and children and whatever supports it, if only I could sell moths to people. I know what Nolan Ryan is doing tonight, he is pitching a no-hitter, it's nostalgic, as if everyone idolized poets or read their poetry in a hurry on the bus or subway. Tonight one of the hairdressers went to the bookstore and bought Lewis's book. It was Ken, he was riding a bicycle. I've been seeing these insects with bright red bodies lately, they look as though they're filled with blood like mosquitoes. You can't keep children, as if you owned them, they don't belong to you in that sense. Because they are so blatantly made out of you and another, they are separate and cannot consent to your ideas, it's not competitive but wavelike in the sense that history, though it gets beauty from the instinct for chronology, is literally a way of wasting time. Infants are different, they are like possessions, yet still they are not because they are not dumb. It's not only that they cry out unwittingly for food and attention but they do things and other things surround them than what is surrounding you so though you must own them as they are your own you must also own up that they are on their own. It can happen that the children are born without your even noticing it, without your giving it a thought as if you had been in a sense-deprivation experiment like a Pleistocene woman or man, but it's inevitable to think what will happen to them. The man and woman might not agree about everything though they are in love, it might be this very disparity that accounts for the future in the expression of will subject to destiny. It's obvious that our own ideas of perfection are a reflection of something that exists. My appetites are longer than the meaningless death I would crush, ignore. For example I could say, I surmise this work will not live on after me, even finite as colors. When the heat lets up I can't forget to buy a pattern for Grace's mother. She will make a dress for me, I'll wear it. It is so hot there will be maggots if you don't do something about it again. You will, won't you? The same sworn love of the sublime, an unreadable beautiful writing, that's not their real hair, it's cold in Tibet, the Chinese singing girls are clasping their own hands, the pointed stones mark the graves of women, a cold cloth will assuage your suffering, the Spanish woman treated with exaggerated reverence, courtesies for courtesans, the Welsh women have on their silly hats again and so do Mrs. Roosevelt and the graduates of Smith, they were called girls till they were fifty, remember when that guy we worked for called us gals and said we had to wear bras, they still do, everybody's got to wear something, I've been wanting some African woman's dress and the Korean woman's baby carrier, now we dress like European peasants, half-naked, not carrying baskets of dried grass and fruit, they've got parasols and digitated socks, musical instruments and tattoos that look like mustaches, large diamond-shaped patches of dark blue ash-bark surrounding the mouth and extending in points toward the ears, they wear trousers and a short tunic, girls have no names, a hat woven from the hair of her ancestors on her father's side, they never go out alone, a daughter cannot do this, she will run about wild, learning to write, their tormentors have made them eat bitterness, they pay out their mothers-in-law by committing suicide at their houses, they don't eat together, the toes frequently drop off, which renders the hand almost useless, which likens them to the silk-worm moth, my dear I don't want you to work so hard because I'm going to marry your sister too, the baby was all tied up, now the moth would be pounded to death in the typewriter, she looked like a wild Indian, like a loitering ghost, the bride grinds some flour, she is covered, she builds a house, spinning and weaving like moths, Reggie Jackson got a hit off Nolan Ryan, a guest may ask for anything he wants, the babies chew raw blubber, I wonder whether to give you the lamp, I took your husband and I will learn of you from him, I was in charge of the religion but I was only one person, then I had a baby who climbed up through the fire, it was washing day, the houses were empty, she put a grain of black corn on her thigh to prevent dreams of the lost one, there were different foods prepared, the little girl had on a wool dress covering one shoulder, there were no boys in the book, the father-in-law had abruptly hung up the phone when the birth of another baby, probably a girl, was mentioned. He and I and all these people I've begun or tried to love, absent spirits who cannot fly like moths met at the four corners of the world again, I didn't hide my breasts, he shook my hand, he didn't hide his hand, there was his astonished love for once, he danced like a fairy, he could do things, he was agile and manipulative, he was freed, he needed no serving, he did it all himself without thinking, he held an infant, he was not lost, we didn't have to talk about money, we had vanquished death and its consequent security, his son and my daughter were full of love for him, his wife sat on the real ground for the first time, she ate clover flowers with the children, we thought of nothing, we were practically all women, we were divorced from murderous blue fear. Tell me if in answer anybody said anything.

Two Known Lilies

I'D BETTER NOT MAKE a big thing that is what I am meaning. What I seem to be finding out ends who aren't writers, who species. Are you getting as vital to me as it is and so in letters to you and to these friends, I guess I've even known about! You see I so they are inevitably friends, letters in it to you and to I am just being so sensitive to women and I am having a wonder about my time. We had a visit about sex and may even get an old baby and some dialogue ensued hard, especially on a hot night whether of the baby asked what we being a mother is like being on of time for babies conflicting since none of us ever took and I said I knew you could supposed to, then being a moth she said yes that was what men. Now Carter is making so herself actually had the nerve what I mean is having babies could and if you were a mother aspects which I wasn't prepared were going to be, at least for weave them together with her for saying it. She is a woman to me without any of that, sore always suffering, having a hard mothers I know of the horrible continually coaxed and fussed about are supernumerary when on the other hand our children traditionally sort of thrust leaps in independence, not needing and children exist in a place able to feed themselves and ask is not exactly what happens the only way they seem like a burden do it in the traditional way. I must tell you one great this both from myself and to me I am almost flattered by analyzing it all that would answer.

I always figured I would to say in my best moments I when I became pregnant with ones I am hot and grouchy. Ed because it meant that not only Green and CONVENT LIFE by two girls inevitably, but I was to Clark lovingly found for me exactly the same respective ages when are you going and when will girls, without me ever "planning" thinking as you write it that have broken the spell. Don't worry, painting and each church. I do and it is as if the next step is much but the paintings are further exorcise my mother's now. I just passed through the natural existence in my consciousness. You have a chance say something that cannot even be spoken! Art of rhetoric is lost forever such. Well it will not be sad in the art of the novel, to ass-town, though only for another town everything. My mother may I'm assuming. But something new you have gotten for your book and pieces if you can, I've never seen off reading the *Times*, I can't the literary stuff, it gives you thing. Lewis and I are having an endless idea of fiction, we have both become it, but with thinking about it as understood the instinct for it, in fact pregnant so now I've got to go out and for a while! It usually takes me five pages of a novel it is so that world. Well another whole subject to see more of you, or any of you, Russell and Fanny in New Hampshire, wish me luck, write soon, don't join the convent.

Eine Kleine Nacht Musik

I COULDN'T LET MY HAIR DOWN, the idea came from nowhere, you found a line from Andrew Marvell, a stick hit my eye, you moved everything into your room, played ball in the hall, your mother never taught you how to cook, finally it rained, you dreamed a mannequin had champagne in her breasts in an elevator in the Bronx, I dreamed you were kissing me for just one moment, it was the wrong number, your penis got so erect you couldn't get it back into your pants before someone came in, you pretended it was a backpack, did you ever put your hand up someone's asshole, when what's her name was trying to make me mad she implied you would want me to fuck you up the ass, I mean you me all the time, nothing came from Concord, I wonder what the industries are, you never told me you'd like to watch moths fly between my breasts or that I'd turn into a different sex, now your room is filled with smoke and I fall asleep as if I'm forty-four before I can even kiss the back commemorated in that slapdash poem, why does she keep coming out and bothering me, now she's counting the keys, she's trying to eat me, you were sharing food from each other's mouths, she wants to kiss, now I'm becoming another sex, no I've had to be angry to be alone, to get my way, she says she has a big clitoris, she says you have a nice penis especially when it's big but I'm having a nervous breakdown and my sex is on heroin, my sex is like a hairpin, it's on a hairpin, she gives me a piece of her most treasured thing in trade for staying up, I walk her to the door, we don't laugh about it because of your mother, everyone is that way, they made us nervous about getting any of this love and then we did something terrible, like the gas crisis, all the old Chinese women poets who were young ran zigzag away from their husbands and traveled and drank wine, you're exaggerating too when you say I look old because of the style of my hair, maybe it's a conceit, a poetic exaggeration, it's rhetoric or a false dignity assumed for the public to practice words for the perfection of a poem, to induce them to follow me, to seduce you we never knew we'd run away and be alone, your family complains, mine lacks realism but finds a scary chasm below the same jugular-shaped cliff, all I do is run back and forth between the words, we all blow kisses as often as possible and there isn't the world which never changes anyway to get in between us persisting together in everything and even if there were the world as if it were a business or a temptress or a buttress it wouldn't leave us any less desirous together and still for the moment just missing, I was wondering if the words were as far off as the expectation of sex which is so ticklish when it's too fine, the boys used to lift up our skirt but all they would see would be the tops of our knees, I used to wonder how there could be any saint at all among the fucking living or dead, now we live like hermits, we're crackers. Now that I'm a mother my chances are better for sainthood they say, that's like apartheid, there was this boy who always wanted to talk about sex, he was a lot older than me, he was in college, but since he didn't know anything about birth control either he never came inside me or we left our clothes on so I used to think a lot about this other boy, his friend, who liked folk music, I assumed he would make love and I was right, he got married and had five children right away, I started sleeping with another person and we ignored getting pregnant like saints till I got pregnant and then I had an orgasm, I forgot the orgasms I would have at first with my clothes on, Catholic ones, when I was going to have a baby I became promiscuous, it was like authority to do it, Gertrude I'm sorry about all this, it's half-hearted too, it's not telling anything at all anyway, I never met a man who had a condom on him, even Michael Layton got Janice Luarino pregnant in the eighth grade, and Julia Heuther in high school, Sylvester Hanks never got anybody pregnant and neither did John Hoefferle, that's why my mother liked the latter, he was cute but not as cute as Michael who was older who carried a knife and decided to defend me against a group of Baldies who had decided to call me a black whore, though I'm not black. There was Ludwig who brought me musical boxes from Germany and Freddie Stegel who rang the bell and left a lobster at the door, he had make-out parties, I've mentioned him to you before, I asked my mother if it would be possible to kiss Michael in the tunnel at Rockaway on his birthday without committing a mortal sin, it was embarrassing to go to the beach with all those boys, it was too tough, Rosemary was dating the vice-president of the Junior Saints and there was always the chance one weekend he'd be killed at the gang wars, why we went to the Puerto Rican dances I'll never understand, the boys were foreign to us, they were incredibly blunt and we weren't allowed to go out with them anyway though they were Catholic, it's easier to talk about past sex or write sex into a novel, everyone has written it, the only thing about sex and mothers was they were fucking the milkman, our milkman is old and his father just died and he cannot deliver the milk at all this week, if you really wanted to fuck at Rockaway you consented to go under the boardwalk and brought two blankets, sex is now connected to having children, when Marie was first born I saw I had become reactionary, as a child one has that way of hanging around to see if anything interesting will happen, you could also make love up on the roof, people said you could do it on the subways too if you wore the right clothes, there was only one guy I ever left at the gate and that was the guy from the Red Cross who said he was reading EXODUS, I told you about him before, it seemed like sex was never what it was, what's a poet, I'm preoccupied, there was a reason for it, not having children, we were like cave men and cave women, everybody knows this, there's no reason to be saying it and denying it, the plant is not poison hemlock but hemlock-parsley, it doesn't have the tell-tale purple spots on the mature stem nor does it possess fatal qualities, you have this fatal quality, you cannot cease, it is more than half of everything, if only I could make a character of either of us, I've been unfaithful to the doctor, I am smoking your cigarettes now, the idea of regret is like your dream of H.D., at what cost do I dream we are moving to the end of Manhattan, you would say it doesn't pay, or maybe it's still fool's parsley because it's already so ill-smelling, you should write him, it would be a mitzvah to do it, it's one of the things I don't enjoy anymore, I only look for people and see people in the children, in the new baby nobody will praise us for having, you will see when you see me with another one it's not ironic or absurd, but it's slow, it's not unwitting, I'm beginning to think it's about time some ideas were new, even whole words were, words not a service or a mouthful, these supernumerary words not supernatural, no one can assess the unlucky past with pleasure, 60¢ a word, a dime a measure, thousands of dollars for thousands of stories I'll write if you pay me, you know what I found most offensive in that article was when the guy said why would anybody write except for money, I guess that sounds ingenuous, there's one forbidden letter, I won't write it, it will get better like an injured eye it makes you weep to watch, empathy is strong in children but who gives a fig, your finances have not always been topnotch she said, so what if you weep, everybody does it it says in the toilet training book, not everybody has money or is an invulnerable loan-shark though thoughts pretend to be capital, it's no different than it ever was for us, poetry's a license today to be desired, she says she knows what pleasure is but can her husband do it too, and she admires the woman who's foregone it like we all do, she's a saint, and she didn't buy her father a fancy car, it's just the clarity of being obsessively extraordinary, of succumbing, giving in, being nice, being simple, being lost, the other, where'd you come from, whom do you resemble the most, how do you like to be high, to be exalted, to be free, to be without everything, to be alone, to be full of clarity, to be lost, to be retrieved, to be seen again, to see the light, to be resurrected like they say, to be devoted, to be all askew and at odds with everything, to be confused, to be dying, to be lost, to be useless, to be continued, to be continuing, to be reincarnated, to be too much, to be left, to be alone, to be irredeemable, to be hopeless, to be inspired, to be someone, to be abandoned, to be surrounded, to be at a loss, to be reconciled, to be reunited, to be at one, not to be undone, to be made.

The Prostitutes at the Eldorado Club

TODAY IT STARTED OUT COOL for once and everybody was in a good mood when they got it up. It makes a difference not to wake up with that greenhouse effect. Marie came running out just as the alarm clock got it off. She wasn't sweating at all, she looked pristine and cool in her damask rose gown checked with sky-blue-pink flecks. I whipped up a fast breakfast of eggs but she laid off them; I made her a lettuce and cheese sandwich with her name on it. Lewis just rolled over. I had had a dream I was fired from my fucking job but I could get twenty-one hundred dollars every three weeks in unemployment, if only I could get it up to go down there. Also I had to go get our deposit back on that old apartment in the dream I had before, #12A, the one with all the closets and the view of the zoo. Marie had some nuts and juice and said she saw superman flying in a movie in her dream. When we went down to meet Claire she was looking a lot more pregnant than before and Jonas was laying low behind the back seat as usual. Marie told Claire the story of us going out in the rain just to get wet, we had been so hot, and how she slid into all the puddles she could. Jonas popped up to say it had rained over at his house too, all over the swimming pool. When we got to school Mable was kind of close-mouthed about her surprise wedding party, the one we never made it to because of the rain. When we get back up to the top of the hill Claire always stops with a jerk at the new do not enter sign and swerves around the obelisk saying, oh. We talked about Mr. Yamato's apparent denigration of the female sex of what I think of as his wife's new baby; he was also mad she was born by Caesarean section, so-called because Julius Caesar the dictator was supposedly born in this manner. I told Claire my belief that the most likely reason Mrs. Yamato had to lay down for all this was because she was a beautiful delicate Japanese woman who had married a big generous American man. We talked till it was time for Claire to go see the obstetrician who, we all know, would lay her down flat on a table and feel her belly and also let her hear the heartbeat of the baby with some fancy equipment. Claire feels like she's got twins in there, she says it moves around in two different places. The mail was only a jack-off Penny Saver, a postcard for a show, and a nice letter from Paul's friend saying we couldn't really make it in Concord without wheels and if we had the means we'd be better off buying a house than laying it out every month for the landlord and we could stay with him while we were looking. I was so excited when I opened it it made me mad. I had thought maybe he would say come live in this beautiful house I know of, we love you, the rent's thirty dollars, but you don't have to pay it anyway. I have a lot of trouble with struggling to do things, I think it should all come easy. In the grocery store where we get the paper the counter was covered with slick magazines and the proprietor was telling one of his boys where *High Times* could go. I picked up the paper for Warsh and brought it up to Lewis who was glomming PSYCHOANAL-YSIS AND FEMINISM in bed to enhance all these female characters he's creating in his room lately. We decided we couldn't make it to the Pittsfield library today because it would cut into our time later to work. Lewis threw a few eggs in the pan for Sophia and him and when I went in to get her she was nibbling her toes and singing in between. After that we went out to do our usual perfunctory walking of the streets of the wrong tank. We stopped in the library where all the ladies are so sweet to us. Then we got one of those bottles of milk with the cream they have at the health food store where all the vicious dogs are lying in wait to eat babies and the price of prunes had nearly doubled. The proprietor said she was letting them go for even less than she had had to pay for them. I guess there won't be any free prunes this year. I grabbed a few nuts in there on the sly like I always do. We stopped at the bookstore where amidst the privacy of the shelves Lewis changed his mind about DARK LAUGHTER. Jo was using her most disciplining tones to get it across to Sophia that the children's books were getting dog-eared from her playing around so much with them. I made Sophia lay off them but then we had to go, we go in there an awful lot lately, and we never get it on the line. It was one of those days when the supermarket really stinks and all the vegetables seem to be $1.39. We got some jelly and bread and paid the two-bit shunker who runs the place. He seems so hot in the biscuit for anybody's boodle, that's what stinks. Behind closed doors again we put the blocks to some cheese sandwiches but by the time Sophia was ready to go down again, Charlotte buzzed me and we chopped it up for a while. Then the new bells our landlord just installed started going off without stopping, we had to finally call the bandhouse clipper who runs the place downstairs to stop the thing. I blew one up, had a few beers, hung some more paper and ran down to school to pick up Marie. Mable said she was going to go to Niagara Falls for her honeymoon. Lewis had been doing jamoka all day with his females on paper and when we got back he wouldn't stop. I sent him down for potatoes and lay down with Marie to look at *National Geographics*. We were still studying the wolves and Turks when Lewis came back with a ten-pound bag. I had been fuming all day about how all the legit stiffs think we oughtta have a car and a house all to ourselves, to lay the leg in some more I guess. We all grazed dinner together, glommed a few lip-burners and split back out to the jerk town to peg some more stiffs. It was still as a nut, except for the meatballs directing beefers past the crosswalks in their crates. That same old masturbator was in the park with her kitten, and that jail-bait with her big jelly dog. We saw Dr. Taylor on a bench in his bathing suit with his baby. The mosquitoes were biting us like nymphomaniacs so we decided to screw out home. The sodomites next door were coming up the stairs while we were, they like the kids, who flopped right away soon as we gave them some peaches and juice. I had some lead pipe for a snack and Lewis put the squint on the all-star game. I can hear the stiffs in their gondolas go by on their way back from the Shed like the sound of the drink as I bang this out.

Worse Than the Noon Whistle

AFTER WE TALKED I started thinking of all the things I've gotta ask you, about whether when you were pregnant for the third time your breasts still hurt, I did feel like the milk was letting down once, and to tell about Dr. Taylor and remind you of your image of him and about sex and tubal ligations, too bad we couldn't be having libations together without the infants at the bar like the old times now, devoted to some female cause. And how much time you're having to work or do your homework, the other kind of homework, whether your kids poke you in the eye or not, I'm convinced it happens to me because I sit still near them, I forget myself. The girls aren't really that persistently noisy, unless I've stopped noticing it but I don't think we repress them just because they are girls, our life is sort of orderly and they are turning into obsessive-compulsives fast especially Marie who can't forget not to. I too had been idolizing Sophia's placidity like your Alexander's till recently they've started having screaming contests, maybe that's what girls do, they sound like Arab women who sound like Arab women. Does "Xander" really have allergies? And what did Leonore mean when she said Peter or Gabriel was having learning problems? I don't feel pregnant at all. I planted a garden on the windowsill but the tomatoes won't grow there but the cucumbers and basil will, not the chives. I did see "Invasion of the Body Snatchers" both the new and the old one many times, I mean the old one many times, your backyard fantasy sounds romantic. I have at least two dozen small tomato plants right here on the windowsill that will never become mothers and the carrots don't survive transplanting either, now the sun is setting red over the town odorous with gas fumes from all the Cadillacs and Mercedes driving to hear the high-toned music, there's nothing quaint about it, it's been hot here too all summer, Marie just came out for the hundredth time this time to say she'd found the top of a safety pin on the floor of her room, do your kids ever clean up their toys? I can't remember who it is I see in this town, if anyone, there's Doctor Taylor's kids and the slum kids and the hairdresser's kids who eat candy without ceasing and one of them said she has 32 cavities and she's only six, and Jonas from nursery school and his mother Claire who runs "Mainstream Woodworks." And occasionally Matthew Bookstore's cousin Norah who takes me to Interlaken park where I see Lenore. I saw Lenore's husband playing the trumpet in the Pittsfield community band in Lilac Park. Sometimes we go to the library or the bookstore twice in one day. The kids aren't good in the library anymore and the bookstore is getting impatient with them. It's been amusing for us recently, being down to our last dollars, to see that they won't let you be poor in Lenox, there are no ways to be poor, we haven't even found quarters left on the streets by tourists this year. I think I feel pregnant. We do all our laundry by hand since it was stolen from the laundromat. The toddler playground, besides being dull, is overrun with red ants. Cliffwood Street, though, is the same and Easy Street is moving to its most dilapidated house right next to the big white house that used to be McCarthy's and is now owned by a woman historical novelist whose name I can't remember. Mrs. Yamato just had a baby and no one is any nicer to us now than they were two or three years ago. Lots more trees have been chopped and taken down since you were here last and all the vegetables in Loebs, oh but who wants to hear about that. Sometimes we borrow Jo's car and drive to the Price Chopper which makes us feel both more and less stupid than before. Sophia's nearly two and she has a Brooklyn accent but she still likes to spend time meditating in her crib. Mable admits she is a sexist......a day's gone by, maybe two, you've been here and left, Marie always puts the broken toys on my desk to be fixed as if that's the work I do here, now the job's definite and we may have found a Torino to buy from a guy who lives next to the Eldorado Club in Lenoxdale, that's where you go to find a prostitute in what they call the Lenox area. It's a good thing when people give birth to babies they aren't as big as cars and don't go as fast and can't get better by themselves when something is wrong with them. Cars I guess should be free to facilitate the use of all the gas just as cameras might as well be given away to encourage the spending of the repetitious film. I'm going to write a farewell poem to Lenox which will begin: "It was as if they knew we were leaving," you see it is going to be a paranoid poem (I'm just saying this because I know you hate Lenox). I've been reading Virginia Woolf's diaries where she and all her rich friends discuss their liberal politics during WWI and among them she is the only one who is willing to part with what she has, she says her fire is bigger than she alone requires. I don't know if it's the weather or this pregnancy but I still feel breathless, maybe I am breathless. I found out yesterday that though there are both a temple and a Greek Orthodox Church in Concord, there are no Greek or Jewish neighborhoods but only, as it was described to me, the rich part and the poor part. I was imagining not so much that it would be cheaper to live among the non-wasp group but that it would feel better and the food would be better; even though you are not ethnic my dear I wish you and I could be neighbors again, it was so good to see you. I wonder who the richest person in Concord is or will be; around here one of them turns out to be this more or less patron of the arts named J.D. Hatch, heard of him? We were introduced to him recently at a book signing party for Paul where everyone seemed to be saying to us, oh we were all at the most wonderful party given by a Mr. Hatch, it was the most patrician, they said, gathering we've seen in the Berkshires, they continued, how come you guys weren't there! Also after all these years I was invited to give a reading next year at Berkshire Community College. I suppose if having babies and wood-chopping kind of chores hadn't made us think we had to get out of the woods, plus the expense of it, heating a whole house against those expanses of cold, then maybe we could've just loved all the seasonal lushness of this landlocked place, I do like the lanes and this move to Concord, which means agreement plus grapes, is just an out-of-the-way detail of the hot return to New York City where we'll be forced to make our fortune and I'll take the children to school in a taxi. I never thought I'd become one of the people who sat around saying they were dying to move to New York. Actually I guess there aren't any people like that anymore. Concord has all these peculiar industries that have to do with electricity and dictaphones; does the grape come from Massachusetts? Today as if the corn knew I had been talking about it it was being sold at Loeb's, your favorite place, for half the price it was and we are boiling a chicken for dinner just like Bob's and Lewis's mothers have done and do. When we were in NY, one of the funniest things was, after a big meal of beef where we kept being encouraged, no, forced to eat more and more, Bill's mother sat back satisfied with a big grin on her face and clasped her hands together and brought them to her breast and said, "We have eaten three pounds of meat." I think that was right before the big ice cream fight which also had to do with the number three. Yesterday I ate at least three cream cheese and jelly sandwiches after dinner and after we had all already surfeited ourselves together at that place on the Lenox road. Did I tell you Lewis is writing something about Huntington? I can't say more (Louisa May Warsh). I'd like to name a girl Violet, if only she'd been born in the spring. We already have a Crystal and no more female family names that are any good, just heavy-handed German ones like Josephine, Magdalena and Florence (are they German?). I have a friend who has two boys who wants to have a girl and name her Peggy, I have three friends named Margaret if you count you. I also like the names Ruby and Pearl, but like Violet, everyone says they sound too much like black people's names but so what? That's better than sounding like Jennifer, Sarah and all the other pioneers. Rosemary likes names like Philomena, Hepzibah and Archilochus, that last would be a boy. How about Asclepiades (the Greek poet)? Rosemary was a little shocked I had the nerve to name Marie after our mother, knowing I would have to live with (so many memories of) her. I think Marie's going to like our move because she wants so much for us to have a car, like everyone else. And she craves change. Sophia who is just the opposite way will suffer maybe and might finally find a reason to pass wholeheartedly into what I will consider to be her two-year-old way of behaving. Right now Sophia's even fun to share a glass of water with but you should see what happens to her when we are away from home, she is transformed. Today I'm gonna tell Marie definitely about moving to New Hampshire, so far every time we bring it up she assumes it's to be New York, can't fathom anyplace else, a place she's never seen, and whaddayou think about leaving the two of them with a friend whom they know but not really well for two days while Lewis and I go looking for a house in our prostituted Torino? When I think of Concord I find myself thinking what could be worse than listening to the noon whistle for another year? This town is leaving us.

The Slicing Machine I Seen Through the Door of the Eldorado Club in the Dale

TO WRITE YOU THIS TIME I do have some sort of story to tell though it isn't a story like clean whistling, it's just what happened in this defiant heat of the sun we're having. I can't imagine the crops are growing with so little rain, somebody said there were thunder showers in Schenectady near Lake Winnipesaukee but they didn't come here. The air is so heavy it's as dark as your eyes. First of all I had to have an all-night phone call sandwich with Claire as the meat. I'm explaining changes to shocked people, I wind up having to defend whole states of consciousness to them. Before that the richest lady in town, one of the Stokeses who married one of the Hatches, I mean this lady actually grew up on what is now the grounds of the equally rich Berkshire Country Day School where they say in their catalogue that a scruffy appearance is the sign of unkempt thoughts, anyway this lady gave Lewis a ride home from nursery school with Marie because Jonas was sick, she was all the while complaining about the performance of her '69 Mercedes but Lewis didn't mention she could just give the thing to us as we're in the market for a car and today we got one but not hers, you've got to have nerves of steel. I'll tell you about it. First I had the dream again of the house that is next door to the zoo, only this time the zoo began to be inside the house and the animals could leap over the fences from their cages, someone told us when the fiercest ones did this we should roll ourselves into balls on the floor to be protected from them, we walked out of the house rolling and holding our hands behind our backs as if we were shy and someone asked to shake our hands and the animals nibbled at our fists, they bit us, it was a small house this time that grew large and as we looked into it, in fact it had everything in the world in it, what world was it? Then the thousand dollars came in the mail, our ticket to Concord. We started out into the real world, this one that exists here, to go to Lenoxdale to look at a car, we're driving Jo's Nash Rambler with the hood tied down with a beautiful purple string, we don't exactly feel like that Stokes lady in her Mercedes and it's hot. When we get to the Dale we have to find this house which Lewis keeps insisting the guy, whose name he didn't get, said had gold siding but every time I look at his notes I can see it says blue, but the siding isn't either gold or blue, it looks white to me, maybe it's just the brightness of the sun. The house does turn out to be right next to the Eldorado Club which I never noticed before has a motel attached to it, that must be where you go with the prostitutes, it looks pretty tacky as does this whole town near the Housatonic River. There's an old red brick river factory that's working and lots of agoraphobic expanses that make the heat seem hotter. We find this guy and the rusty station wagon is in between two parking lots in a yard that this family has managed to crowd up with a big plastic swimming pool for grownups and a circular washline also. The old man has a red face and white legs and a big fat son who could be either the kindliest person in the world the way he looks in at you or a murderer, you can't tell. The car is really a wreck and it turns out to have belonged to a man who died of a heart attack, we hear, and his wife who was bedridden herself forgot about it and left it out in the rain and snow and that is how it became the way it looks, you can't make the same simple explanation for these people who are looking at us. Underneath the car is some queer kind of plastic dragging and flying down under the well in the back in shreds and there are bolts on the side to hold the gas tank on, we take the old gut for a drive and it drives o.k., his presence in the backseat of the car is so unassuming, he seems small, he's almost masochistic back there, we ask him all about the gas tank problem. Lewis wants to buy this car right away because he likes to do things fast but I keep insisting we get the real dope on the gas tank and so finally we get sent to the person who fixed it who's out to lunch so we go eat at a hotdog stand in Lee we once took Alice and the kids to. We sit in the back at some picnic tables under a plastic awning where it's almost cool, there's some little trickle of water running behind a fence next to the tables and some real lonely types are eating the junk food. Sophia's been really good but she won't eat but she does drink a container of milk, smart girl. We get back to the station but the guy's still not there, it's Louie Noventi at Fraser's Exxon in Lee, but I keep calling him Mr. Venuto. We wait and they're digging up the ground to put in new storage tanks for the gas. We call Paul to find out if he knows any good gas stations in Lee in case we could take the car to get an opinion since we are always only going on luck and American cars make me feel hysterical, but he tells us of his place in Becket and that seems too far. Then Noventi and the gang at the station all talk to us at once and it turns out the station wagons always lose their gas tanks when the cars get rusty, it's some long fantastic story but the point is the one we're talking about won't lose it again they say, they sound real sure of that and tell us how exactly it's connected to the rest of the car and by this time they're thinking I'm a certified nervous lunatic, this mother with brown braids who's obsessed with something about a $275-car, a gas guzzler. So we go back to Thom McGuinn's house in the Dale and by the time we get there I guess we've decided we'll take it, since otherwise it means having to wait for another cheap car to come up and we only have a couple more days. Now is when we get to see the inside of the house. Arletta, that's the wife, has to make out the Bill of Sale for us. Well you've never seen in the meantime such innumerable, discordant, hideous small things disfiguring the interior of a place to live, as Virginia Woolf would probably say. And they've got two awful little Chihuahuas one of whom Thom calls affectionately Pepito but he slides over the "t" and makes the "o" sound like an "a" so he sounds like he's saying Pepida and when you see his affection for the dog and when you see his wife for a while, her size and the way she was browbeating him about how you had to have a title for the car, not just the registration and the Bill of Sale handwritten on a piece of paper from the now dead man who drove this heap over 60,000 miles before he succumbed, well then you can see that what I was thinking about Thom in the backseat of the car might've had some truth in it. They said to me to sit down, I'm carrying the baby, and when I pulled out the plastic and chrome chair from the Formica table, one leg of it caught in the seam of the linoleum and I was frozen with fear anyway, I couldn't seem to recover, Lewis looked at me funny and he thought I was still worried about the car. It turns out he was looking mostly at the collection of fancy plates that were hanging all over the rooms on the walls in rows near the ceilings, it was astonishing. Arletta told Drew, that's the son, to get the extra tire and put it in the car, seven pretty good tires came with this crate, but then when he did it and came back she yelled at him without mercy or self-consciousness before strangers that he'd gotten his good shirt all dirty. He's in high school, so I look at his shirt to see why it's good but I can't tell, it's an ordinary yellow short-sleeved polyester shirt with a couple of buttons and a collar at the top, maybe it's new. This Arletta seems like quite a mastermind of misery and squalor of a certain sort but all my training in big Catholic humilities keeps making me say that there I exist in some way too, there are mountains of pill bottles on a shelf above the kitchen sink. Thom is smoking his pipe, he's having trouble staring at the back page of the plastic cover of the telephone book and finally he says he knows the number of the Motor Vehicles Bureau used to be there. Then I speak and tell him I just looked it up yesterday and can find it for him real quick, I do and he obsequiously dials the phone and surprises me by conducting a calm and businesslike forthright conversation which begins with him introducing himself by full name as if they know him or it's a requirement to tell, as if they cared. Meanwhile Arletta is reading off the words on the back of the title slow and guessing in a loud voice what they mean and Lewis is reassuring her we don't have to get the thing notarized, Drew is in the bathroom, this is taking a long time, now Sophia's crying and I split for the other side of the door. I mean this whole scene is neither hilarious nor fascinating and I wonder if it's poverty that exists here, they've got two other cars besides this heap God is giving us. I wonder if they have other children who've escaped that densest house. I mean there's also a part of life in this neighborhood where everything is so nice and everybody's house had wood stoves and all the right appurtenances, love of the land and so on, and there's something sickening about that too. We drive back to Lenox in the Nash, Thom following us in the wagon and Drew behind him in his Honda car and we've missed our chance to look inside the Eldorado Club, all I can see is a big old-fashioned white meat slicer. They drop the car and take the plates and we go pick up Jo's laundry for her and then continue up the road to get insurance and plates. I won't go into the whole detailed trip of it, the insurance place was just too depressing, it was like arranging somebody's funeral and I was thinking that way anyway. I felt like a ripped sheet of clean white paper for a shroud, something about this whole ineluctable scene was reminding me of my youth where you might more often wind up stuck in a place like that for a while, without power over it, maybe because one of your friends lived there, but even then at least you can look it in the eye like a fucking pioneer. Anyway this whole time I'm meditating American junk and feeling scared, the guy who first owned the car was named Lefevre and most of the rust on the car is on this part of the metal which, because it's a station wagon is made to look like wood so it's hard to believe that it's actually an alloy of steel and when metal rusts it falls apart just like paper, they'd put some brown spackle or adobe or something all over the worst rusty parts so now it also looks like some kind of art, then suddenly I realize it's not all the junk that scares me but the idea of leaving and moving away and this car is the first step we've made but seeing that doesn't make me feel any better and in fact I feel like a person at the peak or in the chasm of some ordeal, going up this hot road to the insurance man who treats us like junk. Maybe that place was more like a morgue than a funeral parlor, it was the pits, I called Claire on a phone that had one of those shoulder straps and looked at all the girl's dresses and nylon stockings, no punks here, those dresses they have on remind me of something too and now I'm lost to little bits of memories for the rest of the day I will barely be talking to the people around me because it seems like it's all movement, best without thought, to do things and never exercise the reluctance of feelings because then you might become too weak or too strong to be able to do anything normal ever again at all. Let me know.

Dear Only

HOW CAN YOU CALL ME other poets, it was you who is crying trying to hold up the tent you mentioned though it was me in areas where I am I mean we are both poor and rich though Concord seems like a muscle, I didn't want it to get eccentrically minuscule, life the semi-real school or a nanny. I was thinking maybe considering I should wear underpants when he found out after all I could go on it's just jealous of all people breeding a nice letter tell you I wrote an angry letter protesting the absence of women and when we get to New Hampshire worse cranks with other old males and time compared with us, wagon covered with rust, American house we paid charms but Lewis got caught in a beautiful hell here for weeks him nervous about the car not lightning he told me of lightning hitting a Hampshire. I would like of the academic so if I have nice false letters like essays because each is addressed, maybe to women lately of the day's events and getting quite which of course lacking in commercial my friend the magazine next issue to selling a novel these sentences series like you know what I mean the way it had to be it seems as if he is but I must admit he's the one I try to, as you know. To hear you being some more news, isn't that sort of remaindering part? I'm telling you and explain so much and I are in a fantastic wheel it's less so for Lewis. I think or around here we'll get to report about my poem but I also thought maybe I have no plans. We'll be near the poem now but

I have the last little changes. Hey might be to finally get some foolish guy for this fame and because I'm pregnant though I sometimes nihilism and complaining wind up doing like Charlie Parker it's Mabel Mercer's chair. And yes right away, o.k.?

Pursued as She Stumbled about You It Could Signify Nothing

I DON'T REALLY KNOW if there's anything to mention but I wanted to start to to prove I have a sense of humor about it, you see this guy's coming over and even though I'm dying to have my picture in the paper I hate answering questions about poetry especially when they're about my life. I feel like I live alone in this room, is that the way it should be? I owe letters to Rita, Rudy sent a card in an envelope from Athens and Raphael sent a picture of a girl, I think it was from Holland but Marie's taken it, I have to call both Russell and Rosemary to arrange our trip alone, letters to Charlotte, John, possibly Charles, always Peggy, Alice and a collaboration, Rosemary, Elizabeth, Helen and Bill C., also officially Annabel, Richard and Ed F. but I really have to write Ed B. first to tell him what's happened. I could start phrasing that in my mind by saying, but first I wanna say how hot it is, is it hot there too? to (question marks are not so bad if you don't have to begin a new sentence afterwards) have people reading what you just might say by accident is frightening, even about women, the trees are kind of dry, there was a car door closing but it isn't him and the thistles are covered with bees, the mailboxes with wasps, do they like the glue? The children are like exercises and one wonders if it's a pleasure or not to move one's legs about, we couldn't even get up the street tonight after seeing the doctor's family all so blonde, eating out on a porch in the yellow sun, Sophia's legs became like jelly but it turned out she was just demanding to have the gingko leaf I was waving and we didn't know it. They loved the visitors, there were nine people in the house when what's his name, who didn't seem friendly at all, couldn't get a ride home. Kissing Grace and Peggy at the bus was the best part. You should see the cucumber plant and the haze every night, my life is a mess, to inundate you with writings, it's exhausting, it's grown so fast it is latching on to other sticks or things that are just in its way, not meant for it, it is luxuriant yet the fruits are tiny, you couldn't even tell what they were if you didn't know what they were supposed to be, the blossoms fall off, it swallows gallons of water daily, his voice was just like himself, did he like me? The others are not as great but some do thrive. Those two are even edible already and give you great confidence that they can actually grow. I cut parts of them off and put them in the sauce, but will we have the sun so much in Concord I am worrying. So I can grow more of them, even all winter long. He said it was old-fashioned. They must think us weird or odd or foolish like Good Friday, writing the Chamber of Commerce or something like old hats or old cards or wizening fools, this pregnancy remember I thought might be menopause since I recognize change of life in advance but missed and made a pun of it, this time I am just moving, amazed at how stricken my environment is at my loss but my attitude to winter is after all not much different from how one talks from day to day, they were sitting around drinking wine, as he said, and wondering when we would come but when we come they won't be there anymore and we'll have to be on our own. I forgot to open the door again and tell him I was sorry the wind had blown it shut, I hadn't meant to slam it as if in frustration or rage at being asked the questions which were nice. It's good it's up to him to write the thing, I wouldn't want to have to would you? Did you think of that when you were talking to him? I told him it was only misleading to have given this impression perhaps that you could earn a living writing poetry. And then I talked all about women which would've made you nervous I think, when exactly are you coming back? Is it in the middle of when Lewis's parents are going to be here? Will we see you with them? Will we have found a house by then? Does your income increase because of the oil thing? What does that do? Does it feel like everything when I stood with the children next to the Lenox kids messing around the hotdog stand, I was waiting for Lewis to come out of the drugstore with the stationery and the kids were looking at me funny because as usual they were lounging and looking suspicious even though all they were saying was something about spare tires, also as usual. Is the ballgame still on? I don't feel light as a feather, do you think the will to exist with an electric energy in relation to how one can make things happen and answer to that is important at all, I am saying this as if you were saying life itself isn't important at all but only just the writing because no one can fight that in words and I wish in all my time here it could've been clearer what kind of generosity can be shared, as it was, but you never let on what you thought of my family and you were even still a member of it, in your own way. They wanted to know what to do next and I couldn't tell them we didn't want to be able to have that much time, did we. Some emotions like these are always distant and the proximity we speak of is only heady, yet when I tell you and I phrase it this way, I am working on my most flimsy book to date, you wonder if that might not be actually the danger I say it is. I can't blame you because I know my way of speaking is awfully headlong especially in person and I always forget it because otherwise, like in the past and remember when we were first introduced, I couldn't say anything for fear of it. So this guy gave me the impression that we were among this union of writers, united, secreted among these towns and others, me in a fly-by-night way, as always, writers who write without anyone ever knowing it, as we do, hours a day in an almost romantic way, not to fault him, like if he could see, or anyone, the constant rip, I was going to say tear, in this paper and that one, a series of ripped sheets I am using, it would be amusing for him, but he is also an intellectual as he would have to be, consulting Milton and so on but he had no idea about women and I used my eyes to tell him how furiously I felt. I wonder how good his memory is, is it as good as Marie's who at age 3 ½ has her whole history down already as if she were writing it, no not that, but rather as if she were not which is why she can remember so much of it. She remembers more things than I do but not like me she doesn't sit around wondering if when her energy flags for the day or night it will ever return and can I count on it. Photographs are so desultory lately like poetry full of people not to please you. Then again the eccentric reckoning with objects like love I was talking to him about and I was thinking but I didn't say it was exactly like love, that exuberance which saves or salvages both the place and moment, or time or whatever it became, is not something that's there anywhere but in poems, I don't have to tell you that, but I often wonder if you think about the end of it and in a way this letter might be more like my half of one of our conversations we used to have to tie up the nights so and render us so much more in proximity, I haven't been staying over for such a long time. I regret that and often think this move might become a benefit in that way, but not while I'm still pregnant probably. Alice was saying in her recent letter how I was becoming a paragon of whynotness in relation to the babies and that was praise but for the sake of not leaving the room and doing things as fast as I can I'll say that I know you think of them as just interfering with the work and I must admit I never thought I'd have all of them, like when you asked me if I thought it was o.k. to just have one and I defended her state as the only one, among you three, as being possibly a good thing, thinking that the thing, situation as it was was fine and had no harm in it and of all the only children I knew who seemed terrific why not but not knowing then it was a volatile subject and how it could be for women too who wanted to devote a lot of time to having babies, I'm sorry I had the nerve to give my half-assed advice which was full of holes. But everything else including about writing I've ever seen done has been shot through too and I don't think I've ever said anything and anything that would be considered to be (struggling) important without turning around later and winding up doing or thinking just the opposite of what I might have said. Because when I was first trying to learn about the world, I remember it clearly, I realized easily that I couldn't apprehend it all at all, I was amazed compared to what I thought other people my age seemed to think who seemed to already have opinions and thoughts and I decided the only thing to do to be able to speak at all was to find another person I loved and respected, find out what his or her opinions and way of attacking I mean acting about the thing I was wondering about were, and say they were my own. So thus I could find out in the talking from the words what thoughts were because I couldn't find out from my silence truthful as it seemed. There's a word for that, not catatonia, but something that children do when they won't speak, but always there is thought to be a reason. So I got the habit that way to experiment. To, like the other Alice, see what I would say. Which is also why I never could believe you or anyone could take my writing seriously because I knew I was just trying out for a world, even of words, everyone but me was the master-mistress of, at least apparently. The old hodge-podge double-indemnity I'm-not-responsible dodge. Part of that bores, psychology, and part my mother's inherited humility, but part is maybe a smart recognition early of how everybody learns something, except I saw the structure of it so out loud it made the learning seem false. So I never could understand how one could have political feelings before all was understood or feelings about groups of poets even, that were true, and I became as if obsessed with truth and its clarity and then that became something I could only admit to in writing, that and the energy to find that life allows me—accounting for what just happens—to be identified consistently as Bernadette Mayer, or the person who looks like the person who has that name if you knew it, which is also not allowed because you must not have a style if you don't know everything, which means you are existing in the past. Other people like those one lives with and loves are still influences unduly, it is improper, possibly unjust, I love the idea of your looking up words in the dictionary and I wish I were there to watch you, there's no reason for it, it's an exuberant love or pleasure of youth described perfectly in some novel or poem of Sappho's you or I am reading but we no longer feel that way, it is like the past and the fascinating idea of writing about it, like knowing all about death from seeing people dying and then dead or people vitally living and still young who then die; seeing their corpses is like this shame of all real love, at least we know. Which is why I love to converse with you, oh god I'm sorry for the imminence of my own narcissism, after all you can be sure if anyone is quiet for a long time—with you and with everyone, almost at my will, whenever I want it at the spare beggarly behest of a still secret living love, I am so ashamed of. I can't imagine when we get older, very much older I'd hope, and we will be writing to each other without knowing if the other will live long enough to receive the letter in the mail, but it's unseemly to say that, not only that the whole life is an assumption which I guess just goes on like walking in the woods with a friend and intimating you may faint at any moment and have to be carried home, you can't say that, just forget it, it's unfair. So the delicacy of our work I know is understood and its heart is too, the blatant mysticism even of everyday life can't be lost to any of us, we are even now attending love like that but what we promise to each other we cannot remember because otherwise it would just be crazy all the time, and that being crazy all the time is just what I know you don't like, you drastic person, like one I'd imitate when I couldn't figure out something. Still I still am left wanting to say there's a difference, and still one, between being a man and a woman now, and I know you can cultivate your images of thoughts and even opinions, if there are any to be had, easier than I can, because you've been longer and better at it, you've been given them, and perhaps more generously, no you've gotten them without remorse, and gotten used to them and don't mistake me I know when you're writing you let them fly (away) but in the end it makes no difference that we are different, even of sexes, if we can survive the liveliness of it which I don't know how you feel about, you pretend it isn't there and that is nice, like a nice question. From which anyone can go on who, like we do, would wish to.

Dear Ed

I WISH YOU WERE A BETTER correspondent and now I too am catching the disease, my only excuse being I've been waiting to find out absolutely what is going on with me so I can tell you so you will not have to hear rumors and now I am rushing to tell you that we are moving to New Hampshire which is not so much to say as to say, also, I'm going to have another baby and it was funny when I was in New York I was joking with you about that and now it turns out to be true and all I can say is I just cannot seem to cease having them and I always thought once I made it to Lenox I would find it impossible to leave because I would make it impossible to leave but we have no money but I don't want to be a teacher and don't tell anyone I am one, just say it's an odd job like any other and you would love our new car, we can get a quarter of a tank for five bucks and it doesn't exactly hug the road either and so we'll be moving at the end of the month of August in the car and tell me when will the movie be on t.v., it is so hot here and has been for so long it's impossible to think in the daytime but I am feeling fine except I need ice cream and when we go to find a house in Concord N.H. this week it'll be the first time we're away from the children and Rosemary and Charlotte will be taking care of them and someday soon too my picture will be there in *The Berkshire Eagle* and strangely the tourists seem less like dandies this year because of their cars and just because of that their cars don't so please let me know what you are doing and I sure wish to reiterate I wish we would be really corresponding because otherwise I don't know how to do it, let me know.

A Proem Added

I HAVE FOUR BOOKS BEFORE ME: THE LETTERS OF LADY MARY
WORTLEY-MONTAGU, THE SECOND SEX, LUCY GAYHEART
and THE HOMERIC HYMNS (trans. Hine). I also thought the weather was cooler but when you move around at all it's still not, I don't see
the moon. I'm tired from listening to the heartbeat. Who would care
about any such dalliance anyway, the dreary reportage of almost equalized daily events in a style that is merely leftover from what was both
freer and more controlled, now I don't even come to an end it is less
than a form but what form can we expect to be about anyway. Poetry is
filth with its coveted endings, is there something I don't know. Cars, big
ugly wrecks, are going by, we have one of them now. Ours is parked in
the space under where the thunder knocked down the dead tree over by
the Golden Needle. The burdock burrs are blossoming but what is that
blue thing, it's all over. Sometimes the doctors seem wide-eyed as books,
other times sultry and often too young, this one had a bad eye and was
taking white pills which I almost thought he was going to hand me, he
seemed so thoughtful about them. He's wiry with brown skin stretched
tight over what I guess are his Anglo-Saxon cheekbones, now I've gotta
go find yet another one in another type or kind of land; active women's
movement, he kept saying, Feminist Health Center. Midwives are legal
in New Hampshire though they're not licensed. Doctors are so fucking

busy, fuck them, he didn't look in my toes, I will beat them. The black woman's son had a funny way of walking, I'm sleepy, love is hopeless. I think it might be a rattlesnake-master, one of the parsley family again, intercourse.

The Day Thurman Munson Died

IT'S O.K. WHAT I SAY in writing, nobody could ever object to that, even the moon is almost full again over my left shoulder like all learning, no ending and salt. You see this light is kind of an interim night and suddenly what we thought of as life is something different, not quiet with time to write and stuff but interrupted and also still so hot. A lot of people said, first of all, it was unfair to make the comparison, with even reference to the O'Hara poem, but since this thing isn't one, as if it's missing one, and the questions of likes and dislikes is lost anyway—the fish jumped—I guess it's o.k. I always liked his name, its distortion of forgetful letters.

Even the Chinese people now are starting to give up smoking if it can be believed. There is the outside of a person and the inside, almost that.

What it was was the trip to Concord. Shit, it started out great with us riding out early like men dividing the trip in our minds into four neat hours that were quarters and also roads like the four corners of the world, we even got to buy some blackberries. Then the heat came up after our excellent breakfast of lost thoughts in vinegar with Heinekens, along with our hopes. Dashed in Concord, full of epithets against the numbers and activities of human children, brought up again the next day in Henniker, only to cause our hearts, or at least mine, to beat too fast in the very act of calming them down. We had already seen our coming house and shared a beer with the mad man. In fact there was a lot of beer and we had gone to stay, because of the cats and dogs, at this methodical place which even though it said it was one thing and really was another had a nice man at the desk, I mean at least he wasn't a snotty or beefy kid in an imitation waistcoat forbidding you the use of the pool but when we got to the room there was a hideous buzz but eventually it stopped. It said George Bush on the top. Tell me, what is the value of paying for anything.

And they do play up Hawthorne and Pierce a lot on the trail to there, especially Pierce who was born there, Hawthorne's pal. What did Hawthorne have to do with it.

I'd be scared to fly my own plane.

I missed the store it was closed. Anyway then I had a few attacks but I didn't collapse but the thought of the trip home at the end of the day like this green bug flying around was unbelievable. Do you know that all those men, or boys, seemed so fat or stocky or healthy but not swarthy? Hale.

The fish in the lake nibble at us and wait for food. Nobody thinks anything is quite right. We saw that awful man torturing his children again, also at the lake.

There is an object which exists, in duplication, all over but it is neither here nor in the lake. We saw these obnoxious boys today, they pulled up to a hotdog stand on the road and took great pains to replace the ice melting over the case of beer they had all wrapped in plastic beside the ice. It wasn't much beer for so many of them actually, the lake is full of weeds and when you swim you get entangled, it isn't pristine, it isn't pure, it was funny to watch but I am not looking forward to teaching about it.

I guess I've broken a few of the rules because now we've got a family and that means everybody thinks they can tell you what to do.

It worries me that sometimes I see you might be feeling deferential to this world, those fish are not minnows either. Let me tell you about the accident. Even while the moon was moving behind the thunderstorms we wound up sitting stock still in our car among a thousand others, three or four abreast, stopped still on the big turnpike both ways because something had happened up ahead. I was dying to get home and see Marie and Sophia and let Charlotte have time to get a ride from her friends, it's like the time I showed you the picture of the view from my house and thought you were me and could see behind it.

Even then, after a few minutes everybody turned off the engines and lights of their cars, it was spooky, Nancy said like dead bugs, and they said and started to walk around up and down the lanes between them and the people with CB radios began trying to pretend to inform everyone but all they were saying over them was fuckin and fuck, these men sounded crazed.

Then after that we had to drive real slow between storms because neither of us could see the road or signs we were so tired and there was a chance the road itself would just take us, it happened at every exit. It's a sexuality that is sort of hysterical like the diary of Francis Ford Coppola's wife, or Anne Frank. I mean we've stood on our heads, I wish I still had our Brooklyn accent, like what's her name does.

So we got this place from a platitudinous psychiatrist and if I didn't say it was nice I'd be kidding you, only thing is it might turn out expensive because of the heat and it's a secret to say I'm scared of it. Then again what's his name told me tonight the midwife actually lives in the next town over, won't it ever get cool or hot.

And we'll have a pond, rooms to rent, gas burners and an electric oven, well water I suppose, and the perspicacity of our notoriety no. The idea of the truck running into the two cars is too much.

There's no wood stove and it's all oil and it's not insulated at all though it does have storm windows. Leah was the wife of Jacob who expected to get Rachel. I don't understand the expectation, like people, of constant traveling, it makes no sense.

There must be something I've missed though and also beatific because of my own fears. I don't forget about you is my problem even after all these years.

You said you don't think it would be a good idea to marry me because it was just too embarrassing to think about and also I forgot to grab you and you were still already married but then again so were you. And in a way it was the same thing for both of you.

There's something about myself that reminds me of the rest of your family, did you ever think of that? You might be able to see what is wrong with me, like that x-ray, but see you did me a minuscule damage. So, as with something missing, if you get mad again because I'll have fallen asleep again by that time, I don't know how to say I wonder which kind of mother that might be the result of, not doing it.

If Mr. Fink was such a mighty oak why didn't he separate the heart bill from the other pension measures in the first place? You see you can't forget either, so you both have heart problems and actually have the balls to talk to me about dying, because of course you trust me to take it. Like in Concord I must admit there was no way of breaking the faith and just freaking out because of the danger of being elsewhere and so far from Marie and Sophia you could feel it.

So now the things to do are pack up, entertain and go. Without a thought?

There was this at least it's not a fire station or a lighthouse, just more gratuitous than here or maybe less. I can't figure it, is that the label?

I have to really bite my lip, I don't understand it, never happened before. What's he doing?

Millions of daily but it's only paper clips, heart of dereliction, it doesn't fit in to an image of a man or a woman in love. Nevertheless it's just crazy.

And this image is always nothing. Like the streets of a loony city some miles away today. I hope you don't forget me.

Dear Peggy

WRITING ABOUT MOVING seems to make for some dullness, I'm sorry.

Just now our new landlord called and we found out the ceilings are not high enough to support the bookcases for the books, we'll be moving on the first, so you can join us.

Only thing is Nancy wants you to come up the weekend before for the baby picnic so why not just come for the whole time?

I hope I didn't seem hazy as I felt on the phone with you, it seems Simon had, just before that, induced us to smoke some hashish and I didn't think it had any effect on me as I only took one long puff, thinking the Beardmore Glacier might not take to it, but then when we stopped talking I realized not only had I complained a lot to you but I was also left with the feeling I had never gotten to the point though even now I don't know what it would have been. Jonas refused to admit we're moving and keeps insisting Marie will be "only three minutes away" and the nursery school, synchronously, seems to be falling apart, one of the teachers quit in some kind of rage and Marie's other friend is moving—three new nursery schools have opened up here this summer. Russell Banks' daughter, who goes to the college, is interested in trading us a room for babysitting, and we were thinking maybe we could rent another room to pay the heating bills. I keep sitting around making calendars of the days left in Lenox and trying to figure how many of the nights of those days

I'll get to do any work and I keep coming up with numbers like 4. So next time you see me I may be a lunatic and this full moon of recently was a real pregnant one, having that remembered effect as a result of which I got to watch it setting around dawn twice now and one time when it was rosy like a sun behind the branches of some trees in Lilac Park and it looked like it was dividing itself up like a pie or peeling like rubber balls or broken, it was spectacular to see. Lewis has started packing books and papers and is utilizing his theory about work that one does a little at a time; I have a feeling my theory may turn out to be the opposite of that. I can't face the clothing none of which seems worth transporting, except for the jogging shorts. Simon was here and we cruised around in our car, he filled it up with gas for us with an Amoco credit card, and we ate out, went swimming and dropped in on people. Dash seems to have decided in a childlike way that he'll pretend we are already gone and that he's got his mind on other more interesting things. Simon brought us some Chinese notebooks; it turns out he could have a girlfriend living in China with him if he wanted to so I suggested lots of people I know would love to at least share his rooms but it would change his identity. I have this overwhelming sleepiness, let me tell you a story. I've been reading the letters of Lady Mary Wortley-Montagu, I was reading in the first volume of her correspondence at random, it is proper and spirited and kind of nothing, when I found myself reading a letter written to her sister about a trip to Europe, to Holland and the letter suddenly seemed to me as if I had written it myself. I had read it over and over till I saw it was the very letter I had read, about fifteen years ago, in a funny book Rosemary had given me about ladies' etiquette, 19th century, and used as a source to write this work "The Sea" which is in the NY POETS ANTHOLOGY. For a while it was like thinking I had reason to believe in reincarnation. Sophia's in a semi-rage sometimes lately but it never lasts too long like Marie's rages did and she always winds up still easy to put to bed and loving to meditate, I was realizing my whole schedule is to allow me, not to work as it turns out, but to have time to lie around in bed meditating till 10 am, just like Sophia. Neither Lewis nor Marie can bear to do that kind of lying around, it makes them nervous or it makes them worry. If I didn't have to have so much sleep, or time in bed, maybe

I could be a painter.

If it weren't for winter I think I could move into the new house without fear. I've been reading these novels by Willa Cather (who lived in New Hampshire once), the novels mainly take place in the midwest, so full of snow, of being snowed in, and they are great. Lewis is inspired by Sherwood Anderson's DARK LAUGHTER, a book Joe Brainard praised to us. I feel fine though I can't stand to eat anything I cook and only want to eat out, I have already absented myself from this house and so the care taken to do anything seems like nothing, like a dereliction of love, as if this space of life must be artless and the food we eat in the new house will be new food. And to make things a little bit crazy, we never buy any food because we have the car, so Lewis goes out at the last minute to get what we need, corn and tomatoes. Rosemary and Charlotte hid cookies (for themselves) all over the house! I still cannot write poetry but only these letters and the other letters. Marie is wonderfully comic lately. Has Grace left for Paris?

Dear Rosemary

WE HAVE A HOUSE and it has nine rooms! It's in the country two miles from the college and it's heated with oil we have to pay for. I didn't call because we can't make any more calls but I do want to thank you for the work with the children who loved staying with you guys, thank you! I heard you were exhausted! Too many cookies! We felt hideous physical separation anxiety pains and we were so dying to get back and then we had to wait on a super-highway in a traffic jam for one hour while the authorities cleared away some amazingly complicated and no doubt horrible accident and Charlotte of course was convinced it was we who were involved in one because we were so late and we nearly were I guess because we were so tired that the road kept driving us off the road, I mean at the exits we tended to drive off into them if you know what I mean, but the car seems o.k. and we do drive like retired people. I think we're gonna move on September 1, a Saturday, and that's all I can think about so it's dull. Our house has its own pond full of frogs and Lewis's parents will be here this Sunday for a confusing week (hey, you should've talked to Dash, or at least admitted you were here! I got tangled in a big web of lies!). Now I keep wandering around the house looking at all this stuff and then taking to bed or desk to read a novel or write one—anything is better than packing! Concord is horrible, ugly and hostile so we'll be living in the town of Henniker, the college is cute. All the male students look like they eat steaks. No dark-haired people around. Concord is full of people who don't like to rent houses to children, I mean people with children and, strangely, we met Patti Oldenburg on Concord's Main Street and had a beer with her. Our new address is Flanders Road, Henniker, New Hampshire. Why don't you come up before we go?

Dear Grace

YOU HAVEN'T GONE TO PARIS yet have you? Here's the schedule (you'll like our house and the pond too, you won't like our landlord, he's a psychiatrist): we haveta move September 1ˢᵗ or 2ⁿᵈ. I think Peggy's gonna be able to come up then so you'd have company conceivably. Otherwise I was thinking you could bring somebody else with you, to accompany you if you want. I guess we'd load the truck on Friday and drive on Saturday. Whaddayou think? New Hampshire has a funny character, it is a little close-up and a lot tight in a spatial way, everything seems to have lost its normal depth, there is this mountain practically on top of us, no kidding, just a tiny mountain, the whole place is nearly below sea level, there is much flatness and few distances and the ones there are aren't far enough away. Maybe it'll look better in winter. I've got hayfever tonight, an excuse not to pack. Next I have to write a letter to someone who wants to remainder MEMORY. Lately I fall asleep at ten and dream nostalgically of the hairdressers. Listen, let me know your plans, come up anytime, as soon as you can so we can have some fun, I mean packing doesn't take up absolutely all the time and I still get to go swimming in the lake every day in my new car—do you think it will harm the transmission? Love and kisses.

Lady Mary Wortley-Montagu's Letter to Her Sister

YOU KNOW I WOULD CONFIDE in almost anyone and when I'm pregnant the wine doesn't even affect me that way, it's as if I feel lucky to have a forgetful glass of it, without worrying. She would take my pen into the woods with her but then she would bring it back. It was nearly that sort of perfect day except for the fact that one must do something to fuck it up. Your letter was the one I'd used to write that poem "The Sea" which is in prose though I didn't say what I'd meant to say, especially after smoking the hashish I had then, it's really like a primer, a book for studying, a reader, like a detective novel written by someone greater, a good book by a good friend of hers you accidentally came upon, something we never knew about, a discovery, I wonder where the lines about Esterhazy came from though, another anonymous letter I presume in the etiquette book, it must've been some joke someone was playing on me giving it to me, I think it was Rosemary, I've noticed other people have given me books like that like the vitamin cookbook, also full of wrong information from the 1930s, what will people think is true at all or of all fifty years from now also. There is always the thing, like in the remaindering of memory, of writing too much, also that no one wants an old book on a momentary subject, 5¢ among the secretly suddenly available valuable ones someone else discovered next to me. I know all these people will suddenly say how much they love us or you in town and will miss all that even though we don't kiss much on the street. There is always a new chance to die away among a new way of speaking, maybe the nursery school will teach elocution. The basil plants the best luxury are thriving while the others seem to need more room as if an herb were naturally small, like a word. I put the fragrant mint in Charlotte's package because I knew I could rest. It's great though to get to watch the leaves unfold, though you know you're already hungry, in seasons that are not still spring, I think that's the main pleasure. And they do it fast, it's not like houseplants, I wonder if we'll have sun in the upcoming rooms and sights for Sophia's meditation practice, and for study. I know there is a field and I could see that the snow would be up to the window in a day: the swells of time are just men and they need them. Oh god if you can imagine all the terrific machinery that still exists while we just leave ourselves alone writing poetry it's no wonder the faulted alloy falls on handwritten sheets of paper anyway. As if there could be such a thing as ceasing like a tentative quickening turning everything into fear. I've got to take Marie to see Jonas this weekend and we'll send the security too.

Niagaraphobia

EVERYTHING ALWAYS CHANGES in this way that has to do with saying I used to have to type out copies of poems and other things all the time, to make corrections, and now I never seem to have a reason to need clean copies but we will be able to earn some money anyway, this time by teaching about it. Perhaps it was because it was summer. I had dreams caused by speaking and caused by eating, it was easy, this welter of affairs. Marie was packing fish in cans with pieces of fat added in like a Vietnamese person, a transplanted person, I guess I had thought I was like a refugee and, like our trip to Concord, we left on a reading tour to Harlemville where the famous anthroposophic doctor is, the one I'd like to see. There were no cars on the road, only people, and Bob C. was the entrepreneur who paid us thirty-five cents less than we were due, for his trouble he said. And it seemed like a lot of money anyway, it always does, and then it turned out Sophia who's 1½ was a poet too and she showed up with her poems under her arm but she was still acting like a baby and had to be contained in my arms. And then Lewis became gay, and then Grace did too, then I did too, we were all gay like some phone ringing and then I was watching the women and what they were doing and it was all passed off as being rehearsals for a movie or play but when the women would play with each other they were excited in a real way, and for rehearsals it was going a little slow because of that; I can't remember why or how he became gay because his parents were here and I couldn't write it down or speak of it before I forgot. I mean I couldn't have said, hey why was it I had a dream you became gay and who was it with you, while we were eating dinner at the Red Lion Inn which cost seventy dollars, I had duck and so did she; he had steak and so did he. That couldn't have been it, could it, like a man whistling out the window at night? Or a woman who lives here who's gay who jogs and has a big dog but she is not at all gay. I'm sorry, he was sorry he said fucking when the electric window of the formidable car closed on his hand and his parents heard him. We try to get away with as much as we can, in fact it seems rather passive of us, why not curse till the dawn. Then there was the scene of the poet we picked up at the bus station. I looked at him, he was a little bit mean, he had a blue face, then he insulted women. I asked him if his face must be blue like that. We had this strange white apartment and a big baby carriage I got into when they began insulting women. The poet turned around, he was hideous, his hair was like a mountain and all caught up in steel stiletto curlers to make him look like Tutankhamen, he was mean and there were others like him and we were devoted to him and to them. Who would push the carriage? I can barely do my own work much less read other people's. We had to swim in such a typical flooded backyard, like a resolution, I saw an image of a girl, one of the regular refugees, she was swimming after it and then drowned, there was no way I could not do the same thing, but I was only falling asleep in water over my head, like no love lost. Then there were the long walks through the city, again alone, taxicabs, the whole thing, meeting you, you taking my arm and saying nothing, we never spoke, we couldn't even say what was needed, we left out the most important part together, I thought a lot about it, I said nothing, I was never able to speak then at all, you led me back up to this huge house, a loft or something, one woman mentioned what her job was, to annihilate something, other men doled out the beer in a fair way, you got lost, she said she was me and then she took it back, to prove it she had recited a line from a poem, we remembered everything, we worked fast as if we were younger, we couldn't speak then, I knew I had to pick up the white car, it was the old car, but when I saw it it was the wrong you that was there, was it a you I was wishing for or just a man I remembered or one I was supposed to remember, out of an obsession, a speaking to friends, like a love or hope for that tree to observe for a while, to be given back to me to write about, to need to breakfast absolutely, possibly the way we used to, why not except that it is too confusing, but the tree is not, never is, would not be, couldn't be, is rooted, doesn't move, like we might wind up wishing we didn't either, we couldn't we had no feet, just that kind of trunk, instead of the rented truck, two feet so stuck in one place, that resilience in the wind, not to run away from thunder storms, to be cracked in two if need be, or uprooted, sawed and chopped and carried away if threatening, sprouts easily and the afternoon of nothing, with that grace. Well the old tree or trees don't think much about death and they were here, it's all jokes about coffins and cemeteries and all the serious stuff is about having the best; they will often say about someone, praising him or her, in relation to an attitude to a child, well she only wants the very best for him, or for her. Still it's a sweet secret what their primed minds think in those bodies, they smell good and clean and never do what's dangerous, what we do, then they don't love me. Then we must be like them, we almost are them and when we are full of fear and unable to do all these things and no one praises us because we are lost we will be the same as they are and we will go slowly and ask to be driven because we've asked for it. You just love them anyway, everyone has a watch, they cannot say I love you you are wonderful, well who can. It is only that it will be I will say you can have whatever you want but secretly I'll mean you can't because I have a secret desire I won't speak about and just as it's unfashionable, it's not kosher, to wear bright clothing like the natives and have it be red and pink and yellow all at once just for pleasure so it's not allowed to say I want this or that or even you. Because it's safer to please everybody and then make them feel bad, I wish I were better at what David used to do. He could make everyone love him for expressing the instincts of a baby, yet it was a grown-up because he could say oh that is just boring or stupid and we want this. But who cares, and they are dull and we only work and do something else and look funny and so there are judgments. Now I've gotta call Grace. I must admit I can never get it through my head when the cheapest time to call is. I mean I do work at this the way my father worked at desks, to kill either himself or the piano. Yet I didn't know him well enough to tell and I have to survive longer than he did to prove as much to my kids because this time I'm on the complicated end. It's my job or it isn't my job but my mother died younger than he did without doing anything to prove it, I mean you could have said it was his fault but never hers, she just died, she didn't even smoke though she refused to learn to love him. That's my indictment, which one I am, it's probably wrong, and can you believe these local fireworks just went off because I'd guess historically they played the 1812 Overture locally and that will never happen again when I'm in the environment. Maybe there are things that will never happen again, but how come people die anyway so suddenly, I know it I have proof, remember the causes of God like the telephone—it would be good to receive with your phone bill Aquinas's list—parents think and act the part, so important, so unimportant, still as the blue steel stiletto you drew, I saw you, it was an act defending me, sexist remember, it was silly, swimming anachronistically in the observed pool, the smell of that same food cooking cooked by the lesbian wholesale entrepreneur, won't she ever learn not to mix the smells of the baklava with the spinach pies, I can taste it in my mouth like a permanent wave, she must be stupid or have no room. She's the one who went to Mrs. Hall's school around here, ah if only she knew my theories. I might call you at one moment and you will not be home, well why should you be, it's Friday night, and I only love you and am afraid, even though I know you are all screwed up by the illnesses of your mother and father, just like so many people lately, that you will still want to come at the last minute and I'll have to say you can't, even though I want you to. We never walked down the street not speaking. Now I haven't talked breathlessly to you defending love lately. Will you let me let you do whatever you love to do. I have it secretly in mind, many to women, especially to you. You are a changing observation and it's silly, that even as the cars go by the fireworks are still going off as if they all left early to be sure of getting out. Please send me some more works to hang on so many walls otherwise we may just fall. This love and that shrill whistle, though they may be too purposive or even prudish or too much something, signifying as if it were rosebuds turned in all directions on the design of a lampshade Nancy got for us, with buds and leaves too, still will be a pattern like that design I can trace, still will hope to be us, accustomed to be told we'll be shot on that day or this, because we have so many other things to do on the other days and nothing was perfect though we know what that is, it's as if confessional, and better than this, an impression. I'm done, I wouldn't miss it for the world, I'm practically a policeman or policewoman, it's true I think the trees might laughingly fall each day as the same joke that might mean we die or that they might suddenly speak, and say what they want, revolve upside down into revolution, love then they talk freely though they're old about the beauty of writing books, too many lovely books without rancor, irony, prose, a book like an abacus, these ignored fireworks, for traffic, sweet stars, can't see, love too much used turning over on me, of the sonnets or some other book, how come there are so many of them, does that mean we have to die too.

Anacolutha

THE DAY IS DIFFERENT and each day slows it down, I'm not that old yet, babies in the chairs. There was a spent grace in what you offered but the only thing was you didn't know I would use it over and over again without ever buying another one, a new one, I just liked yours or the light on it, I thought it looked good that way. There have been millions of men and women living and not studying, not even noticing what kind of light it is. Cotton, silk, wool, denim, argumentative socks. Didn't somebody say something to the effect that I forget, am I losing my mind again? I met them and he and she never think they are losing their minds at all but they totter in public, stand stiffly, do not give way enough, I hope they don't fall down. They're old, are you my friend, they say. Just in case I'm not great, I'd say if I were they, I won't be great, it's the risk. Don't get me wrong, I don't fault them, Kerouac or Hemingway. Who are the great American women novelists, I don't even have a saint here, there's no field, Willa Cather. The old film got stored, we couldn't afford to develop it, there's a chance you can keep it in the refrigerator in film cans, it's o.k. for months like wheat germ, libel, practicality, a plot, as long as you remember what you said. Did you promise to eat it? Is it raining, it's raining, it's been raining all day, for days, the rain makes it cool, it smells good, it's not so cold that any of us can't get her head wet, you might lean out from under the tent, children do, to catch drops on your hair. People frown when children make noise and look at them as if the rest or roast were silent but when Sophia crawled between the people's legs, trying to buy records, they were just stunned. Then Marie crawled too because that's what she does but she's too big, beauty is only skin deep. It was something about a flat tire on the Volkswagen and favorite black clothing like working suits. The serviceable jacket cost more than a hundred dollars, the classes will begin in 3 ½ weeks, what shall I say? I feel exempt and also as if you could draw me, nobody'll ever see it, like pleasure, I do it whenever I can. Do you think someone, like the quest for possessions, notices us. Maybe they will begin to in this new town because we have this funny hair but it isn't particularly curly, wrists, even with watches maybe, veins, feet with soles still on, children even if they are something you have, more of them, eyes, black leather jackets, yellow jackets, the page I turned to had, on both sides of it, an odd red tape that had assumed the words themselves onto its transparency so that, when you ripped it off, you were left with a torn red empty page and a beautiful diaphanous tape which said: by the and in the one hand and its noun of phrase in a lie! How dread difficulty investiture like quite a sufficient, a no different, another raid of coming times, to die fighting for measure which with military text order to make Westminster respect no Westminster finding place in more telegraph. Will not do; we the sacrificing sly an unfair verb supplied tense, did, but have (make). Un-man and so.... And then on the other side the mysterious tape said: Ability to hand only use it older experimental against is inequality and his judgment at grows older, none at all, although worshipers at many pass'd be right in like is a man who speaks an incarnate blue merit of the book problem with and with a disco decessor. Time has an opinion which tell you are all creation, on the other man' man's or the following is a natural debt is a confusion e'en...and, and acorn's choice Russia has, Times. Ed to choose bend or the expansion have in that sub which abolishes minister Gazette. Question lies be sense that does...But nobody cares; who, in Europe, at least, would forego the delights of kissing (which the Japanese by-the-by consider a disgusting habit)—without embraces—and all those other endearments which are supposed to dignify the progress of true love! But when I dreamt I was visiting your commune, where the one woman said, "A man, young lady! lady, such a man as all the world—why, he's a man of wax!" and no one was kissing anyway but there was a song on and since it was a dream I can't remember if it said, do do do what you did did done last night, or else it was, do what you did when you did what you done last night, I think that was by this guy named Thurston Harris from a song called do what you did when you did what you done last night, pretty baby, or pretty one, I think the flip side was I'm asking forgiveness, oh there's that fucking whistle again just like perfection. 22 feet is an awfully big truck, that's almost four people. Anyway your commune was, uh, a little dreary, it was just this place where people including me I think were fighting over the sizes of the cans of beer they were getting and sharing and we hadn't brought any extra because, uh, when I met you on the way there after my surprising journey through the New York City streets looking for my so-called car only to find out I was living in the wrong decade with myself, you, uh, couldn't say anything at all, you couldn't talk so we just walked, maybe the way we used to, I don't know, actually I used to even refuse to take your hand because I didn't want to be seen, I thought it would look like you were leading me around like a girl because I couldn't imagine our being just friends because of the differences in our sizes and also you had implied you had all these girlfriends, why would a lesbian want to become a midwife, unless it was a form of desire, like our silence which we didn't know enough about, at least I didn't, in fact I still don't. I was afraid you'd make fun of what I said. If you're not home at nine you're not going to be home at 11 are you? Come back around 3 and there'll be nobody here then, I must've answered the bell because I thought it would be you, that was about 13 years ago so you were thirty, does that make sense? When I saw that other poet with the stiletto head and steel mind I didn't undertake to believe any of us were supposed to have the kind of father the third man, possibly the man with the blue face, implied later was a trait he would most admire, when actually everybody thought he was queer, at least part of the time. There weren't any women around except Diane diPrima whom I didn't have the nerve to go up to, and later another whom I took for rich and thus to have no feelings then. I mostly saw Rosemary who was on speed and my old girlfriends each of whom was very mixed up or accidental, or the girls from New Rochelle who thought I'd gone crazy, I remember this girl I picked up, along with a group of people from the Cafe Figaro who needed a place to stay, they all slept over and then the girl turned out to have communicated syphilis to one or two of the other men, and the man Michael I liked from that group of people who came back another night later and swore he heard voices coming to get him through the open dark window of the piano of my room, all he wanted was a piano, and the sailor from the ship who was a cook, it was fun letting him off at his dock somewhere near the middle of nowhere on the West Side Highway in my car, it was Rosemary's car, she used to dance a lot with the men at Stanley's or the Annex and when she took me with her we all drank port wine on ice with lemon and the men never let you go they held you so tight and they always had erections while we danced, John used to persist in playing this hideous Bob Dylan tune on the jukebox every time we went to the Annex, the one that says she's an artist and she don't look back, what a hateful tune, one night I saw him on the street when I was living at Frances's near MacDougal St. and he beckoned to me in the most peculiar way, sort of like Vito hiding in the dark like an animal. On Grand St. there was the guy with all the braids, a Rastaman who would lie in wait for you and not let you get in the door till he caressed you with all kinds of threats and you couldn't unlock the downstairs door because there was nobody around so you had to talk to him and tell him you couldn't give him dinner and a fuck as he put it, on York Avenue the guy actually pushed his way into the house, he had a cashmere coat on so nobody would suspect him of something and I slammed the door on his fingers because I got scared, then I felt I had hurt him but I got the door closed after that, Ed, who I wasn't sure was there, was in the bathtub and thought my screaming was a joke, and somebody I wish I could imagine had stolen the five dollar gold pieces I still had from my mother who told me she saved them from some great gold collection and her diamond ring and took everything apart and took my uncle's perfect though ancient Royal typewriter, and then spit on the floor. It's easy to remember thought and nothing more had happened, I never fell, once a man hit me, once a man was kneeling and I was like a stone, I was fleeing, like the night now each event in words is as laconic, simple, obsessive, grouped, the tiny kitchen, the one window that was smashed when John turned the oven on without lighting it and it exploded, there was a concert with atonal saxophones and we wondered how it would affect the baby no one would harbor, Yoko Ono gave out strips of paper about kissing, we sat on a field of folding chairs, there was a woman such as all the world—why, she's a woman ripped of straw!

Jobless Petty Criminal in 20s

IT WAS THE PERFECT NIGHT for something. John Ensslin was robbing a bank, he got stuck in the vault, couldn't get dinner. Those vaults are pretty nice, like expensive cars. Then I look at myself and saw my self had gone and I was another. Although we were dancing I was dancing with the feet of another person, a baby. Had I forgotten to eat? Had I wasted away again? There was a time like a fat person of intellect writing poems or a bright moth walking under the drawer. The other thing is it's good it's dulled. Because what is this feeling? And if I got sure I could write any sentences, well it wouldn't be bad but—what a woman she was, and that sort of thing. To learn a new form, to use it three times, to be shameless. Like a thoughtless diver, it's a good thing. What will happen in this mix or mess? Sometimes the man or men of the world or situation seem suddenly different or even unaware, I think this has to do with lovingly handling the children, also in this situation which this time is this society they say. The men may bicker with themselves on this one issue because they're forced to feel forced. Then again this isn't everything, but like everything it seems so. You went overboard again they would say, you did too much, that used to be: you thought. Now all of a sudden it's hilarious to be giving birth too much. Nobody faults it as much as thinking. Nobody faults or fathoms both. Because there has been one, or no one. Hey where do you think the Xerox might be in the new place. It might be less than wondering to create a fantasy as a burden to one that might take up even some more of the time, you know how to do that, it's better than watching television. Or dreaming, the abstract insufficient dinners of colors, caught from these fraught moments, with apologies. What it was perfect for was one thing, which, ending, detracted as it must from the whole rest, so that it could no longer be allowed to be perfect. It was timing like a headache or fun, I'll miss this floor. A thing being appropriate, or a good arrangement, is different because it can persist. That may be perfection too, it may have something to do with it, and only that can be becoming it more as an end and in other words it may work. I could say that that I can write this now as a part of this means its form came appropriately to be used now. It's not fair speculating, but then I guess I could change it. I know that real tree could fall or a tornado come, even in New England but still there are so many people in the world now, that's how we know what our chances are. Sometimes the papers are telling us how good all this profusion is, just like and while some men and women are saying it's too long, I can't read it. I even read they said too much writing was being written, and Lady Montagu saying the tales told never intended to be published had the only truth in them. She said too love of war, like Homer's, was forgetfulness. Well it's simple to see the simple truth in something but is someone doing us a service by not writing something, I can't see that. I guess I still have to learn to be good, what they call better, like a ringing phone elsewhere. Nevertheless it is not myself who matters but this diet, duty and exercise that has to do with wiring writing which can then go into the thick of the soccer game, or whatever it is, and we can still hear everything. But not pretentiously either, like special ones, but just as it is. But not so much as it is that no craft or love adheres to it, or even no self. But who acorns, I mean who cares. We saw that acorns last a whole season even if they're scarce, even in my pocketbook. You may be in a lousy mood, and you may not forgive me for saying this, but you also know this, then again I may have made it too simple. Just because I liked the fucking sun today and it's been raining. Sweet hope that I haven't set it up, or you don't, that I still will have to save myself to see, in the sense of believing. Or because it is all too much, too long, too many, too difficult, too structured, too unstructured, to tell the truth, and with this desire. Anyone could do it it's true, but I began to feel bad when I called them all up and they were watching polar bears on television, or what. Well what else is there to do. It was as if I lived here in order to write that poem, now why am I winding up going somewhere else. It's not magic as if the magic could be tomorrow is another 1440 evening, as well. Rose travelled and now she is home, Susan and Larry will travel on Friday, Grace and Harris, Greg and Steve, will travel up here; all of us will travel over there. Harry and Ray travelled home from here, Rosemary did too: Charlotte went back to the colony. We'll be travelling through other strange towns where one, if one were stopped there, wouldn't be used to the life and it would seem strange. Thinking about it you get used to it, like the day ends, we didn't die. I thought I could do all this very fast but it's taking weeks and meanwhile I've got no desires. Nor could I tell anything that happened short of needing to be fixed. I'm married to it, even though we'll never have any rugs, or wake up. Last night I talked to Harry, Ray, Hannah, Susan, Larry, Grace, and Claire. I always think you're fooling me when you say you can't do something. When we move Grace, Harris, Greg, Steve, Clark and some of Mr. Hatch's students will come to help us. Claire hasn't even used a babysitter in months. It's scary to go out at night. I can't find the gold polish for you, I must've thrown it away. Life is too fucked up for words. Homer couldn't have said that, too busy visualizing battles and who was who. A girl may marry a female (invert) and live with her for years without suspecting anything. Phrasing things, also a sort of disease, led me to write you before I had answered, and this timing is frustrating in other ways too, working in the living room, having to have a fight with Marie every night so she'll finally stay in her room, I don't know too much, people running in and out even till nine o'clock, then exhaustion only comes with peace, did you notice how I'm talking backwards. About leaving this place I feel leaving it is too busy, so much more busy than living in it ever was or is, and sorting through all these papers is dull. Also it reminds me how forgetful I am, and do you really lie? You sounded so vulnerable because you said things so transparently, like a letter to everyone. There used to be so much accumulation for the writing of one book, now it gets closer, all the stuff, to the size of the book in the end, what does that mean? Will we do poems about nature the incessant chant toward or against the elements again, this huge house we're going to, three floors of a mind to account for, plus all the other spaces of the house, we're only renting part of it, will we have to account for the psychiatrist's apartment and also the barn and storage space how many amps does the machine draw, and I forgot the two porches and the possible clothesline and cellar. You might say Bob writes a letter more like a speech and Bill refines his to such a degree you are sometimes guessing at it. On the other hand Grace and Peggy can barely put pen to paper with any endurance lately and when the second version of Susan's letter arrived after the first reputed to be ten pages had been stolen by Steven Sandler, it was only an excerpt—two typed pages, which I cannot even answer as she'll be travelling to Europe for two months, they must feel crazy too. The librarian, the one you like, the one you describe as "the fat one I like," turned all of a sudden and said, "Are you due again?" Lady Montagu says the education and what she calls the disposal of four girls is employment for a lifetime, she was telling her daughter not to have any more kids. I forgot to tell you she had dinner with her again and in a way neither of them hardly ever sees anyone lately, except she has people she works with. What would each of them be if she lived in China, outer space. Sherwood Anderson has this peculiar way of leaving out the verb in a fairly long sentence so that the sentence just falls, almost anti-climactically, and you never get used to it. So that his work is full of many statements. But I am reading the book so slowly because I am always falling asleep that I can't get more of an impression of it. I hated that device in the other book of indenting every line of the dialogue, that made it too easy to read. Is it a mistake to write a letter to Dr. Incao? Why are there always psychiatrists around now? I don't know of anyone who likes Lenox except me and in a way Nancy and Clark. Everybody thinks we'll be a lot better off leading a more complicated, expensive, normal life. I shouldn't speak this way because it is like usury. That book by H.D. on Ezra Pound seemed lousy. Harris used to be a teamster, he drove a cement mixer in California. Why don't people tell you things, I don't mean for Harris to tell me that but for you to tell something like that, analogous to my information. You always say you can't think of anything. Claire has trouble being serious too, just like you and Mary, she laughs when she doesn't mean to laugh, then she has to say no I was serious all the time. Sometimes I think that this has something to do with Jonas's anger but then what would be the trait in me that has to do with Marie's. There hasn't been much peace lately and when we put Marie in her room it makes her all the more enraged and it seems all wrong. Then again, like in the writing of one, I can't imagine what else would go in a book. I know it could be a fiction: there's no way of forgetting that but Mary took Jo to the store. When they got there Jo started acting funny and nervous because she suddenly remembered her accident with her foot Mary didn't understand this so she questioned Jo about the recent bank robberies. Then Tillie came in.

"I heard your husband's leaving you and he wants Mark," she said to Mary.

"Oh please, not in front of Jo, she's already freaking out," said Mary to Tillie.

"Don't worry about me, I'm going to go home and read," said Jo, and she left. "Goodbye."

Mary and Tillie now had nothing to do; the only reason Mary had come to the store was to bring Jo and Tillie had just walked in because she saw them. It was a grey day.

"Let's walk to the wildlife sanctuary and back," said Tillie, thinking Mary needed the exercise and then they could have a long talk.

"Oh no, I'd never make it," said Mary, "I'd much rather wait and see if Suzie comes by so I can see how she's doing with her new camera and her new car. Then we could all go to her mother's house while she's not home and have something to eat."

"Of course Sherwood Anderson didn't write novels that way," said Tillie, "he actually made them interesting and many pages could go by of just thoughts and impressions, even descriptions, but his characters still had those kind of novel-like names."

"You mean WINESBURG, OHIO?" said Mary.

"No, of course not, DARK LAUGHTER is much better," said Tillie.

124

"Did you ever read WINESBURG, OHIO?" asked Mary petulantly.

"Actually no," said Tillie defensively, "you see a Japanese boy once gave it to me to read, romantically, and because of something I can't say here about him, I couldn't read it."

That kind of impatience might be difficult to trade for what the rest of us might call a normal life, Mary was thinking as she ripped off her clothing and begged Tillie to make love to her but she didn't and then, remembering how she had always had to trade this perspicacity about feelings for the ability to express anything at all in words, so that some interpreted the possession of the very knowledge that made her naive as slyness, still she could only say, "I love you."

"But why dear," asked Tillie, "I'm a woman and you're married anyway and you know I have a fanatical devotion to Jo who, although she is always saying she needs me to be constantly by her side, keeps running off to be alone. Between the two of you I'd be a total lunatic if it weren't for my husband and family and my love of my work."

"Tillie you are so lucky," said Mary, trying on a new suit of clothes—the jacket fit perfectly but the pants were too tight for her—"even though you forget that no one understands you, each of your problems ceases when the day ends."

Tillie now said she'd give her life to get out of this store and if only Mary would walk her home she would kiss her. But first she had to walk Mary to get something sweet at the grocery and by the time they got there there was someone else coming in, I think it was the beautiful lawyer Mary had decided she could trust to defend her in getting an equitable divorce, which meant, for Mary, dealing with a lot of money and property and of course keeping Mark out of Peter's hands, because although Peter had a lucrative practice he had also joined the Hare Krishnas and meant to live a double life, hiding his wealth from the sect which normally forced people to share or submit it in some way. Even the firewood they chopped and left lying on the road by the nursery school wasn't meant to be picked up by anyone who didn't believe in them, and consequently people were afraid of it. Some even had the theory that the whole reason they had chopped the trees down was because two of their adherents had been killed a while ago by a dead tree hit by lightning which fell on their parked car. The only one I had seen stealing any of the wood was the Director who was distracted because she was leaving the next day. The lawyer at the grocery though, had the reputation for being a little stupid and doing everything wrong, or else twice over. Mary didn't care because she liked well-appointed offices.

"It was not a farce," said Tillie.

"No," said Mary, "I'm afraid it was made of that regretful kind of irony."

"You see, Mary," said Tillie, "you haven't completely lost your intelligence."

"To sleep? To sweets?" Mary queried.

"To the unanswerable dusk of this still life of attempts, this mess of everything we have now," Tillie said.

"It's easy for you to say that," said Mary, "it's routine, like the work of this grocery checker, he doesn't even have to figure out the change anymore."

Mary always got queer on lines and Tillie's response was to cease speaking, lull herself with the looks of faces, and shake a little bit to remember her own liveliness but this made Mary feel she was being made fun of so she wanted to steal something.

"Hold my place in line," said Mary, "I forgot the tomatoes for Peter's brother."

"She'll be right back," Tillie said to the checker, realizing she had to create a diversion, so she knocked over the chewing gum and then while she was bending over to pick them up she bumped into somebody's child in a cart and had to do an about face to apologize and by that time Mary came back but she was white as a sheet.

"No tomatoes," she shouted, "Simon will be furious, what shall I do? I mean they have tomatoes," she smiled at the clerk, "but no imported pear tomatoes with added puree."

"Don't worry Mary," said Tillie, patting Mary's shoulder generously, "it's really fucked up to even care what that cocksucker wants. After all your husband's leaving you so maybe his brother will just go too."

"Do you want the cart to wheel to your car?" the clerk asked because Mary had bought so much, but she said no.

In the aftermath of saying one thing and another, both Mary and Tillie felt they had lost their identities but still they had no car with them and they had to carry the stuff home, but Mary only lived across the street but she had no desire to go there yet and begged Tillie this time to come with her to the park so she could help her carry the groceries home later. So they waited for Will, a mutual friend of theirs, to appear, because it was lunchtime.

"It's impossible not to visualize what you're familiar with when you think of a word," said Mary.

"Also a story has that same disadvantage, as a genre," Tillie added. She was anxious to move around a little bit more than Mary seemed to want.

"If Will comes, let's remind him that when he writes a letter it's wonderful how he ignores everything that might be unpleasant and changes it to pleasant or at least interesting things," Mary suggested.

"But Will will just laugh at us and say how pretty we look today or something like that, even though I know what you mean, but you know how he takes those kinds of things as possible criticisms, because he is so social and he hasn't been writing," said Tillie.

"Oh you are just as obsessive as he is, what will happen if just as he comes, the scarlet tanager shows up too—you see the bind history, sexuality and our times has put us in!" exclaimed Mary. Just then Will came, along with Mr. Mole.

"Oh God! What is he doing with Mr. Mole today?" said Tillie.

"But what was he doing yesterday?" asked Mary.

Will and Mr. Mole caught sight of Mary and Tillie who were the same age or older than Will but both Will and Mr. Mole shouted in unison, "Oh there are the girls!" and neither Tillie nor Mary even noticed it anymore, but Mary did say unconsciously to Will, "Hello boy what's up."

But Mr. Mole was so boring and talked so incessantly about inflation rates, mortgages, investments and taxes that by the time Will got a chance to say to Tillie, "Do you think Mary would like to get married again later after the beautiful lawyer frees her from Peter?" it was time for everyone to either get home, to school, to the hospital, or just on the road, in the case of Mr. Mole, showing off houses to people. Will, it turns out, had not been trying to buy a house though, but finally getting to discuss with Mr. Mole the affair Mr. Mole had had, years past, with Will's aunt who had been Tillie's mother's sister-in-law so that in a way she had also been Tillie's aunt but since she had been so little a part of Tillie's family, not because of the affair but because by that time she was living in Hawaii and had only been married to Tillie's mother's brother for a week because he, a military man, had suddenly died, she had never been thought of as that, Tillie's aunt. But she had gotten pregnant and given birth to this person who was now running for state senator from California but, as many people said, he hadn't a prayer. And it turns out Tillie's "aunt" had just bought a vacation home a few miles outside the town. And not only that but her son's wife was threatening to leave him and come live here too, with her two children, because he, the aspiring senator, was about to be involved in some hideous lawsuit, somehow depending on the outcome of the election, just like that one in England, and the rumor was if he won it it could be suppressed by his being able to offer the complainant a particular job except for the fact that this guy's brother, the main witness, had just disappeared in Europe somewhere so there was the chance it could never be brought off. Mr. Mole of course didn't know anything about all this, but both Will and Tillie did, and naturally Mary did too.

"Mr. Mole studied to be a doctor you know," said Tillie to Mary, as Will and Mr. Mole were leaving the common, "but he never practiced, I mean he actually got his M.D."

"Why?" said Mary, picking up her things.

"I don't know, probably because he wanted to," said Tillie.

"No, I mean why didn't he practice," asked Mary, annoyed at the whole thing.

"Oh, because of some depression, war or idiosyncrasy," said Tillie, "no one knows why, it's the kind of thing he would have done, I mean it was like him, when he was young."

"I read an article in the paper today defending the army as a good place for poets," said Mary, "and another thing, you know since my life has decided to be changing I've been hearing from so many people all of whom have gotten older and so they have changed and they tell me things and I get angry and they are platitudinous and the people I want to hear from, because it's me who's making the change, never seem to call up as if I were changing in the way all the other people are, gee perhaps I am."

"Oh we don't have time for speeches, my love," said Tillie, "let's carry your groceries home in a hurry, half of which, I daresay, you do not need."

"Yes, Till," sang Mary, "I will and we will meet again tomorrow, willy-nilly."

"Yes, tomorrow, on the road to the vegetable stand," Tillie answered.

"And now, to there, till then, with you," Mary.

"Get up then, let's go, yours, Till."

Don't Film

FOUR MORE DAYS in Lenox with nothing much to identify us, Marie cut off her hair and I am not routinely anywhere so I cannot be still and I can't bring myself to get ham, I mean film, there's all this roast beef in the refrigerator because Nancy gave it to us as a going away present, can you still defend me and will you? There's not much more time I can't remember the rest of how to feel the whole of it like nursery school and the Schenectady anchorwoman Sharon Smith. And the sportsperson Liz Bishop. Of course everybody moves before school opens, that's not our phone. It was great having dinner at your house tonight, I too am devoted to my manuscripts and the camera has a ribbon now with the spectrum on it. Pretty soon all the pictures will wind up coming down and Memory will have to be wrapped in plastic. It seems like too large a truck to have to have. And by the time I let you know where I am it will be naive to be further away. But tomorrow I won't have a chance to think like, naively, what's under the couches. We can joke how to phrase things but what do you think I shall say? It was a pleasure to talk to and look at your daughter and to see her as being yours and yours. I hope the other daughters will be just as enamored of basketball, a saxophone, loafing in a chair, being lithe, baking the yellow cake. It's amazing, after contemplating so much soft skin, of course we do look old and the way we look at each other is also denser. And, how little the two plants resemble each other, not as an image or analogy, except for amazement, the one that has enough soil and the expansive leaves have that same pleasure in them. To eat with someone. I was telling Summer, as much as I could, how the expansive leaves, no, how once you have babies your way of looking at men changes in the sense of survival seeming less desperate but men don't change, the secret sex poems. Now since everything's been done and that's been learned—but that man is suffering and feeling old because he is to some extent forbidden to work. No luck for the moment, like a swimmer. It isn't like talking, it's not the same thing as talking, talking isn't as good though maybe it serves like the summer sun. Do you have to pay your bills before you leave? She was sort of saying men were almost only good for sex, as if to be kept like the old days and no man ever had, I can't go on, as if one ought to refuse to teach because of it coming out of stubbornly being a poet like that guy who admires John Ashbery so much, as if he never lived before, and he says he doesn't need the outside world either. We spend too much time with all these guys, they have no curls. Less to carry. Not only that this or that way of speaking or writing isn't based on reason or even the sublime but on the curling abstractions that have to do with our time, and this right to be absurd or his to be flippant though generous, and his to be completely occluded—it's all a form of torture! Is it not? Wife and mother are general relations hideous Hegel said, individualized desire renders her ethic impure. I only said that so I could throw away the paper it was written on. I'm sorry, that is true. It all fades away more slowly, suddenly choking on the salt water. It would be nice, there's no reason not to have to. Still as the waters that still still speak, like that lake we passed, in winter, imagine. Stilled by being frozen but you're not sure it's safe to walk on. Or living past eighty, it's too fast. I wonder if it's blacker, it's emptier, the town is like a torch and we'll sit on mattresses on the floor, we'll be beatniks again, professional lovers of, I have no thoughts. Dear Dr. Incao, Enclosed is dash. I'm sorry it's taken us so absurdly long to finish paying our bill but I didn't forget about it. We are moving and this fall will be teaching writing at a college in New Hampshire. (Is it worth while to do that?). Also we're going to have another baby due in January. I was wondering if you could send me prescriptions to order Calcon I and II and

131

the Gentian Anaemodoron from Weleda, so that I could take them during my pregnancy. When I begin to receive my salary, I will pay the rest of the bill. Meanwhile, if it is possible, please send the prescriptions to my new address. If you can recommend any anthroposophically-oriented doctors in the neighborhood of Concord, N.H. for our family, all of whom are well, please do. Thanks. Yours sincerely, and my best to Betty Peckham. Is it too old? The gnats and wasps are flying all around. In two or three weeks it will be cooler. Tonight in the park the sun was already going down. Susan said the trees were getting older and shutting out the view of the mountains but Celia thought it would be wrong to cut them down, she said it would hurt especially the smaller trees. We're still packing, still maintaining our equanimity as the house is beginning to look sad. Never to take a book from the library again! There's nothing interesting about taking down the pictures, it's a chore. Giving birth to babies is a chore, maybe fraught with more interest than this, yes. Time flies of the man is wine. We have to get a present for Mable, we didn't look for boxes today from the Lemon Tree, we won't have to live in a place that says Shear Design over the door anymore. When I water the plant the leaves spring up or stick out once again, big leaves, broad ones, cornflower plant. Their house was so green around it, lush, but they don't like it. We're sharing a suitcase for our unpublished manuscripts, why bother? He said he never could paint in that house, Paul showed us a letter from him where he says he's sold some paintings to an oil company. Summer never shows up when she says she might. Actually I guess it's safer to put a six-year-old on a plane than on something else. A plane is like a crib. Thanks for letting me use this book, we're off to the new life in a few days, will keep you posted, what it is or what it is not. Have not prepared any classes yet. Crickets chirping all night, the pond, lots of frogs. Overgrown grass, sort of a hairy monster of a house, old barn to play danger in, basketball hoop, spring water, gas burners and an electric oven, no more loud voices, Main Street or smells of pie and permanents, a lot of people filling up a large space, I'd like to pay this bill. Then I'll have enough children, or habits, not a business, your head is small no it's not. Flat boxes, plant food, drawings and pictures, a truck big enough to live in, swept away by the winds like tape. The blue mirror and the valuable hooks, the shepherd, the farmer doesn't move so often, the apartment, the streets, the field, the house. Still recognized by humans like the design of the hill growing green, cultivated even, like the design of the frame, too grand perhaps for these windows, you can tell it's not a farm, will the house be dark, too distracting for that dotted or Impressionist painting, postcards of it like hotdogs in reserve, in case you expect dinner, dark laughter. Marie found a pillow and says she will use it, to be alone for weeks. The dust rested next to the Eldorado Club where some of the police went when you couldn't sleep. Peggy seemed tired, perhaps it is anger, Susan enjoyed talking to her. How much David always loved her, will I ever recover. If there were another woman, who was myself, who did everything I wished to do or as I would wish, would I imitate her then and then have no fears, would I feel I had to be like her if she were real. These bugs don't know what they are getting themselves into, to lose all structure, all memory, to come out of dying, to be resurrected, to emerge from the tomb, it depends on the times at what age it might strike you and then ten years ago none of us suffered. The doctor was scattered, he couldn't find his papers. I haven't been reading the medical journals well, I don't keep up, but living with other doctors has helped me. I can cull opinions of my own from what they say as if they were my parents and I was still too lithe. There isn't any black and blue checked shirt is there? Will I be able to be in front of a window, seeing that field pile up with snow so we can hardly see out. Snow is intangible, it doesn't exist now. Here, with the remainder of our things, exists what they call a household, a possible one. I know this attitude is against the poem like a crow just sitting there in the lilac bushes, not moving, rustling the leaves, scaring you. It's hot too, you wrapped the wild cucumber in leaves so it wouldn't hurt you so I knew you knew something, how to do that. Once we couldn't bear to. Where are the doors?

Grace Drives a Twenty-Two-Foot Truck

THAT'S OUR TRUCK, we saw it again on the street, everybody around here is money, everyone is moving, it's lonely, there are no faces on the blondes. I finally read some famous poems, I've got to get rid of these dreams. First off it was your mother telling me mothers are different from sisters, like yours. We have to get rid of these dreams and have supper with her so she can enjoy the children or else it's oh do what you want I don't care whatever you say goes it's crazy. I had been in the corner, on the corner at the edge of a religious ceremony about turning, a ritual of turning but I was watching Group Two though I was a part of Group One, Gruppa Seventy-three, and then, rolling rock! I kept turning the wrong way, distinct from my group, it's like heil Hitler yet you jeered at me for scoffing at religion, don't you see it's the same thing. Anyway it was only my dream and it doesn't prove anything, we've just moved. It's beautiful here, hurricanes, rainbows, mountains, lookout towers, heat, cold, minnows, chipmunks, frogs, crickets, outdoors, indoors, big house, psychiatrist landlord, divorces, clotheslines, no washing machine, loneliness, no faces, no Clark, Nancy, Paul, Matthew, Susan, Claire, Mable. Grouchy New Hampers putting up with a whole town of new faces, students, worse than tourists, all old, all young. To create an excessive dependence I pretend I need you so much it's unnatural so that it becomes natural to ask your permission to go to my job, and so on. The auditorium, gymnasium, full of noise, no basketball game, the hoop, gates, the gates, things. Trying out for a movie I can the false surrealism but you let Joey the sailor in for a tryout first, at least you call him, he's not there, he's queer, we'll wait ten minutes to see if he shows up, how interesting it will be to see long lost you. He's trying out for the part of the First Precise Commander, it was as if they knew we were leaving. Spaghetti and beer might be a title for one. Is this the hurricane David that lashed the fierce coast of the Dominican Republic of Francisco Aybar the piano player who had already flown. These window frames are not complex but the shape, a narrow rectangle, small, has charm. It is much like seeing a cow in the woods, lost between trees. The paper ended like a square nail which does not fart, I made another note. He must work hard, he is rather impersonal, is he plagued by something, something having given up or lost it. Is he obsessed, sad, distracted, though it seems to be in hand and there was from it such a big garden, all the vegetables he gave us, it is just we are new, and quite unnecessary, are we disappointing. We finally got rid of it at the neo-Fascist Newport dump, it was so badly broken, an eyesore, an uncomfortable couch, an ass sore. Perhaps I could say that man made me feel like Demeter, it turns out this place is beautiful, the Miss America pageant as they call it is on, perhaps I could show you Sesame Street and we could visit the ocean together in a car. Does no one like children, are they deaf. He is I am sure deaf in one ear. We had had to go to the Claremont Ryder which was called Taylor and as I was falling asleep I saw the name of the place and that was it, I awoke and we swerved in, the giant truck right behind us, tailgating, would we be killed. Greg and Steve made it easy, it was not so much of an achievement for them as for us, that trip was long, stopping, remember the women lunching before Encore Shoe Corporation on only two benches provided them in the sun, working women, does she have a right to paid maternity leave. Parturition, this flying ant, and it is cold. Will it be so cold, what is the field. Mostly it was astonishment of the facile kind at the faded dresses of the past in the window of Hooz's of Concord where someone may shop, may have been shopping, may have shopped. Was it dangling or incorrect like the memory of a similar place, only the dresses there were expensive and there was so much space in between each one, I loved the dresses, certain ones. Certain stores, all stores, objects, so much needed, so full of them, oil heat, the factory and all around here the railroads, elevated down by the river with houses under the unused tracks, charming ones, both things made of wood, old wood. Are there any dangerous outlets still exposed in such cold as this, how did this happen to us. The old hotels, wonderfully dingy with glasses set out as heavy as candlesticks like plastic baseball bats, is it enough yet. The people retired in Florida outrageously ousted by a hurricane named for a Jewish boy, no joke the fear of being blown away or even drowned in butter and ivory. Turn the butter back to cream if you will, there must be an audience for poetry, Walt Whitman and Frank O'Hara and the image of speech this way, just a clear expression but succinctly everywhere, no mixing with the mind for a second, just like a drop, one drop in alcohol, essence of the silver moon to acquaint you with torment, the hair of the dog, the same moon whose total eclipse was overwrought by the storm, the already high tides fed and as they call it lashed. Some of you guys are having fun at a dinner party, there were hurricane parties at the bars, an excuse to drink, to drink even more, to speak French while drunk, to be better at it, to cut through the sublime just as the storm was taking off and when it was cleared away, back to business he said, no it was even more dramatic then, recovering. This is the difference between the nights and the days, we wait for morning, the dream of the test you couldn't apprehend the meaning of, what were all those initials above and below the buttons to press standing for, then you said don't give me away, I'll get in trouble, just like school. She was only a barmaid in a false delicatessen, so perfect to depict what memory is, everything's changed, what am I doing here. For the place I was born to turn up in at all is incoherent now since it has ceased to exist, as if everyone's different and you and I look. It's so cold I brought the plants in, this is rapidly freedom, just what I wanted years ago. But now the age of the day demands circumscription if that's a word, it's not my family home, nothing ancestral, it's gratuitous, it happens to be here, so many other places do and not one single person we could chance to have known already, how huge it seems to become then like this fucking cold, an envelope of twisted plastic on my knees. Some of the bottles wind up in the garbage and others, because nothing is that ordinary and we couldn't bring ourselves to close the windows that had been open since we came here, because we are new, carry deposits in their heaviness, you can apprehend it, so they'll be returned. Still everything is new, everyone called us before we left the old place but no one can call us now when we need it and there was no welcome from the gorgeous parting like a fight, the picture of the park was so old it was beautiful, now it's a paved parking lot by the river, they must use it for college beer parties or something, it looks that way, one piece of trash. Sweetly unimportant as it is to go on forever, I can't defend it, you see I don't think properly, I don't know what's important, losses, and what's not, for our times. If I tell all you will see it as a symptom, it's only because it is so freezing, the air is big, smaller rooms would be warmer. In midwinter it will be all the same, how come you're so famous. Two pairs of stairs, rendered fanciful by the knocking down of walls between them. The great stone earnest cellar with the old wood-burning heater, not in use. Do we all hate snow, I want to be high. Perfection is an action not included in white bread sandwiches wrapped in plastic for the faculty. There were cookies too, I forgot to get you some, I am thoughtless. Will the days watch us like chapters, will it be heading toward another season, is a story from a dream because I must relate it, I feel impelled to and I want my family to both return and advance in time. Warmth as from bodies, machines, wood, fuel, under covers, to sustain us, it said many of these families never saw other people for months amidst the barren land. They never bought flour till later. There is nothing tough about it, it seems just stupid. These dark faces with their stolid certitude, their opinions so frightfully written, their stolen dignity, their waspish cruelty to the new, their misunderstanding of women, their hatred of blatant and finicky freedom, their determination to rule, to feel powerful, to be right, these faces so white. They are not noticing each of us has eyes and the order of things sometimes prevents us from fucking in the snow, what an awful time to have a baby. That glossy woman in her clothes, she looked like that funny actress, I can't remember her name, in a movie called the big something, I can't remember, they were fucking on a tombstone but then when the movie was on t.v. the scene was cut, what was it. My grandfather was right, I should have ale in the winter, now I'm going to catch cold. I hope warmth is allowed. It was by that director who began the football movie, "Paper Lion," what was his name, Alex March, he worked with giant dogs hanging around all the time, then he was fired. The big something. He was mainly a t.v. person. Oh god, I don't want to get sick, what a drag, I better sew up this forbidden cigarette with coat thread and make some tea. It's hard to do anything right, there are always matches lying on the floor. I'll never forget when I said to her I think I've bitten off more than I can chew, or something like that, all she said was well it's only going to get worse. I guess she was jealous. Another she is exuberant, and seems fine, I hope she is dutiful, we are somehow providing her livelihood. Mothers are different from sisters, long walks in the woods, every place is circumscribed because of seeing it, do people think t.v. shows are like friends. It's too blunt and direct, he was a much more airy poet than you ever remember him being, Frank O'Hara, he didn't exactly write about things, ethereal and beyond it all, intelligent for words, words I might see circumscribed like the forest, no boundaries, lost in it, abdicating sense, will I never get back, well one must live in the world, everyone walks in the woods, investigating the edges, to see only trees is magical, no one does, what events can be there, what imaginings, you shave on the porch in order to become another, the willful bearded professors make their wives work hard, it will illuminate them to find us working, soon a studied transience is over, she just made tea anyway so what was all the fuss, you have to be somewhat planted, at least at night, like a rooted tree, always everywhere in one place, and they can do things. "The Big Bounce," Leigh Taylor-Young! No, I don't think so.

138

Pregnancy Mask

HOUSES ARE COLD. Practically wherever you are refrigerators turn on. Have I lost it, would he or she have said that? I don't know what's happening to my face, we just moved in here, but it doesn't seem to get any darker except around the edges in the September sun where it is all too brown. Mystics don't use themselves up, they cease. Some others don't either but the lack of use might be wasted. If it is the only money we can get and it's a little too much, we'll use it up rather than save it. I don't mean mystics are saving, it's not the same as money, where am I? Like a squirrel or other animal I still would like to accumulate piles of free things, leaves, sticks, stones, bones, even yarn. Don't mix the sticks with the leaves because we are signifying something human. This nest however is a mixture and the sentences it implies might learn or tend to be complex, if only the words understood how nothing is ever clear, but once it is, almost like a story. The moon was a mixture of this air of too much notion, it was all too still that night. We thought people were looking in on us through the dark windows, maybe even monsters or adamant bears. Men, I have to make an appointment. Ann Meyers wears a t-shirt under her uniform and the men can't get used to knocking her down and so they mention it. Sometimes it is humorless to say so like counting what's left of all the money, forty-two dollars not counting change, that has to last a week and a half. Whenever we buy some food it disappears right away, unlike Jack Kerouac's food. At least though he lived to be forty-seven. Soon when the men and women see that we are going of our own accord to Contoocook, they'll see that the part of ourselves we can't rest or retire would rather be grateful for the finality of these new surroundings, among the star-crossed memories of Indians, redskins. My skin got too brown, it's from being pregnant, no one will ever be the same again. They're full of all these new-fangled ideas about everything being bad for you, even the forest and the moths, Little Red Riding Hood, the whole fucking deal, even Kerouac had warts on his penis. Walking and using or being used equally, like people. The windows put up inevitably slam shut. The Chinese women said they wouldn't be free till they had washing machines, I'm sure they meant laundromats though and not one in each house like the people have here where it's hard not to think about school, what is it? The students all say they miss their cars, telephones, horses and dogs. It may be fun just to throw words around, perhaps, consequentially though nothing comes of it. I am often bereft that the houses are and must be becoming so cold, no one would dare turn on the heat yet this year when the trees are not nearly even noticeably yellow, but some are red and you can see the ends of the leaves toughening. They are, not ironically but surprisingly, losing their soft crispness at the same time the chlorophyll filtering out will allow the carotene in them, eventually, to turn the leaf absolutely crisp, and then it will fall I think. At least this is what has happened every other year since Demeter swore off her curse. Leaves are as instinctive as grammar, what a boring thing to say. Now there's only twenty-three dollars left. It's just a few blocks to walk independently, do you mind that I string the stuff together this way, without insisting you walk me? Someone said what happened to the love poems and I must admit when someone says something bitter to me I remain embittered for a day or a while, there's nothing for it, we could after all buy kegs of it. I'm just like a student myself, I drink beer, sweet satchels of beer, some of it's bad beer, after all you could tell them to read anything. Sometimes I feel like I'm teaching things so simple as to defy all the knowledge of a college, yet if I were teaching that it would be more mysticism, now you can't confide in him because he is so nervous, like an appointment, I thought this might be an opportunity to do a lot of eating out, there are so many wasps around at this time of year, I mean real ones that may sting you, they're half asleep, numbered by the cold but it's not cold enough to kill them off, I wouldn't miss them, will the crickets get killed off too, along with the pollen and the first subservient trees, the ones along the open spaces, I call them subservient because they are subject to the earliest frosts just as valleys are colder because of their pockets though someone said this about the leaves wasn't so and there's nothing to it, they just dry out. Frequently women are left without pockets, I don't know why, maybe it's because pockets full of stuff would make bulges and you couldn't see the shapes of the women then. It's just as hideous to have no pockets as it is to wear a tight skirt so you can't move your legs around. Sophia was in a swing today for the first time, it was the kind of swing that forces your knees together, you feel like you're in a tight skirt, perhaps with a kerchief on. Students are so fragile, so precipitous, this house is an old log, it exists, it still bothers me to contemplate the barn, unused. The barn is so functional-looking especially from the back with a ramp for the animals to come down, the pastures overgrown and ready for another goat, chickens, a horse, an abdication of the distraction of living here so apparently uselessly, day to day. It's a shelter, you can climb up on one of the biggest rocks and see even more of the mountains. I have no illusions about the local people and their wisdom and when I find myself loving to stare, I know I'm being identified as a tourist, a student, an interloper, a person who could be from anywhere, a dark Indian, one who doesn't fit in, it is not a university. I'll never wind up writing about people in the town here, functionaries, because, I myself have a function. I've never been identifiable before, in New York one is nothing and no one, one is just one, tough or tougher, vulnerable, just walking. In Massachusetts I was an observer, I was a mother and I was also no one. I was known to the people on the eight streets of Lenox as a visual subject whether I disappeared or not. Now I've got to be part of this college, instantly, there's nothing more to it. In this town I would like to be the streetwalker in red, I'd like to find the lowlife, instead I'm a consumer. We saw the Converse All-star factory today near Contoocook across the street from the guy who orders books from us. Contoocook is a rich town like Lenox, full of perfection, I have no impression of anything. I am acting like a person who has lost her lover and I will not look around, or I look without seeing and I have what they call the distinct impression I can never learn to understand this neighborhood. Even the local trees confound me, they don't go fast enough, they are not with me, they won't be slow, they're not lush. The original impression of beauty we had of this place seems dazed as it is and the trees hardly there, not looked at. Odd things happen, someone seems to be building a house in the woods practically next door, there's a clearing full of tractors and backhoes, it looks like a foundation's going up or frozen food lockers, you can't tell what it is but I saw a family playing there last Sunday so maybe it's to be their house. Marie said they were just building a new road. What I pay attention to most is all the insects, myriad kinds, we saw a fantastic yellow black and white caterpillar today eating milkweed leaves, I put it in a jar to show Sophia and snapped off a few more leaves so the thing would be able to continue eating locally and the milky juice covered my hands. Let's dig a hole, let's live in a cave, let's climb the rock again, I'll teach you to drive the car. People notice each other's habits so much that they begin to annoy each other, this is the first time I've been working while you were in bed. Someone might say something like, survival is weirdness. Well Hawthorne complained a lot too and began to hate his mountains but at least the Hawthornes could get fresh milk. Now that we have to go everyplace but the woods by car, we have to rush. There's a dairy the other end of this road we might be able to convince the owners to sell us some milk if they like us, that's the way it is in New Hampshire everybody says, you have to be liked, you can't just be a person. A poet's never going to be liked, no matter how pregnant she is. I want to study geology, it's the best department. Maybe all the moving around both inside and outside the house will amount to something. Nobody knows, I haven't made any phone calls yet. Everything is always closed here but there's a good playground but no kids in it. Let's eat a few million tomatoes together, let's wait and see what the new life brings, closed quiet up here on Craney Hill, let's go into the woods together, c'mon let's hurry let's run out of the woods as fast as we can, there's a wolf, let's see what the atmosphere of the place is like, let's feel the stunned caterpillar we find to look at, it stands out in the landscape, let's observe that big bug who looks like a stick, camouflaged in the sand, I haven't seen one of those in years, let's poke it to see if it jumps, there's a spider who's caught a grasshopper in its web, now they're fighting to-gether, the spider seems to be taunting the caught grasshopper, now the spider's hiding back among the stones of the old foundation, now it comes out again to hit at the hopper, the grasshopper's done for, there's no doubt, should we help it out of the web, you say no. I'm scared of that wasp, it seems so slow-witted in this cold you could step on it easily and then get stung, put your shoes on, there's one of those great yellow but-terflies that look like the sun, everywhere I step grasshoppers leap up at me, they can jump high, let's poke around with a few of them, let's put one in a box like a jumping bean, lookit that black and red spider on the rock, you say it looks like a ladybug but it's not, it can't fly, oh god, there's the hugest brown thing I've ever seen, and it can fly, and its wings are black what is it, close the porch door, don't let any of those things get in there, you put clover on the table, shit there's a bee on me, I'm so scared of the wasps I forgot to be frightened of the bees, that wasp is just walk-ing on my leg, I can't believe it, whaddo I do, there's a wasp and a grass-hopper in the pool, when we take them out they're still functioning, you say you don't even like black ants now, there aren't any red ants here, I bet the grasshoppers eat them or all the spiders, I saw the biggest spider in the world, one of the furry big-bodied kind, there are lots of the spin-dly small-bodied ones around here too, I'm never afraid of them, I saw three wasps in your room this afternoon, two of them were kissing I swear, standing facing each other, then we saw two grasshoppers mount-ing each other remember, what were they doing, when you look at them up close they are so complicated, if it weren't autumn I'd read Fauré, and those black beetles who crawl so slowly, everything's slow at this time of year but they're huge like carrots, if you pull away some of the growth right next to the house you can see millions of them, moths mass at the screens but somehow like the flies or unlike them they can never get in, we even have fruit flies like the city and the rodentiferous chipmunks who have such long fingernails, these guys I'm afraid are our relations, it's not like we live in a valley where we can hear momentous owls hooting, and really the cries of the bluejays are so far off, this mountain or hill is just insectivorous but still and yet blessed with butterflies at least, monarchs come around and also the white ones but only the brown moths and larvae and pupae and cocoons and chrysalises are to be seen everywhere, along with the myriad milkweed pods to feed them, no flowers but a few clovers left, some pretty low-lying evergreens from trees, just sort of being on the ground, the soft ones, invasions of ants our brothers and sisters you suppose, no rabbits but in the books I read to you, we were warned of a pack of local dogs who'd raid the garbage but I don't believe in them, and if it gets colder the deer might come here in the morning, I was dreaming of Matthew and Claire. Sweet insect things that I see here, adore the difference between my face and hands, and picture me as I see you, a thing, a thing moving, in back of the house with one's species' grace surviving, but I need a box to put my clothes in and one for my books, thanks, and because of my size I guess I might live longer than you, seeking out my complicated food and shelter in the cold of this coming winter where you leave the residues of your heirs, they might become components of my sweet or scary dreams, these things but still people are different, you can see it from the way their hands hold their children, in a painting.

The Notch at the Flume of the Gorge

I'D LIKE TO HAVE a dilapidated house in a warm place where I didn't have to pay anything to live and I could walk everywhere and even if the house was small you could do things outside of it, Jack Kerouac was a better spontaneous prosodist than I!, I'm not bop enough. I never think a flume's a flume, I think it's going to be a geyser, something gushing, where is everyone and where's the flume? A rune. A book of runes. You see I'm afraid to say what must be said, I've left it out, the problem with prosody is it's verging on clarity at least in life I was in the middle of doing things I had called chores from the Middle English for a turn or job, a piece of work, and trying to keep Marie in a good mood, it came up, they liked adjectives a lot that's what spruced it up, it came up to go down to the mailbox but the mail wasn't there so we decided to die, to wait halfway on the hillside in the lonely cold country to see what the man looked like, ready to sprint down and scare him with our exuberance for anything written on paper, by now we're here two weeks and we're dying for letters, by now all of Kerouac's books are more or less in print, it's amazing they do exist for us. A good course in American writing study would be Hawthorne, Whitman, Kerouac and Stein, see how much each did for the sentence and the line, what queer attitudes to sex they all had, Hawthorne the stiff-backed fantasizing Puritan who was so cute and had such sensuous lips, who walked and had a neurasthenic wife, two religious daughters and one dutiful son, who said after his third child was born, no we will certainly have no more of that but he didn't say how; Whitman the man autoerotic who was nearly perfect, the wanderer, the fucking mountain; Kerouac the crazed, a retroactive family man who wanted work; and Stein the expatriate lesbian who loved her country and a big fat woman Donald Sutherland the critic said you trembled with sexiness when you shook her hand, another talker, food lover, I wonder what Hawthorne's and Whitman's voices sounded like, you can imagine, family life. I like these guys better than those half-English dolts Joyce and Pound who made such a tight-assed mystery of their love and the horrible head-heart problem, I shouldn't say that, my love is unsettling. I hope I'm like Whitman, exempt. Oh and I forgot William Carlos Williams warning us about all the bastards, he and Hawthorne and Stein had devoted wives, in fact everybody has a female but Whitman so I can think of him as a woman like me, and Emily Dickinson who had it with everything, what is a woman's experiment with memory, tell me. Lately I am suddenly a woman when you are a woman you don't exactly have to be one too much of the time in our time because to be female is corrupt now, I wish I could include Flaubert with the Americans. Corrupt because the classic, no careless past renders us lost to memory's images, so put in our heads, we can't be like that, we can't be like those ones as they would say in Brooklyn Steinese. What was expected now can't be had, the sodden lack of purpose in seeing the days go by, in being an angel in that (fear of prostitution!), watching the wash or something, there's something to it. Dear love of images since I've been a mother I have one image of women I wanted to mention, it's a woman in a house without trees in a sandy lot, a brick house of one story like a spaceship in a wasteland where everything consumed purports to have a purpose but it isn't needed, there is no action and no wonder at the arcane show of distant life where there is awful need, I'm not talking about women in the city though I got this image from the spaces of Brooklyn, it's connected to the walking through vacant streets, streets like Cypress Avenue and Underdonk that led to other wastelands on the skirts of the town, you would walk them and find you were looking at your shoes, flat dull spaces around places that exist everywhere it's flat, going for miles, it doesn't matter, it could be in the country or near Concord, to plant a house down and enter and exit, most have cars and get in them every day to go anywhere; today I saw a woman wearing a housecoat, know what it is, we were driving to a town we'd never seen named Weare, she was walking on the road, it was weary, nothing there, not even a hotdog stand and on the road back we saw the woman still walking, I tried to identify her house among the places we saw, each one with a story for families, for related or non-related people living in the same dwelling, she was carrying the mail, American flags out front of every one, the dullest flag, flag of stimulation full of greed and just wars of a nation in luxury and ease, everything is justified, broken machine, paved widened road in good condition, dilapidated conscience, which house was hers, were her children at school. At first I thought she was barefoot but when we passed her again I saw she had what Marie calls flip-flops on, rubber sandals, she seemed to be walking a long time a long way, she walked with a critical stance like women walk in hospital corridors and she was dressed that way, not the corridors of the fancy mental hospital you were in where everybody was obsessed with the Jesus Christ Superstar album and the patients who had gotten the "right" to wear their own clothes lately looked rich and snappy, but the hospitals of Brooklyn and Astoria where, so completely among women, it seemed to us we'd rather be men who could at least maintain the tension of teasing the nurses with their fragile sexuality but the women all walked in a beaten isolated way, maybe this woman never got home, maybe she didn't want to, maybe she got some bad news or was waiting for it, what age was she. I used to hate thinking of being with women, in hospital, school, prison, the presence of men seemed to enliven, or lift the irreducible sentence from its gloom. Now I don't feel that way. My father died and left a family all women, but who cares about psychology, his return. That's a humorless stance, I did wish to be a man, it was better to be one. Imagine knowing you could not bear children but could conceive them and they were your own still. What fun! I'd go around conceiving them every chance I got. What a confused reason to be fucking if you could find someone to love like a giant child of the gods planted upside down in whom to conceive your child, then she would give birth to it, I can't fathom it, is it yours,

Curse and fight and smoke, this harsh alternating New England country my parents showed me, summers, with love, a poet in the family house, if there was one, its value. What's strange is this, reading to fight the energy of writing to save like in a bank the value of excitement for the baby in the belly, setting oneself straight, wanting to create the illusion of a heath that exists anyway, wanting to wake up in pleasures of the child like the poet who works at writing. To be a mother, and with father their endless intransigent transience, their chores, unless you like making things clean and neat and to eat all the fucking time, becomes shared with poetry the pleasure in the others at their ages as they are human without reason, we don't exactly need people right this second. They continue and in all ways. The anger inherent in mothers and fathers, she said to me the only thing you can do is keep them comfortable and dry, she said I don't like taking care of them, I never did, but they could hear her, she felt she was better than that, was meant for better things, and we heard them say, the woman was saying to the man, she's spitting up on me again, he said well what did you expect when you had another baby and then they went home, it was their second child, and she said to the child don't you ever do that again, how many times do I have to tell you, all focused in rows of the neatness of love, locus of affection like a fucking orchard, cultivated food, then all the parts of the plant come up in one season, sprouts, buds, leaves, fruits, gone to seed, you have to be hated and also hate and shout. Like the smooth uninhabited nature of the moon as it comes and goes, even, for that reason and unlike that, to draw applause every month for its attractive reticence. Children are wrested from nowhere, count the claims from the beginning in order to come in waves and nothing much too quickly, don't mistake me, I'm not putting down the tidal effulgence of a natural night-light, that's why everyone confuses them with immortality, and men and women, at some times, want to shoot them. Or throw them out the window as a fear like the fear of stepping down steps or falling off cliffs and into gorges and flumes, driving as a family (or perhaps not) along the vertiginous edges of everything on roads that should never have been made, please take the children back to the room. I thought I never thought about having children and I was thinking of having children all the while because I knew I could have them if I could, and if we did and if we didn't, our names are gratefully our names, change them for me, almost that's all. She's not a she, she's a he, she doesn't bear children; what I meant was if all began as female. The children were drastic people, soft skin, before I was able to feel like an animal, now there are causes.

The Great Stone Face, The First Frost

THIS MORNING COLD with a big purple cloud over everything we sank
like visitors into cold chairs on the porch of this big house, we have too
much work to do, babies, washing, students, papers, studying, business,
reading, writing and now it's freezing. Just a light one they said that will
cover the living plants with ice, ice which will have to melt in the morn-
ing, it will freeze the clothing hanging on the line, frost the windshield of
the rusty car, shiver our timbers, don't say that. The ice will be nothing,
it isn't ice it's frost, frost on the meadows and the pears still hanging like
rocks on the pear trees, why won't those pears get soft, we baked some
in a tart and they were tart but good free pears, we need a cook. If we
could have three more people living in this house we'd have all the help
we need, babies, food, a secretary or helper. I never really valued inde-
pendence at all like free matches, did I tell you how cheap cigarettes are
in New Hampshire, cigarettes and beer and the well-paved roads, all the
American vices, I wish somebody would write me a script for the state, it
would be interesting to discover new things or forbid them to be inter-
esting as a word or be alarmed; though I'm pregnant I'm daring to drink
a boilermaker like other New Englanders. An esoteric history of the po-
etry of the world, we have so many bills to pay. Marie got shit on her
shoes so we couldn't go out all afternoon, luckily the shoes dried by after
dinner on top of the car so she could put them on again, it was too cold

to be barefoot this time but we ran through the grasses a little in socks but she kept sliding, why don't all of you come live here? You and Ted could have one of the living rooms for a bedroom and Marie and Sophia could sleep together and Edmund and Anselm in the other bedroom upstairs, only thing is they'd have to go to the Henniker school but the school bus comes right by here and there are so many doors, we'd have no trouble. You could share our teaching and we'd each have half the salary and we could get foodstamps, thus we could live easily. Maybe we could even get what they call a fuel allowance, but we'd have to share the car and we couldn't all fit in it together unless the children could float in the back. But you would be bored here and the winter winds would whip our tails; then too I'd have to have a baby and that might cut into our privacy and admittedly the other half of the living room has no walls and you guys wouldn't have any private work spaces unless one of you could work upstairs on the third floor and the other in your bedroom, we could get some fancy Chinese screens to screen each other off and then scream, we probably couldn't agree on what to cook or who would pay for the pork chops that day, Lewis will not eat pork because of his religion. All I'm saying is it would be a lot more fun having you here than not here as I think of you always with love and this is such a big house and there is so much space around it too and Simon, no it was Steve, said you were broke. Greg is a master of the big rigs, he drove our 22-foot truck so fast following behind us we thought we would die. You could get him to drive you too with all your possessions up here to this per-functory gratuitous isolated place but there are no museums or even many other people. I forgot what I was saying about the frost, we can get free xeroxing for our classes it's September 19th, everything's the same. The heat comes out of these funny things all along the bottoms of the walls where they meet the floors with metal slats in them, it's some kind of steam or hot water from oil, it will make our magazines curl. If I ever get a National Endowment grant I'll buy a cheap mobile home in New Orleans where there aren't any colleges. I guess the frost is here, I hav-en't seen it, Lea our babysitter had makeup on tonight and got the star-ring role in "The Hot L Baltimore." Now there's been a noise, maybe it was a mouse come in from the cold, we'd have to get a bigger table, do you think I'm a fool, that was why I never used to speak or speak up, also I didn't like being a woman then. We keep dreaming of our old homes, even Brooklyn and the Bronx, Lewis was dreaming about his Uncle Sammy and that he had gotten a job in Miami and had to leave us, I was dreaming someone said my father, in his job, was superficial, just an introducer of tourists to the culture or something and I got mad, then the new baby was born, I hadn't nursed her yet, and I took her to a room with a coffee urn in it where Marie was living, I didn't like the set-up, Marie was like a student in a college I guess, she has a sink in her bedroom here for some reason like a whore, and in this room... oh forget it, it wasn't that interesting, there are all kinds of grapes growing around here, today I saw a house covered with roses and the people covering them with plastic in preparation for the night. It isn't easy to excerpt ourselves from daring to proportion practically everything even the potatoes which are almost free among the ends of the sane heads of lettuce, I'll never forget you told me once you were eating dinners of lettuce and potatoes, we often eat spinach and spaghetti, or the same colors and families. Bill said I was sly but I don't think that's so. He and I were having a conversation in letters and we were talking about which of the poets were good or bad people, it's a thing Bill likes to talk to a Catholic about. First of all when the students did say they'd never heard of Jack Kerouac I started wondering about it, and when I read to them from "Old Angel Midnight" they said he hadn't a good ear and they couldn't make sense of it and I'd thought I'd read it o.k. When I teach them I sometimes get confused about what they don't already understand, as if they were not children anymore, which they are just past being but they don't like to think about it. They like cars, beer and skiing. Now the house is cold but we will not shiver. They don't know fame or remorse, no matter how little they drink they say they have hangovers, it's their favorite word. They are fresh from their parents, it's an odd thought. Meanwhile the moldy baroque bindings of my Hawthorne books are just as bad as that and I have no remorse. Pregnant I think I should be as unused and immobile as a tree, in order to feel good. Moving around and doing things is so dangerous, so fucking dangerous. We thought when we get paid we would get a lot of English muffins. The absence of love must be like a frantic turn-around, just like for the mice this frost. My pen is old and it is always recuperating, things go too fast, I want to sleep long, every window needs something to hold it up or else they slam down like a shot, sometimes on your fingers. Too bad, I was thinking, I didn't make friends with Diane diPrima when I was pregnant years ago when I used to go idolatrously to her readings but I couldn't speak up. I got an amazing letter from Dash to which I have to reply tactically, it's like an exercise of total intellectuality. THE GOLDEN BOOK OF WORDS got a review just as we were leaving, in *The Berkshire Eagle*, the Pittsfield paper, they said it was "rambunctious." This cold air is flooding my lungs with tactics and I have to reform and drink tea with it, the absolute bottom line of the frost, someone might have said, is this mirror-like reversion to change, tightening up for the culture of winter which has got to be noted like a faction in a game. The whole rest of the landscape will still rest in a pleasure for a while with those famous trees on the edges of roads, the ones we can see, performing their own habitual drying out. These landlocked trees on the Persian-carpet mountains, as Hawthorne would have it, still pick up all the colors. Lewis can see some of them, others he has to guess at like Milton or Buckminster Fuller. When he makes a U-turn, boy sometimes you are nearly on the continental shelf. I covered my eyes and when I opened them it was dark and was it cold. Goodbye.

The Red Paint People

WHEN WE LEFT YOU we got on the wrong road for a while and came close to colliding in a minor way a few times, I had to explain to Lewis again about the so-called blindspots. It was sort of a long meandering time. We almost didn't go to Newburyport because we thought it might be easier to go to this place called Salisbury Beach but then we got on the road and it just kept going, through the quaint and set-up clean town described as historic, past the tiny bay, the water blue today with white boats, over the Plum Island bridge to where suddenly we were driving up onto the sand and we ran from car to where sand met the sky and right there below us was the ocean. Darkest blue with crashing waves, cold wind, waves that scared Marie and Sophia so they wouldn't get close to it, an enormous driftwood, part of an old tree trunk with smoothed-down roots, we were sprayed with salt, we took turns approaching the ocean while one of us played with the children who shuddered and held onto us every time a wave crashed, the waves rushed up to get our feet wet, it was surely the ocean and still the same. There were people and dogs running around against the cold, we hovered as a group in the hot sand underneath the wind, we never lay down but we should have, it would've been warmer. Sophia's pants were wet and she was getting cold, Marie was a little nervous, filling her new yellow pail with real ocean sand and the few white shells, each with a tiny hole in it, to be found. We took some sand and shells and went off to drive up the horrific coast. What we saw after that was all the Coney Islands of New Hampshire, I didn't know they were there, they made our hearts beat too fast, you could hardly ever see the exploited ocean again after that though we were on a road right next to it, traffic jams and hotdog stands, it was weird. At Great Boar's Head we started going west getting lost on little ancillary routes like 101E and the bypass of Exeter, it was endless. Before we had gotten to the worst part of the ocean's human appurtenances we had stopped at a roadside stand, I dared to have clams, our food was done by a depressive person and there was no bathroom to go to. Also we had stopped at the Great Independent Potato Chip Company which was a second-hand store that sold typewriters, old ties and homemade potato chips in waxed bakery bags. The rest of the trip was just getting there, Marie and Sophia were screaming so loud in some game we screamed back at them, then when they stopped screaming they fell asleep suddenly until just after we missed the turn from Concord to go west to Henniker and then we had to go back through the city to find our road but the sun was shining so brightly in our eyes we went through a red light on South Main Street and got stopped by a real prick with black leather jacket, motorcycle and all who couldn't make legal sense of our Massachusetts car, New York license and Henniker residence, I hid my beer, it was the Molson, the Octoberfest you gave me hadn't been bad either, I kept thinking this guy was going to drag us off to jail or something, what a welcome to this location we now seem to be calling home, it was odd to come back here after a trip thinking this is home, home is just the inside of the house not the outside, anyway we got this big ugly pink ticket and then oddly enough we immediately went through another red light, I don't know how, nobody saw us. Concord on Sundays is flat, too bright and empty, there is nothing familiar or cute about it, we had gotten stopped right by the ancient dress shop called Hooz's, they've got dresses in the window that must've been there thirty years, it reminds me of my mother and Ridgewood. Then we began to see the mountains again, on the right road, and we felt better. When we got here we came down Flanders Road and sort of cruised over to the mailbox like we always do so we don't have to get out of the car to take out the mail and this time we almost crashed right into a something coming up over the little hill. When we got up the driveway intact our landlord was cavorting with his girlfriend whom I've begun to think must be the same person as the wife he is divorcing because these two women, if they are two, have the same name. This one, the one we see, has the worst shrill voice you ever heard and we told them we had been to see the ocean and they said it had been a hot day. Now that the crickets have gone away the birds are more in evidence and after we ate all the wonderful pasta with pesto you gave us and the kids had fought over the ladybug a little we sat outside the front door which is the door that faces away from the landlord's part of the house and watched Marie and Sophia jump off a snow fence under the maple tree in front of the big view of all the mountains that look like the ocean in the dark. I made a girl-scout campfire of broken sticks and we talked about this place and your house in Boston. Then Sophia had a tantrum because I wouldn't let her sit on my belly so we tried to go for a walk in one of the further fields but the kids didn't want to walk they wanted to climb fences and tiptoe over old boards lying in the grass they call them bridges. By this time we were behind the barn and I noticed a tree that had real red apples on it but when I looked close they were rotten and hard. We came in and Marie had a tantrum because she wanted to drink a moldy cup of tea, they were dancing to Elvis Costello and even though we had forgotten to feed the fish before we left which we remembered on the road they were still o.k. so we realized the children had to go to bed. Sophia wanted one last apple but she was distracted by a truck. We had also eaten the Brussels sprouts from Wilson's Farm. Lewis took a bath to soothe his leg, do you think it will get fatter and swollen? We read all the mail which was letters from Dash about his book and from Alice and some from some Massachusetts friends you don't know, Meg and Matthew, and a hundred dollars from Harry and Ray for Rosh Hashanah and a MasterCharge bill. I took a bath and read the news, scanned a book on the White Mountains which kept using words like lucubrations and meditated on all the possible ways of giving birth to babies and the nature of that activity. It's like heating the house in the sense that now that we're here it just has to happen. Then I picked up Colby's history of the New Hampshire Indians and it said in there that 10,000 years ago this state was covered with ice and shortly after that you could look around at all these mountains and they would just be sand and gravel with no greenery but the Indians came and found a lot of salmon to eat so they stuck by the river and where we saw the ocean today was where the Merrimack runs into it and we crossed the bridge under which that happens. Then it was tundra and birches and later the pine trees and then all the rest. About 8,000 years ago there were these people living here who made tools out of something called jasper, a very hard stone they found in a cave, and they covered everything they made and the inside of their graves with red ochre powder, they are called the Red Paint People. I thought to write and tell you some of everything, it's cold here tonight and the windows slam down like salmon down the river. It's still pretty green but the milkweeds look different. Last week we found a broken chrysalis and the broken seams were filled with gold, the rest was turquoise. Thanks for that visit, I'm so glad we came, could you send me my boots, I think I left them lying in the kitchen, I had brought my sneakers along so I'd be able to walk in the sand, much love.

The Vanity of Mount Hunger

WE HAVE MOUNT HUNGER and Mount Misery here, we have enough money for once but not enough time, there's too much happening and at the same time too little, if we buy paper for the magazine we see we can't pay our bills but we have plenty to eat. Some families are just nervous like epochal letters, the Howes are a nervous family, I met Susan and now I've met Fanny, their mother is a famous woman who ran the Abbey Theater in Dublin and she married a lawyer from an old American family, can you imagine coming from a family like that like a movie. We're a nervous family too though it's more anomalous to have emerged from the saintly stodgy Germans with nothing to do with that, no tragedy or drama like the Irish and little fragility among our nerves. Sometimes it seems our nerves are not continuous like the nerves of others but simply either absent or deadly as if there were, always possibly available, a state of perfection we could have, do you know what I mean? How come you aren't writing, I mean letters. In the midst of all change it makes me feel disconnected to you, is it the result of so much isolation this summer or are you just starting the cold weather's work, I feel kind of staid tonight. And fat, I can feel the baby moving, we've been eating a lot, a lot of fish, isn't that what rich people eat. The kind of time I need I haven't had yet here, it's a kind of absent time, probably what you've been having, where I can do something or nothing but without having to think the way you think when you have to do something else next. I like having nothing I have to do, that's why I liked Lenox, I tried to explain to my class today how the word "Henniker" sounds and it turns out there's a Dutch word "henneken" and it means the kind of noise a horse makes when it's whinnying and also the laughing of a silly girl. Marie says Sophia's new name is Sophia Fifi Sunflower and she calls herself Marie Ray Fifi Sunbeam. Those two have a secret language and when one of them says a certain word, like "tedemone," then the other one has to say, "Don't say tedemone! Say Daky-doe!" and that's how the game goes. Sophia can say everything now in imitation (I forgot to mention tedemone is also the name of a game where each of them wraps herself in a baby blanket and they sort of skim about the house as if on ice skates pretending they're kings and shouting "tedemone, tedemone"), she can even say "I'm hungry, I want breakfast, but first a diaper change." Meanwhile, down the road, in a field above a house at the corner of Gulf Road and Flanders Road where they meet with Ramsdell Road which is the road that goes along the river, the Contoocook, a wide river that curves around in circles all over this place and runs right in back of the Main Street of the town of Henniker and many other towns around here with endless dams and bridges existing because of it, covered bridges even, numbered covered bridges, this river is a whole civilization, and at that intersection of roads in that field are three llamas. Marie had been saying for days she was seeing llamas, just the way she used to say she saw monkeys on the windshield of the car when she was a baby, then we saw them too, two big ones, a white one and a brownish one, and one little one. Do you think that living in Henniker will come to mean we'll have drunk llama's milk? And llama cheese, cream and all the rest? Llama curds and whey? A field of llamas, sometimes they run. What geniuses the people who keep them must be, to have known we were moving here. A source of wool, meat and milk, a mammalian animal much like a camel but without any humps. A llama for us or above us, is life really too simple or free, is it a sin to see a llama. I still am smoking Triumphs (llamas). It was Lea whose real name is Leona who turned me on to Triumphs, she's Russell's daughter and when we were in Boston last weekend Russell kept saying he had found some mini-Guinnies, meaning little stouts (little llamas, babies, writing is so much like love) while Bill C. is always saying, do you want another brewsky bernie? Around here in the neighborhood is the Converse All-Star Factory and did you read about Ann Meyers, she didn't make the team but it was inspiring to see her in the uniform. These pants I'm wearing right now which Ray got me at "Lady Madonna" in Pittsfield were not made for a skinny person who has a big baby, you're not supposed to be skinny and get big with child, you're just supposed to become fat all over and so the pants, as the baby grows, are too tight, there's room for me but no room for the baby in them. I remember the woman who sold us them said when you're pregnant you're supposed to look awful and puffy and ugly and wear baggy trousers that make you want to commit suicide because everyone is making fun of you and also you can't dance. Like llamas? The New Hampshire accent isn't an accent but just quick clipped talking in a certain tone of voice, you say a lot of things in a hurry, maybe about the weather or freezing in low sort of growling tones, not bad tones but laconic and succinct and sufficiently slurred to be alarming, and then you stop and be ominously silent as if you know everything. Then you say something really slowly and drag out one particular word, like, "Here's a quahhrrr-ta fer the paper." It's different from New York State's yawning A's which Massachusetts inherited. And they don't call them cheeseburgs here, they leave the "er" on. On our way back from Boston we went to see the ocean at Plum Island and we passed where the Merrimack River runs into the sea, that's the river that runs through Concord and Lowell, Kerouac's river. I'd better stop speaking so much about him, Kerouac, Shakespeare, Bernadette—how pretentious she is. In the biography of Kerouac, this guy who wrote it said he thought Kerouac was crazy for thinking he was such a great writer and talking about it all the time just like they always say Stein was a megalomaniac. However it does seem like they *were* that great, Kerouac loved Proust and did you ever hear that story of his reading *Henry IV* outloud with somebody and then the other person realized he was doing it from memory, remember when I did that once on Demerol with NAKED LUNCH? Oh fuck this. Kerouac died in 1969 while I was living in Great Barrington, I would barely see you then. Of course Hawthorne is up here too and wrote three stories about the White Mountains the foothills of which I am in, one was "The Great Stone Face" about the Old Man of the Mountains, and "The Ambitious Guest" and "The Great Carbuncle," all about that part of the mountains around Franconia where we went when we were kids. The Indians were fishermen here and they used jasper for their tools. Contoocook, Penacook and Suncook are in the local phone book, along with the English Chichesters, Pittsfields and Washingtons, and even a Bow, a Boscawen and a Waterloo. A famous woman photographer lives in Deering and there's a town called Hooksett. Marie has poison ivy but for some reason she never scratches it so it hasn't spread, it exists as these peculiar bumps on her legs and she says her ass itches and would I scratch that for her as she can't get at it with her sleeping suit on. After the last ice age began to diminish in New Hampshire, first the hills were bare, only sand, all brown all winter, then tundra and rushing, the tree-less plains of the arctic regions with birch trees on them, these beautiful birches that are now adjoining the barn in such a perfect adherence to form as we learned about it, then the pines and evergreens which grow here like the myriad of bottles in a bar, then the rest of the deciduous trees, all the varieties but of course mostly the maples which hang over the house with solemnity, brushing against everything. Here the apple trees were planted and the other fruits and grape vines around the barn in such a way as to make you want to weep for necessity, its former or-derliness and the use of everything even in a climate like this one in the overgrown fields we now look around in where someone who never thought we'd move in here all of a sudden in some season, renting half a house from a child psychiatrist, arranged all this. Our culture is more in between the store and the wildness all this has become, and in keeping a car, no horses in the barn, no milk either, old weathering sleighs in the field, old boards to play on, paths between stone walls, a lot of stones to make them with. Were the people who made all this and put it together plagued with as many wasps and bees as we are this year? And crickets, overwhelming us, now beginning to dissipate and make room for the winter birds. Will the field mice and flying squirrels move in? The land-lord, this psychiatrist who's never here, who's reoccupied this place, gets *Playboy*. I can notice the slightest difference in the fever of the room, fever of the field, it notices me. You can sit on the porch which has a screen on top, a sort of ceiling, and look at stars. I wrote this for you, mixing together love that's briefer said and all the rest of everything, views and names and stuff, that's why it has a title.

The Men's Men at Women's Words

WE WENT TO WOMEN'S WORDS in Contoocook but then there
were lots of fights and disagreements and the whole day for a while took
on this pall and it was graying, Dash and he can't seem to be nice to each
other and he acts like a bad baby and then disappears for a while and
when he comes back he says something like what Ray always says, to
make you feel bad, I shouldn't interfere, that sort of thing, I wasn't going
to say anything but and so on, but then I guess I shouldn't interfere, it's
dull, it makes me feel about thirteen and shy or stupid again so that I just
want to go home and be alone and avoid fights and hide, I don't under-
stand why they have to act so much like lovers so now you can't even
celebrate anything but that it's all of a sudden becoming entirely fall,
even all those words seem ordinary, remember the movie "Two Wom-
en." If he's always saying he doesn't want to do anything bad I'd guess
that he does, the landlord wants us to lock all the doors before we go out
and keeps calling to see if anybody's been snooping around as he puts it,
maybe his ex-wife, his fantasy, the one he's divorcing, he makes us won-
der if we're in some danger, like will she blow the place up or shoot us
through the windows. Now we're doing the book, I might be writing
one, we run one off on the machine, I'd better begin to eat lightly. The
exhaustion of the day is like that bell, to know everything. Bill said Dash
wasn't happy, Gordon's book is very bourgeois in a way you never ex-

pect poetry to be as if he forgot to lose something before he sat down to it, to lift off a part of the big head, or maybe it's just too new, like the pill or something dilating the pupils and giving you half an hour of being nice or good like the chemicals of a good child. Jonas used to do that same thing, he'd lift the cover of the angry pot and then look to see and when he saw you watching him, he'd without knowing it grab onto it with the strength of a thousand men even if you never tried to take it away, and later whining about it. Somebody said it must be the food of the twentieth century, one side of beef to every page, you're on call. It's 9 pm, balmy and raining on the brightening leaves, I'm not on my way anywhere and I'm not not happy to not be being there though I wish these guys would straighten out and act like people together so I could be sensibly inspired. It was a real big boring day and I miss Grace. He laughs outloud at his own old words, it makes me mad. Having the new baby will be like a performance just for Marie. Why the fuck do these guys bicker about everything together like old married people. I can't stand it any longer, I think I'll go down to Sal's Townhouse Pizza Parlor and get in a fistfight direct with the blondes just as dumbly as the pickup trucks go by. They talk a lot about how each is becoming or being just like their fathers, I can't see that, so together they can be free to be small mean or shy though they don't try to make money or anything, I'm sure I shouldn't be saying any of this in public but I can't think of anything else to say, women's words. I was just doing something, maybe you could learn to talk better, there's always the threat your mother won't like you, Hannah even called and Lea thought from the sound of it I was talking to my mother, the closest thing I have to a parent though is David who won't hear from me, answer. She sent a childlike letter about western civilization. When they see me on the street they must think it is very odd and flat, the way I felt. The crickets' windows are held up by boards with nails, when you tip over the land it falls with you in it, no poem got written, it was what they call a long haul, you can't get money in the woods, there's no bank there, just a sheltered pond where the air is warmer so it's still summer but for the freezing water, you can't go in. Today I saw everything, the graceful tree, the inside of the woods, those low old reeds and red weeds I dare to remember from before beside the staghorn sumac trees, I didn't photograph your face but all the trees and leaves around you, I'm waiting for that tree to become something. He and you and I and also another one are all so alike in one or two ways, she isn't. I know you wouldn't want to be me at all just gliding on this sea in an open boat assuming nothing awful will happen again and counting, daring to count it all up already before it seems like nothing. These books all around are a temptation but if I read them I won't know nothing. Sometimes you make it seem this way, but I shouldn't say that, you just got here. The camaraderie of the pills is beyond me, besides I'm pregnant. Old friends are different, look at Peggy too. Except it's not the same, how shall I sit on this chair now? How shall I be exactly sure of the end of being pregnant, every woman is frightened, of becoming the other. You could become the child, the other woman, the man, a dead one, you could be transformed, a freak, freak out, become someone different, a totally crazy one, a deaf or mute one or even the mother of a freak, or one's own freakish mother all over again, human, or so much not one's own mother you are crazy too, or just so much a mother you are all lost, or you lose your talent or your beauty completely, finally, that would be a relief, then you would be a tree and at last or even a mountainous season, moment, nothing, space, a place, not a person, you are that now already, you have a being inside you which is not a pebble, stone or monkey... The feeling in the house was dead and there was other work to be done, silly baby. I never did tell about the fair and now I've still to tell about the midwife and how it's raining. To achieve perfection in any way might be better than being dead, maybe I was all wrong about the above, it's just that I couldn't stand the feeling of it, it didn't feel right. We always all called Betty the midwife but it turned out she wasn't one, now this one is one and she is young and full of vitamins and with a back-up doctor and you can page her while she's in her car. She reminds me of Katie Schneeman which is very comforting. I'm only as pregnant as I thought I was though I am always wishing I were more so so as to be closer to the end of it. A lot of women say they prefer being pregnant to afterwards, with the baby being outside, I do not feel that way. I find no relish or what it is in being physically so big and hampered like a covered bridge or gargling with marbles. There are a lot of Hell's Angels who're fatter than I am now, or am going to be, and they have a purpose too. Dash doesn't understand how weird he is and then he tries to make you feel guilty which only makes me feel like an adolescent, I guess I said this before and I could feel more free if only I wasn't supposed to take sides then, too. The thing is he doesn't let you look him in the eye directly, without any meaning. There was something about the rain that connected to all that but I forget what it was, the indulgence of it, it's changing the colors of everything, making the tree bark black. Often people mistake a kind of attention for misanthropy. Now I haven't had much peace in a while and I can't calm down, maybe the winter will take care of that, I'd like to find objects in this new world. I'd like to pile up rocks in a construction, let the rain be like valium, diapason, no something higher. We never even talked about poetry with its sacred scarves, jackets and jewels, its emblems and worn-out paraphernalia, its pejorative near-loving and near-overcoming of everything including funny ways of thinking about other people that make no sense, seem off, lose something like information does. This one last time to have a baby, did I really need to spend part of it at the Deerfield Fair where wizened drawn whites derailed at poisoned food stands all over the place, kids on dangerous rides, the loudest noises in the world, parking lots so endless though in the middle of the woods everyone was running lost Dantesque in them, some joking, some panicking, and the not so inevitable two-headed cow taunted with a stick to act by a fat woman who felt desultory about the animal in general and other freak animals, a horse dwarfed by its own legs, a giant monster with an extra casement, a poor old limping dog, too many toes. They made you pay to see these things in a tent, another fat woman collected all the money while she nursed a big girl. At least there were also, later, the normal animals, all shampooed and groomed to be in contests, clean goats and sheep and a house full of chickens, the drastic merry-go-round, log-splitting, horse-pulling and the rest so serious you had to think you were neither here nor there, I mean a person from Brooklyn though my grandfather slaughtered chickens and as a result would never eat them, shouldn't even look in on all this. Fanny had stayed home baking pies and to be alone, there were twelve children of four families at the gathering after and it was funny to feel you didn't know who they all were. Then we were told and we were not told either this or that, one wonders what, the whole rest of the company might be brewed or imported like a beer, why am I having so many children? To get from here to there, as if you had to store up something to do it. Homeostatic people like the oceans, the gradually changing grounds. The sad looking woman Pontormo painted, silly faces of the babies, babies squeezing out of the bodies of women, big fat bellies over them, giant breasts, three big balls, dark nipples holding birds, the old father knowing everything, everyone is there like at a devotion, I owe you something, babies still being born, you revolve around, you recover, the baby recovers askance at birth in the house of noise, the average ages, intelligences, kinds of love, the food at a feast, consuming food, the end of recuperating from love, you don't have to do this, you could just not do it, you could merely help to deliver the love instead, you could love its being in your charge, too many writers disdain this birth, as if it were history, it is her history not to give birth, it is mine, no one does, fighting writing, exegesis, the rest of sudden movement, the breaking up of the day. They say each thing must be rewritten and you cannot do it only once, it's stopped raining but it's promised it will rain again tomorrow, better and stronger to knock out the fucking leaves. This ace or plant is not planned and with such love, it's an anomaly, the smiles of women in stores with babies. One said I'll have to spank you. It's like being in a box of cigars or sardines, like your father said. Speaking justly of what you need what is determined and what can be said. I have to have a bath and the frantic will, did you have the measles? Just tell me I am doing it well and I will, old force of cures, home deliveries, Dr. Williams and the force behind the rest. Women, this time, fierce love, what exists, hiding. Also is history and I can be like one. Not to have lost a place under everything above and a ground or pavement. Circling around and all the words for things. The things and prose and even poetry. Music and the people in the place, plus the complications and the rant on death.

Gargling with Marbles

I HAD A DREAM I lost the box many things of yours were in, don't laugh at me, I had forgotten I was in the city again and everyone steals everything, now the dream is gone too. I'm ashamed. Every time I start to tell you a dream you change the subject, we don't have any life here, we are a wreck, we don't know anybody, everyone is hostile or indifferent. I know the pioneers never see anybody else for the whole winter but winter isn't here yet. Now it's October, no one writes to us, no one calls, your father's in the hospital, we have nobody to talk to, I don't know any women here, the children have no friends. I can't drive the car, I'm scared of it, I can barely eat my dinner, there are fights, the food makes me sick. The pictures of the fetuses scare me, I pretend I'm not frightened. No poetry comes, the moon is full. This place is awful, I can't see the trees, there's no good bread or milk or cheese. The only liver is pork liver. We have some money for once but we can't get anything good to eat. You don't like it either, we've already circumscribed this world. It is this place everybody wants to leave, every weekend everyone does. Nothing is familiar, I can't see through the trees, the trees are absent, the weather is wistful, the papers are full of horror, I have no strength of mind, I care, isn't anyone thinking of us? I don't mean to make you laugh but my chair also collapsed. I am a fool, I should've noticed it was weakening. I can't even talk, I am breathless. At the poetry contest Allen Ginsberg asked me where I live, I said I live in New York in your room. He said, get outta here. Back on the bus to my house near Troy where Harry is sleeping, I talk to Susan about Clark. I fix the poison sausages and fight invidiously with Harris over his poems, he's made so many corrections we can't read them but when I ask what the words are he gets mad. I throw the poems to the floor, I think the word was *mirabile* or miraculous or mountain. I go to the hotel which is the center of the school and just as the lens flies out of my glasses I break up with my boyfriend, nobody shows me any praise here. That you might be bearing children beaming and hanging, having nothing else to do, assuming you might live forever as I do, I never do, you have to know about religion and how it could harm you but telling you about it assumes I'll live to. There's a rotten old fish in the can. Maybe a man's love has more to do with love and a woman's has more to do with love. House's hours go by, then the baby is born, how many hours was your labor. You say, the real part? Some Indian women and so on, telling all that they did, even alone. If you really want to get me a present see if you can find a cloth to hang in the house, something colorful, or a bread maker which is a big pail with a handle to turn to knead the dough and in which the dough can rise. I wouldn't want much more of this night to occur, you're a Hell's Angel, though your friend says everything is falling apart, innings in any sense, did you miss another game? People don't die that much because they are trying so hard not to, however it's hard to, like a t.v. that is sadism though I never knew it when I saw it. We pay our rent to a man who has a door, he is behind it in the middle of the night. I wonder how it is you wind up doing things the way you do. The family is not sublime, there are chemicals in the beer, books up to the ceiling, yes that is exactly what Agatha Christie was saying. I think to remind you to be William Saroyan without any notes, W.S., Will Shakespeare? I restrung my necklace like Carlton Fisk, my heart like his elbow out of whack, I'm scared to death. Some of the beginnings of poems are so blank as if all the words could be replaced with others, it's not a cold night. The back of the broken chair looks like a book or a door, the seat in an airplane crash. Everybody says everything will take two weeks, I'd prefer to do the driving of my daughter and that the pictures be sent directly to Kodak. They are giving this course in assertiveness training for the women. Lights of car pass behind bended trees, it seems to come up here and it might be the lord. I'm sure there is a chance that the real Lord might walk up through the fields like a deer or monster—in blue and white? In school colors? The fields seem to say so. I'd never thought to be so invaded. Greater winds cut through here on the backs of these seasons. Nobody says anything, nobody has the leisure. I wouldn't want to be that age again, they say, forgetting to stand on their heads. Jack Kerouac did better than that. I want to tell a woman something. I have to feel this bad to walk in the woods. The road is beautiful. I might do paintings. He doesn't use the pain for anything, I need more room, Grace's mother used to build cocoons for the babies before they were born, nests of gauze and netting over cribs, like the womb. Once she didn't like having the baby at home, someplace like Rockaway, she said it was too sandy for a baby. It's not like having an operation on the kitchen table, though you don't even get whiskey. All that air breathed in and out, I wondered if anyone knows about it, what could happen? There are some people who always say something pathological, men more or less stay out of the conversation, maybe they're jealous, I guess not. I'm not working, I'm not having to arrange words, I don't know if you notice, it's more like combing your hair. No one could be expected to lack the same structure I do. It is better to marry than to burn or something like that. It seems like it is either talk shows or the Pope, in what can be read today. I never read books during the day, I'm taking care of children. At night maybe I write and then later I read, or I read the whole night. You could even eat hotdogs if you wanted. There is this funny scene at the health food store in town. You walk in, you pass the boy who looks like a girl sitting on a chair outside, he is very young, about 13. He gives you a mean look, then he follows you in. You ask for something and he snarls, naw we don't have that. Then you look around in wonder at all the junk and leave. At the place in the college where you go to cash checks you get yelled at and treated like a child. No one looks you in the eye, the winds are distracting, or the photographs of women giving birth. No one says you are transparent, the barn is in disuse. Think of the barn, meditate on the pattern of the curtain. Touch up the wallpaper with magic markers. Buy a few old rugs. Tell me where to go. You say you don't know of any good doctors around here. No one is young and no one is dark. When I think of all those blonde people breeding I panic that I am still alive. I'd like to see "Bringing up Baby," or a Ma and Pa Kettle movie right now. No one writes me, people assume religions, we are lost. I am not as smart as Gertrude Stein was, she simply lived and died, she seemed to enjoy the feeling of herself, she drove her Ford. She was rich, she ate truffles, she smoked a woman. She learned everything, she delivered babies but she didn't have one. I wonder what she thought about that. Was she horrified by them? She lived with Alice and that was what it was, no second-hand drama. I am not as smart as Shakespeare was, he did many things, he moved about, conceived children, lost his name somewhere, owned property. I am almost as smart as Dante in this exile or Freud in this bind, but Freud was Freud and thought twice about everything while he dandled the kids for fifteen minutes on his knee or knees. I'm not as smart as Agatha Christie, I won't live to be a hundred though I don't like her writing either but I do like oysters. I don't like the way Saroyan talks about talk shows, as if he is scudding. I can't apprehend this place, why were the men so silent when I asked for birdseed in the farmer's exchange. It was cheap and now the wind blows the old men around, nothing is good for you. I am invisible, we have no mirror, the students sneer at everything, there's no place to publish poems, no one to read them, they're all too long. What will happen when we get into bed tonight? I'm supposed to eat that dark bread and those sweet apricots but there isn't time. It's not a fit subject, don't listen, I wish I could divide myself in half, I miss our rooms, I'm ashamed of all the deaths I've witnessed, and how little I ignore it, each present writer has a past, maybe they love it, some dumb America, those fucking leather shorts the German boys wore, forget it, get rid of it, go to another city, take an airplane, forget about children, it's too something. And then you have to defend that. Take nothing from me. Don't you be a fool, eyes and convergences, the news. The projects of food. Flies on it.

Pear Pie

I KNOW IT SOUNDS HOMELY but the tree wasn't, well it was but it was homely in a striking way, it had been struck by lightning and cemented back together as a stump or a trunk but then branches grew out again sprouting leaves and buds and pears it looks like, and that's where we got the pears from, they were hard as a rock, then I thought maybe these pears are going to be psychedelic and we'll have a psychedelic pie, what if the traditional family of four, plus I'm pregnant, got higher than kites on this pear pie, I thought at first they were quinces, they looked odd, I wanted to get excited about something, even just these green pears which the fear of makes more interesting and if and when they do ripen, as a few have done, they turn more yellowish than green but I cooked them green and we didn't die but we didn't get high either, we just had a pie, with cinnamon, ginger, cloves and an egg yolk, honey and molasses and brown sugar, practically everything we had except for the crab-meat cakes, now what does it sound like? When I was sitting by the split cemented thriving tree with Marie the other day having a picnic with the year's last real tomatoes on sandwiches and beer and cider for her and a cigarette for my pleasure in the tall weeds, we had put our picnic on one of the many boulders embedded in the fields and then I knew I heard the sound of a river or a brook gurgling and flowing, no need to say anything, so we ran across the field, after I saved the other half of the cigarette for later, Marie fearful of the thorns in her flimsy flip-flops which damage her toes, you see there is no way of saying anything without implying something, I wish there was, there used to be but it turned out to be too loaded just like the idea of doing whatever it is you please which works meditatively but not well otherwise and if you are alone, but anyway the river which was a stream was not too far in and I made Marie wait and let me explore beyond her though she was afraid of my going so far she couldn't see me and I got my old feeling back of being world's fastest walker in woods though this extra fifteen pounds I've already got with the new baby was unbalancing me when I ducked under branches, then I took Marie as far in as she was willing to go through the trees and we stood on a cliff like primitives to see two streams converging around a small sand island. There was barbed wire running right through the stream, who would have bothered to put it there, it had fallen down into the water, old boards you could see it used to be attached to, rotting and lying all over. I would like to know what it feels like to be another person, getting hot, it's a hot day, later it will be cooler, do I even know that? To be unassailable, to never have thought about death, to need a dictionary badly. To love a businessman, to love a man who crushed his hand, to love an actor, to love to cook. To be wizened with brown spots on my hands, to watch television, to call your son a cocksucker, to be called by him an old whore. To be discreet and rich, to be invited to dinner parties like Proust, to be white trash, to live in a trailer, to give birth to babies unknowingly. To inherit a fortune, to buy racehorses, to drive off from a famous mansion in a long sportscar with a long scarf tied about one's neck, to die, to be greeted by the servants, to walk the long hallways, to be served the game like in the movies, to be down south, to never be cold, to be in a daze from the heat, to be first mate, a homosexual, to be a half-blind peasant, to be Milton, to be sleeping at the fire without thought, to be a man cruel to women, to be a dog, to be the recuperative pear tree, the resilient tree, to be the fattest person in Henniker, to be the crazy man in Hillsboro, to be the person living furthest off in the woods around here all alone, to be freezing to death, to be going to the opera all the time, to wear a mink coat, to be a judge in ermine or sable, to have a coat of arms, to live in a sandlot house, to be a housewife, to drive to the arid supermarket in the station wagon, to want to have knickknacks, to be a basketball star, to be the most famous person in the world for a while, who was that Elvis Presley? Not to be the pope. The pope who spends his money, wherever he gets it from, perpetrating secrets, big distractions from anachronistic poverty and his own sodomistic wealth. To be a leader of state, never, unless it's a state of being, never to be spoken of. To be a teacher of something, purported to be that, never. To be a father though of a hundred children in a harem, I would have so many wives I'd be thought a genius. The woman you see could never bear all her husbands as many children as the myriad and tempting wives, so no matter how virile and fascinating all the husbands were she was always all caught up in something else and couldn't do it fast enough, even today. Moon's just past full, I hope I can sleep, I dream I never sleep because of the image of my daughter falling into a hole in the ground, it's nothing, you must swell with pride and keep the windows open, count the sciences in books and know we are different, lost like a number. Love is the same and does not keep that name, it's fucking love, somebody said not to say fucking, blasting off in paragraphs that kill wandering, walking, the door swings open, the wind is a man or a woman, the still pictures must be a movie, remember me, this astonished stone, a breaking stream heard from this patched tree, so seriously. And then forget love like a city and become the country's anger as an experiment, a loft, no hallways.

Lighthouse

IT'S COMPLETELY BLANK. It's October 11, it's snowing, a Wednesday. Why are you so incomplete? I dreamed you were my daughter or that a woman had a penis so that I must be becoming you. There's not much more to be said, there isn't even a title. Something you understand might seem less fearful, more deadly. There were some other things like the bright light that seems like a fire near the floor. I'm not used to this place, to its heat and nature. I even thought the doctor was you. What would be a form of perfection becomes something sad or stiff or still or missing. No one would approve of it like chaos, it's funny. Nothing fits, like vanity. How come you never taught him, showed him a few of life's arts? How come you were afraid to eat the raspberries from the branches? There's no mistaking raspberries, natural things are not so dirty, how come you are still so jealous of him as not to praise him. How come both the men and women are so strapped in, like having your third and forbidden baby in the People's Republic of China. If surviving is the main thing, then I guess that must be all, is that what you're thinking? How come it still must feel like being a bad child, not as grownups talk together in the off-limits kitchen—too many babies! Are you too a Maoist? As we get older you are getting even older so there can't be that much time left, can't you hurry? Odd that he knows none of the things you know best, is it an antagonism? To be great is something else, not like any of this. Poetry is always too much so I'm not surprised at your alarm. Still we are not going forward yet, still in sensuous delights, wondering women. Still the pleasure of the day, spent arranging moments with time and things, still the precarious attitudes, the acceptance of everything that is, the denial of both our plain immigrant accents, ones we may have had in common opposites, and you become young again but too young, already being back a little girl. Sweetly you can't sit on the floor or walk downhill, it's all in the handbag or giant pocketbook, contained like his hand, refusing to be offered even as a friend to a stranger, there can be nothing new, it's all too new. You're better at old age than I will ever be, I'll be yelling and shouting and dying, I'll be tearful as a baby, you managed to stop going backwards maybe at age ten, at the age where a girl begins to love herself and can do things, even apprehend the logic beginning in everything. But to be irrational or even crazy like one of your brothers, or even worse like we are, always has this swerving or falling danger, getting giddy, losing it all for once. I've got to be careful what I say, it's a difficult time for you, and because of what's going on I feel a little shaky too, I can't even write any poetry, nothing comes to me just like being borne by another hand. You have no vices or bad habits but that plentitude of fussiness we could talk about within which you refuse to admit to love's vulgarities though like the girl again you seem to be aware of them like everything. Oh you'd better watch it, you'd better have that taken care of is what we hear when we're tearing out the door we can't come in anymore. Everyone does it one way or the other just the ways everyone winds up writing his or her poems who must, you have a love for him and he has informed you yet he's the one who is mistrusting of everything. It's a mystery to me, all this suspicion, I never met it before. It may be a heritage and also New York and a sense of triumph over everything fought and security in money too. We don't have that instinct and we are lost to our pasts of lives on the momentary plains, now tundra, now something else determined by the presence of conifers, other glacial happenings we've seen and you have not. I wish I had spent all that time knowing you so I could've seen what you were doing. Years and years seem to have gone by in your lives that I know nothing about I guess, I often feel much the interloper as one might say, often I wish you would turn to me and say, you look just as you did when you were ten years old today. Whenever my parents are talked about, you say well that's all over, we don't need to think about that anymore. I used to wonder what you meant, did you mean it was unpleasant, and to change the subject fast or do you mean my unnecessary sight of death may in fact be bad luck. Whereas it's you and he who are always reading obituaries, not me. And he even reads the columns of lists to see if there's anyone you might have known in the unfamiliar past of keeping everyone at arm's length who might have died and the odd thing is hardly anyone ever has. I don't fault you this, I am even getting into the habit of doing it myself, reading them I mean, now that I know it's something that can be done. I know you read everything else in *The Times* too so you must also see a picture of things as they're depicted in there, same as we do. Forgive me for drawing so many comparisons between us and trying to find out and mention some of the things both of us do, it's impossible in my case not to. I know you like my ability to speak and be clear or even glib, you think it interesting coming from a person from Brooklyn who was brought up Catholic, I won't mention my being German for which I am sorry and for the coincidence that not only I but your daughter's other husband is a German-Catholic too, and practically from the same neighborhood in Brooklyn! Sometimes I'm surprised you ever gave me the benefit of the doubt, this is something of our times. I wish love with all its overtness were more forthrightly coming around to be by us for us to enjoy anyway since I have a sense of time being brief. My children are good-looking and pretty smart, at least that is something and without them I'm sure we would have a feeble connection. Part of my orphanage might involve my making friends too quickly, even instantly, something pretty foreign to you. Don't forget about him either, he is also involved and so there must be something because you and he are so alike, so contentiously tense, so atavistic in your sense of movement, so manipulative and stubborn too! You and I share to be women in a moment, you can't deny it and if I didn't have so many children perhaps I could better prove it. Children for you to begin a line again like me with maybe. Though you give a sense so strongly of everything ending with you only. Do you do that in a narcissistic way? or is it a denial of the need in this for me? Is a son so much the same as his mother? And is the mother not lost in him? I won't speak of daughters and the fearful poles and the sense so strong as anything that it is you again, and the fighting all about it. There isn't enough time to tell all, nothing answers and now I haveta go to bed again and maybe have some more dreams. I hope you wake rested and feeling good as one who doesn't smoke or drink, I often think, must feel in the morning. Please think of me when the light is out and wonder if I'm feeling the same as you this cold October night of fall, me with my periphrastic name.

Lewis Stapling Books and Watching the Series (Pittsburgh-Baltimore)

IT'S MUCH LIKE THE '50S, people call you a health nut if you eat whole wheat bread and they use the word gross a lot, the men say dick a lot, the women say it figures. We have to go to Concord tomorrow to have Lewis's leg x-rayed and today this cold rain dilapidating what never quite made it to a traditional fall makes me feel like everything is crazy. The UPS man who looks like that famous guy who trains animals in the circus, I can't remember his name, and smokes a big cigar, that's the UPS man who does, a really smelly one, delivered a big package today from the outside world, he'd gone to every house on the road and nobody in any of them or at the college had ever heard of us, what was that guy's name, something like Werner von Braun, that blond Austrian guy who makes love to the lions, he wears a wig too, he leaps on the backs of elephants from a seesaw. This is my William Saroyan imitation. My lip hurts and I feel guilty. It is so dark all day it is practically steaming. Big mists of steaming cold rain rise up from the fields, the thermostat doesn't work and the landlord is so concerned that the well's pump might be on the verge of breaking he walked into our bedroom this morning. The cars look like squashed food. I've really lost the feeling, summer's over and the wet stream is a funny mockery. Everybody's life goes on somewhere else beyond the metal mailbox we can't put our names on, property. This prefabricated house in the field nearby is pitiful to have gone up thinking so much about its two-car garage within a huge stone foundation, then the rest of the top, the roof today, just slapped on there. Harry has something in his lungs they say might be asbestos, from the public school where he was principal for so long, there's radioactive stuff in the smoke alarm. The furnace rumbles but you could walk to town from here, it's not far, maybe two miles, down the road where the cars swerve off onto your side all the time past the llamas and toward the town. But you probably couldn't make it with the children, I'm getting tired of always saying the same things to them. Anger in this extra flesh, what would I feel like if I weren't pregnant. The news about women is dismal, their voting in Japan, the new prostitutes in China, the female doctors who can't find the time to have children because their husbands won't help them, all the disapproval of having both babies and abortions, the expensive sterilizations, all deduced and argued by the vainest males of choice. Don't read the news, fuck it. Evening devotion to art and so on but there's hardly enough of the right kind of time. I need a vacation in an old place from this new place. Struggling along with the peripatetic babies makes me feel willful, and you always act as if everything's so easy, eating caviar at the Russian Tea Room and so on. Then when I see so much stolidity and backwardness in the day, even in the falsest trees to the season, bitter and brown on the black well-kept road between two towns, the stony doctor under the hateful fluorescent lights in the furniture store waiting room with all the blonde but not so pretty women, the harsh receptionist who won't even tell us how to get there, the artesian well-driller who won't tell us who to call to fix the pump, that lion tamer had three names I think, I wish I were you facing the wind alone in an avoidance of dreams on Long Island, without moods. We are critical because we are windows. A few cold moths came rushing in to the light, there aren't any more winter coats, I don't like fixing them, I wonder if we could make friends with the people in the prefabricated field. I remember tweezing my eyebrows and having an image of what they must be like. Actors, acorns and ancillary actresses don't write good prose, like the Black Mountain school. Lea doesn't clean up the dishes she uses anymore. I guess I can't write you tonight. It's Gunther Gabel Williams. "Mayer" means farmer. But maybe it doesn't.

Dear Alive

I THINK IT'S COLUMBUS DAY, you wrote me on Labor Day, aren't we sweet. This life here in the new place is the kind of life where I think I don't have enough time for anything and then all of a sudden I notice I've got too much time on my hands and just can't do anything but then that's probably because I'm six months pregnant now and when I type my foot falls asleep but nothing else seems to happen because I'm pregnant, I mean all the other times being pregnant was all I ever thought about, except maybe I am getting a little incoherent on account of it? Do you realize how many poets there are named Alice? There's Alice Meynell, Alice Walker, Alice (& Phoebe) Cary, another 19th century Alice whose surname I forget now and you, only to be surpassed by the number of anns (if you count annas) and maybe margarets (if you count marguerites). Maybe there are even some male ones named Alice. We've been thinking of naming the baby Alice. Lately I can't remember what I've already told you, and sometimes others. I think it's because I'm living in the country again and there are no people out my windows. I'll try to be more speedy with the next of my parts of our writing. I liked the list of possible poems a lot and found it most inspiring to get going. I took some liberties with the toilet seat, I'm beginning to like the way these parts of the writing look when they're done, all together, very obsessive in a way, maybe I could induce you through writing to have a sympathetic pregnancy. We feel isolated here, it's a few more hours away from everybody and it costs a lot more to get here, no one visits and the worst part is we've got no place to stay anymore in New York because of too many babies. Also it seems like as soon as we moved here people stopped ordering books but we just did a huge mailing of catalogues and we found a great second-hand bookstore up here where there is a copy of ALICE ORDERED ME TO BE MADE (in the "women's poetry" section, next to all the other Alice's) and a MANY HAPPY RETURNS and also a DREAMING AS ONE and many other ones. I got a new dictionary, mine was missing the beginning pages so I couldn't even look up "adamite" which turns out not to be in the new one either—what is it? "Adamsite" was in there, some chemical. I have a student who is spending the month of January visiting Kerouac's grave. People keep telling us all sorts of rumors about the NEA grants but so far from the telling I find it difficult to believe or disbelieve any of them, I hope you guys have gotten some other money meanwhile, we are finding we have enough to eat pretty extravagantly now and somehow we manage to spend every penny we get almost instantly, I don't know how but at least we don't have to think about it for a while. We've started the next magazine and it'll be done in a couple of weeks. It'd be nice to get fired. I think some poems to write effortlessly might be: (1) you like that colon and the one? I can't think of one. You could write about the shapes of your windows, I always like to write about those. (2) sex poems! I keep thinking we haven't written our sex poems yet, I keep secretly entitling a series of them to myself as THE SECRET SEX POEMS, only thing is they couldn't be published in our husbands' lifetimes, whaddayou think? Then again we have husbands, does that prevent us? Every time I have an idea to write one of them I can't tell it. But then you did well with Kotex…(3) No Rheingold beer up here, they never even heard of it. You could write one of those walking and then drinking wine poems like a Chinese one. (4) A poem about Ted, oh that's been done before. (5) You could write one called "Anselm's Knife." I mean "Edmund's Knife." Sophia is still beginning to look a lot like Edmund. Marie can go to the bathroom now too! (6) The people in New Hampshire are generally pretty hostile, it's as if they weren't real people but you can't write about that. We look more out of place here than we did in Massachusetts, there's too many blondes here. But now I still didn't get to any subjects. I finished reading OBITUARIES and I realized it was just like the book I'm writing except I'm not much like William Saroyan am I? (7) I feel awful. (8) Well I'm sure I've left out all the most important parts but I can't think of anymore. I myself have not been writing what you might call millions of poems but just kind of daily working slowly on this book of prose which is divided up into short sections which are becoming less letter-like and more like essays but when I write poems I find I don't like what I'd call my style, it's too wordy, don't laugh, and I can't seem to wind up getting anywhere plus there's something quite mink-coat about teaching which makes it seem as if it's the ideas that matter so then when I'm writing I wind up saying things all the time like, I am me, the stars are on top of me, the ceiling's in between, there's a mountain there and so on. (9) How about one called "Pretty Short Pants." Well, I'll send you some stamps on Friday, Robert Dash subscribed to the magazine, tell Ted we're not putting his poems in this issue because it's the feminist one, no it got too fat because it's so late but we're to do another in December before Max is born. That sounds unusual, Caiow(?) Manhattan.

Days, Stamps, Stamp Pads, Ties, Socks, Note Pads, Magazines, Glass Balls, Shoes, Gloves, Cigarettes, Steaks, Tokens, Buttons, Accountancy, The Amenities, By the Same Token, Alms, The Single State of Blessedness

NOT ARMS, IT COULDN'T BE arms like loving arms though it could be The Something Arms as in and among the thought of a hotel and packing a bad bag really neatly to go there, slides even, the accumulation of slides, color slides, photographic slides you know what I mean, putting them in order, labeling them, having slots in your desk to do so, collecting pads and pencils, unsharpened ones or ones that are unconscionably all sharpened at once, some things many things never used at all, just collected, ties and socks to match and judging which ones will go with which ones, subway tokens you collect in boxes, you can only buy ten at one time so you have to go and buy them many times to get them all together to give them as a present for Christmas to someone who might feel he or she was being made happy by the accumulation of such a gift, just having them, having all of them in one's possession, having a pile of them, by the same token, many tokens, as you used to say so often, it might be better to just jump over the stiles. There was a crooked man who walked a crooked mile who found a crooked sixpence upon a crooked stile, and calendars and all the days passed one past the other lived together all together in the crooked house with all the consistently crooked things in it, remember that? Count the days, pretend you're in prison, it is like a prison, you have to go to the bathroom every day, you have to take a bath on Saturday and wash yourself with a cloth on

Wednesday all over, there has to be order in the drawers, I wish I could see it, you can fold all the laundry or the clothes for packing in a suitcase, isn't it turning out neat, you can't be a heroin addict because that's too sloppy but you might not be able to forget, on the other hand, enough to enable you to function anyway. I don't mean function, move your bowels or something, I mean just to get through the day normally, you've been reminded of everything too often, now you are quite dumb. There is something about the lovely structure of the gloves the leather gloves on the cigarette that appeals to you, and another cigarette, don't forget to buy cigarettes, amass cheap cigarettes in the closet and bottles endless bottles of mouthwash, your favorite kind of mouthwash, on the bathroom floor, it's red I think, Lavoris. Plan to do the same thing today you did last week on this same day and stamp the day with one of the stamps pressed into your stamp pad, the clean inking of it without getting your white hands dirty, send the shirts to the Chinese laundry every Saturday, have a day for washing and a day for ironing and a day for what, buy lots of chewing gum and store it in the cabinet but you can't keep track of it, it gets dirty before it's used, that's annoying, my, must you throw it out, you can't stand living together, you two men alone but you can't stand not living there either, pay each other a small agreed-upon sum for living with each other and that will make it easier, it's five a.m. time to take in the milk from the milk man, forgive us while we just go and hide in the closet so you won't see we've been up all night doing disordered things, don't fart or anything, here comes Charlie oh no, he's going to ask to borrow money again, let's tote it all up and see how much we've got, it should be fifty-six seventy-seven more than last week except for that thirteen sixty-two we spent on antifreeze and where did that twenty-seven eighty go, by the same token we must know because one-tenth of everything has to go to the church because if we can amass twenty-two plenary indulgences in a lifetime then we're sure of not having to say more than ten Hail Marys after we die before we're admitted to heaven even if we happen to die in a state of mortal sin which means you may have done one of the many hideous things you can do, or maybe more. I've got this huge porterhouse steak, I bought it, it's my heritage, I think I'll divide it in half and save the rest for tomorrow but I was so tempted by the special at Schrafft's that I didn't eat it and now it's gone to waste, I've got to make a list of what could happen next because besides my list of things to buy for the future, by the way always have two of everything stocked up so that when you run out you can buy another to replace the stocked one but you'll never run out of anything that way and have to run to the store in a crazy series of foolish leaps, running isn't good like candy, I also need a list of chancy things, possibilities, I've got to know everything beforehand so I can put that list next to the other list and then I can predict the future totally, you see the blue glass balls on the blue glass table, no the balls weren't blue, not blue balls but the table was blue and reflected the blue color onto the balls, they were cleaned and brought out every beginning of winter and then cleaned and put away when spring came, I don't know why. Maybe it was that the profligacy and freedom of the summer season, warm weather foreboding a kind of releasing of all kinds of unpredictable feelings, or the wind even coming in the now open windows and blowing the delicate glass balls away or onto the floor where they would break because they never did break, not once, not one of them, each of them had a minute hole in it so you could wash them and though water would enter in it would eventually dry out though if you did it wrong the ball would be hazy for the whole season, like a baseball player, that summer was a little bit freer and something as delicate and precious as a plate of glass balls couldn't survive it like us dirty mortals, the glass balls did as I said live forever, all of them did, long after all you guys died. We took good care of it and everything, polishing the woodwork like moths every turn of the season and putting the clothing in mothballs, the whole deal, ironing ruffles and tatting lace, putting stuff in order, cleaning out the shelves periodically, polishing some silver, using the good dishes on holidays, the modern olive green ones and having drawers and commodes and commodious bureaus for every piece of thing, the amenities, the antimacassars, I'm not putting it down, I'm just saying that's how it was and when later the couch became so dilapidated from fucking it seemed like what they would call a crime or a mortal sin and it wasn't a feeling against sex I was beginning to have when I had to put everything in order in turn for my children, it was just a fear of losing control of the structure and order that had been so interrupted by the rift in generations caused by your deaths and the extremes to which they sent me, being so unfaithful and even so forgetful as to just want to be high. So now when I hear the car door slam shut I think that's neat but what if I never get there, I don't forget, I remember every chance there might be for another disaster or chaos, it's a deformation of the attitudes you had so under control that you could keep doing the same things every day of every week for every year and then say as if in a play you needed a change of pace. I don't forget now, I don't feel free, and besides or by the same token something else intervenes to make every moment the beginning of something that has already happened so that this pitiful color of the now dreary October day might be the harbinger of say another death day in October, it looks like something, it looks the same as I remember it looking, cold gray winds, the dirty pictures in the store, if you look at them, well you'll have to confess it, even though they're pictures of women and not men, why is that so, magazines on magazine racks, all lined up pretty neatly, somebody did that, somebody set them out, did they take pleasure in it, not pleasure in that the pictures on the books were dirty but pleasure in the absolute neatness of the lining up of them, the duty, the chore, the job, something you perhaps have to find pleasure in otherwise it's nothing, otherwise you might quit or freak out, there was no freaking out going on in those days if you'll forgive me putting it that way but you could still collapse if you needed to, count what you have left and then go home, back to the piles of things, things amassed and also counted, but already there, counted upon, reliable things, things bought at the store, accumulated at what cost, toted up, dreaded in their loss, how many people do you know, deaths always come in three's, how much did the opal necklace cost, I'll give you a dollar for every hundred on your report card, training of all kinds, don't forget your lunch, you have to go to work every day, five days a week, on the subway, you get into the cars, how many cars are there, you stay there in them, till you get there, you can't get out, someone threatens you, when it's at your stop they won't let you out, it's dark and no one's around, the ceiling falls, a fire might start, a man might climb through the window, what was your fantasy and were your dreams all in order, it's a milk milk thing sometimes, we did learn to swim freely and float on the waves later of our sheets in bed, what was up in the closet, why were those glass bottles there, were we really not breast-fed like the red lines and the black ones in the columns of figures you showed us, breast-fed a little and then to be sure we were existing in the black, given the bottle too? You actually got off easier than your brother, you were less forced because you were a woman, his shoulders grew narrow and he collected so many things, he was a little endomorphic-looking or something, you at least had the carriage of a pride of lions and I must admit I don't know that much more about you except that since I imitated you I still can imitate you dying and many of these cold gray mornings are like the beginning of that scene, what was it, was it just politeness, why was it so detailed, saying the novenas for you assuming that the mathematics of the religious indulgences and the big train into the future of hopeless cases might work out in a saintly way, it's more orderly you said to live in a convent, you were thinking I guess about all the unpredictable craziness of life and even the demand that life makes that you be sexy, or have sex, that love and sex can be a free expression you get for free, you can't predict it in all the disorder in among that, in among the something arms where you or I might be excited and crying out in a rage that cannot kill, knowing another person is human and mute and dumb enough to want to be with you in the anomaly of borders and boundaries that we were so good at delineating with our training, making something out of nothing, adapting to everything like admirable men and women but this guilty feeling that we cannot speak freely in intimacy for fear it will destroy the odious order we've predicted for ourselves among the safe control of just doing o.k. and getting everything done or straight in private so we can continue on, ignoring most of what exists not as things we love but as people whom we cannot count on, who disappoint us and thus though we love them we can always find a reason not to let them have access to what they call the self and we can love them generously enough like saints but never apprehend them or take them to us in all their chaos like people because they are awful and don't fit into the day, the abdomen, the night, in which we are sheltering babies born of them but the babies are not like the cousins who demand money and shake up the scene, or the real babies who make other kinds of demands and also act awful, the unborn babies in our wombs are like the pebbles of monkeys we can control and commune with as if they were not only perfect but ourselves and they are not counted as real yet, we can control them like pictures, we can show them, we can show ourselves off, we can forget everything but our bodies, and what is within them is a deception, only you and I know about that, there is no freedom in it because it is expected and can be finally planned for and the ones who love that sort of thing, well we can seek them out and get approval from them for it, and from the other ones, the ones who insist that life goes on, well we can prove it doesn't because you can't account for that, let me prove my faith your heritage.

A Falling Together: To Make Strong Again as in Restorative, Restorant, Ristorante, Restaurant (Restored by Falling Together)

I INVITED THE MOTH IN, it was a warm night, the way something in a poem brings something else in like ideas of Buddhism, it's one of those moths with wide brown bodies, membranous wings, the moth is noisy, it's all I know, or even the way a poem does something, it usually does, it has a structure, it falls from the light, it goes somewhere, do Lepidoptera hatch? Did this one hatch just today? But this doesn't move, it isn't made like a poem, it falls nowhere exactly, can't anyone write. It must have something to do with being pregnant. I was going to put the letter in the mailbox but we missed the mailman because Marie couldn't get her shoes on in time. Then it turned out that your letter which changed everything but the Arnica tincture was in the mail and, just as I was about to call the clinic back about Lewis's ligament, you also mentioned the name of a more congenial doctor but when we checked the map to find out where Wilton where the doctor is is, we found Wilton in Maine and thinking that was northern New Hampshire we dismissed the whole thing but when I glanced at the Contoocook Valley Advertiser which had also come in today's mail, there was a big ad on the front page for a plant store in Wilton New Hampshire so I knew it must be closer than we had thought and I found it on the map only thirty miles from here and to the south but the doctor's number was busy and then right away the phone rang again and it was the clinic saying they could see you tomorrow and even x-ray the thing. Now there are two you's in this thus whenever I deal with you through the mail, coincidences happen and the same day I write you or send you some money I get your bill and whenever I used to call that place that sends us your herbs and medicines they would always be just in the act of packing the things to send us and I've been waiting for coincidences because they happen in the country. And until this happened I could not feel that the trees around our house were anything but frigid, today we could finally swing on them to get somewhere, and the maples became more yellow, it's not as if anything a certain person does will have to be any good, maybe I'll go to Harlemville when I get old and live with you. Marie woke up all wet, all confused; being a mother is like being a monster, just like pots I mean poets. If there were monkeys in maple trees it would be quite a coincidence, in the month of October or one this cold where all the moths are nearly dead. Those trees are stubborn, they knew I had come in such a fly-by-night way, they wished we would use the farm and bring in pigs and goats and chickens and even cows like the place we got the milk from today, they had gray geese. When a child sounds miserable it's hard to feel human, she comes out and says it's because she doesn't want me to write. To orchestrate the freedom of lives, to make them seem spacious and variable, and it can't be used. Older she resorted to the doors of wars to make her entrance each night, each morning, like the national anthem at the world series. And as it was a day of coincidences I'm afraid it's a night of distractions, I hope that means that Pittsburgh will win, it's not as if I'm at a party either, where people bite my clothing and I am insane. But if things cease to happen it seems like there is nothing and the felt world, like the publishing company that makes my dictionary, disappears. I don't learn anything, the curriculum falls apart and I am vulnerable. There are some things I won't do like complain about children, the bitten scarf of fashion, the punks, the therapeutized, the religious, or even the president and his wife and so on. But this is not a coincidence and the night has changed all that to invention or necessity or something. You have to be slow to let coincidences happen, like the itinerant cigarmaker, also a joke, like seeing all the flying saucers in the sky, you can't be in a hurry and you also have to make a number of things happen, it can't be entirely nothing but it must be close to nothing which is why living in the country is conducive to this phenomenon. Black balls of fire in the heavy quiet sky blinking red and green above the hovering hills whose names are Foster Hill and Goves Hill, Windsor Work Peak, Colby Hill, Wadsworth Hill, Proctor Hill and Craney Hill all named after people except for Mount Misery, Mount Hunger and Mount Hope and Liberty Hill, Bear Hill, what a funny dull neighborhood, there is a place called Slab City and a Sodom Hill in Deering, also a Bible Belt Hill or something like that, there are a lot of fat Baptist churches in this green-glass grassy muddy pleasant upper lower and long loon east west north branch place. There's a lot of forest behind our house with nothing in it, no roads, houses, no nothing just ponds and rivers and lakes, no deliberative gibberish, no unintelligible chatter or jargon of the alternatively equally fast and slow New Hampshirites, are there any special days when you're likely to have milk and eggs, oh I forgot the trees in that forest, and the brooks and streams, it's a watery place, and the chipmunks squirrels and concatenate bluejays, and that little bird that hangs around, and even still some robins and goldfinches and maybe some deer, bears, bad-luck woodchucks, how about moose? And just over the hill of course are the llamas but they are not in the forest, they're in the town, and unless they're being bred I guess they're not even giving llama's milk which people may drink. The milk was a dollar a gallon and if you can get up and around this mountain I think it's a bargain, so full of cream. There's no overabundance of pheasants and turkeys in the woods like there used to be and I'm sure you still would persist in dating the farmer's daughter, just don't let her take you to the Deerfield Fair to see the two-headed cow and the half-dead snowmobiles on exhibit there. Why is that dead spider being blown in circles on top of my books. I used to walk around just another female derelict though looking neater on the pavements, they never told a story to me. It's 10:45 p.m. everything's quiet now, it's 2 to 1 Pittsburgh, bottom of the eighth but the Orioles have a few runners on, Dr. K.'s just driven up and he's sure to complain about the water pressure, these distractions are conducive to becoming more coincidental, now Lewis is moaning. I was beginning to be thinking when I started off writing to a you I have forsaken, the harbinger this Wednesday of my ability to see the trees. But now I've got all fucked up, surely there are ways of not really working like so-and-so or someone to avoid all this, and what would be the point in all this light of another big banging on the door, lights out we'll hide and not answer in the dark then the pear tree will be hit by lightning again, it's like summer. I have always been prone to becoming more dark-skinned, once a doctor even thought I had peacock's disease because of it, now I smell a skunk, conversation can make the poetry cease. It's a big sloppy thing full of the cottages of Americans and among the secret journals consult the reasons why we cannot write these things, I know the plants are dying for some normal sex, I will exhaust you methodically every night that is the night before your classes, are you of the classes? Every day you look like a different person, hugged in red or amber or just brown, even when you take someone to the woods to cure him of a chronic disease. That gnat is orange, I can see its two dark eyes and the famous membranous wings, it doesn't make me strain at a gnat to think about you, now this other man has come in, you look at the map you can see all these millions of places that might exist, that you could exist in without stories, a place like New York City never told a story I'm sure of it, it's like a habit and people are separate as a ruse of it but to make something of this story of a town even in snow it will be is a dog barking at my writing as if I were a skunk or sunk as a skunk or whatever that phrase is, my father said it but a family history is not always a country story and the fall being daytime or night doesn't leave us anywhere because a draft of writing is too logical for this unfulfilled play where nothing in your language happens and the air sinks into our lungs as if it were disaster, the man in the grey flannel suit or something, I heard the car turn in, are there no weird sisters? Are you ready to go, I can go on past the normal time, Marie says she's bored of everything, the breath of talking, will there be breath, there isn't in this pregnancy, being blatant in another concatenation or coincidence of giggling laughing as if we were girls cutting classes because they are the gibberish of unrelated forms as if they were ideas, not like the woods, I sprained my ankle and fell, it's 3 to 1 now and it looks good for Pittsburgh but Baltimore can still be up at the bottom of this last inning like a ruler. For me when I read your poems it's very definitely hit or miss,

now there are three of you, what shall I do. Shall I be able to love some-
one or is the winter too cold and my belly growing bigger I will become
bitchy, demanding ice in my fresh orange juice, thinking everyone is out
when I want them now in, or they ought to be out more, a still swarming
collection of my mistakes is brought here and I can see them. Sometimes
children are nervous and need to drink from silver cups to slacken the
bite of it but they get that from me but they don't get everything from
one of us do they. Sweet something of the time, it's four to one now and
the pretty red Orioles are just hitting people with their pitches, was it
their mothers who are causing this now? It's an awful thing to be Amer-
ican, why don't you live next door to me? Sweet Hellespont of the wrath
of Demeter at the Sea of Marmara, you should watch the end of this
game in your mother's name and not make so much of her otherwise, yet
she was a woman who passed from being young to being old among your
visions I hope, and she didn't envision you being such a person as you
are, she thought you would be more exactly like an unforeseen someone
who was foreseen among pleasures unending and without so much trou-
ble as the coincidence of the narcissistic self who can bring it down to
the end of the last inning in the seventh game, no I didn't mean it that
way with baseball as an image, but there's one more out as I wait, and this
may be the end in this discipline this year for the favored red birds who
have done their scoring but failed! So let's spend Pittsburgh's winnings
together at the Aegean Sea where we might even learn about running
past the hard pear trees to most lost love, I'm afraid we have to though
tonight we might celebrate. The fucking persistent President is in the
Pirates' locker room but Willy Stargell says it was tooth and nail and
tends to ignore him and among the more sad orioles Jim Palmer looks
like Michael Palmer and that is all there is of that.

Equinoctial Tears

MANY THANKS FOR YOUR PACKAGE it arrived intact after the UPS man said he'd had it on his trunk for a week and it wouldn't have lasted much longer, but he couldn't find us, he said nobody ever heard of us so he systematically hit every house on the road and found us last, at last. Those drawstring pants are pretty hilarious and everything is useful but I don't know if I could ever wear that red suit! Except maybe I ought to, I got in trouble for trying to put an ad in the "faculty bulletin" to start a playgroup—another playgroup story, I can't believe it, it's not even as interesting as being thrown out of college for reading Freud! It seems like you're not supposed to act like a person or a mother when you're a teacher, you're supposed to be sophisticated, not hungry or lonely, and to beat about the bush. Also we had gone into this same office to get a check they owed us when we first got here and we had said, which you're not supposed to say, we were broke and we needed it and then these three secretaries and their superior boss, the man, told Russell they had had it with Mayer and Warsh! So I guess this is the answer to your old original question about what it's like to be on the other side of the lectern. Lewis had thought I was becoming paranoid. Well meanwhile Elizabeth Bishop has up and died in the middle of our conversation. And, I heard, she died an hour before she was supposed to give a reading which was something evidently she feared doing. So I started reading her complete works, just like you, and I must say I found the works sustaining and sustained, perhaps in a cold way, almost too good or perfect, did you know she's gay? She was gay, she managed to live a pretty long life for a poet too. And her sestina, as you say, is great. My classes are actually getting better, I had a long discussion with the beginning class about dope, they all use the word "bong-hits" in their poems all the time. My poetry workshop is lively with people shouting at each other and getting giddy and I have one serious writer in it who let me read his complete works the other day. So I am not entirely complaining except to say Lenox was a friendly town compared to this place, even the mailman won't say hello or look you in the eye and he thoughtlessly drops heavy boxes of books at the foot of the hill underneath the mailbox unless they're certified without even giving a thought to driving up the hill so today found me lugging about sixty more pounds than I've got and Marie said to me what's that awful look on your face and Lewis had to walk four miles to get the car fixed because we don't know anybody we can call to get a lift. We found a "family practice" doctor who was nice to Lewis about his leg and put him on a diet of aspirins and Dr. Incao wrote to say there was an anthroposophist practicing only thirty miles or so from here and he sent me all the herbal medicines I took when I was pregnant with Sophia so I can have a good time. Your kids sound raucous, I always think mine are going nuts till I hear about yours, maybe mine are just more quietly getting neurotic. Marie told me today she didn't want me to be her mother anymore, she wanted our babysitter Lea to be her new mother and she hated the new pajamas I'd gotten her. It's definite, isn't it, that when you entrust a child to another, especially for the first time, his or her only recourse is love, yes? …A lapse of three days has happened, we've been doing the next issue of the magazine in the slowest most painstaking way and now in those three days I seem to have suddenly become very very pregnant and also resolved to have my tubes tied if it doesn't cost too much money and trauma and also come to the conclusion that I'm a mother to begin with, what a last few days it's been. I have been sleepless, our petulant landlord is here this weekend fussing about everything and closing off doors with plastic, I wonder if we still have a way out, he's definitely of the nouveau-ecological school—I prefer to be able to enjoy the porch all winter at any cost, hedonist and agoraphobe that I am (callous claustrophobe?) I think we're beginning to go about our business here with what they call chips on our shoulders. Thanks again for all the stuff and I love the hat, it makes me feel "girlish." Now what you have to send me are encouraging words on the subject of having children—an equally huge box of those! Love.

Brilliant Bravado October 20 Night

NOTHING ANSWERS, there was a nightmare of fluency in the dream, the pleasures of autumn, two ways of portraying everything and nothing in two codes, the hideous woman then in her frenetic feast on me was the answering woman the demon the mistrusted persuading sugar of the celebrating food, it was a cylinder like Egyptian tits of the painted brain remembering you turned to me and it was a threat, you were another so I screamed to tear you away, I had walked all the circles of the fearsome library that was also like an autumn construction of words meant to be pictures all on paper, the handsome man or men who live to be fifty, age prematurely and then die, lost to a few, it may be this reincarnation of the program, the fitness program or pogrom, still it was a generous torture and still when you feel good enough you go and do something no one else could do, my location in the universe might be this, I might be learning and there is something heavy on me, it weighs like a tale or foothills a gratuitous place to find out where maybe everything else is but what is here, to be pulled or stuck here, it's sorry to have a reason for its location, it would rather be choosing and then defending the oils and acrylics of some sophisticated painting, the walls surrounding the shut-up doors, give me your paintings back and I will be angry and mean he was saying, a painting exists somewhere that is as confused as stuttering and as ugly as that thing, as the mind can be. There is an ornamental ax in the clutter, it's like money or memory, unnecessary or not used, uncomfortably found on the streets say, you look around, it's a relief to swear off the ugly confusion where the poisonous ocean meets the human land, the nightmare was perhaps a thing you saw, I make you act ordinary and then I'm disappointed, it would be this intimacy we forgot to do, it doesn't flutter, it's not transparent, the clean black ax cleaves it like a penchant for the perfect object, learning to speak. No one speaks to us and the autumn goes awry, an exhausting swelling nothing answers why exist in this world from twenty years to twenty years, why insist that others do because it happens, it's a kind of beauty that has to be sought as though already gone or even dead, nothing is offered and the sweetest statements get jammed with noise, sloughed off and I can't look you in the eye. A better measure of the titles of people might be to say we are doing it all wrong, with absence, with a sort of crooning missing what welfare is, a remark on nerves, we don't know what else, it isn't familiar like smiling or leering, there's no praise for it's all like passing by in the car, the llamas never saw us, we didn't shake hands with the empty tubes of paint before they were gone, the lunar predictions of assholes or multifarious nefarious plentitudes of permanent castings in something tinny like aluminum, the absence of a peaceful pleasure determined to change the size of things. So just let it be, maybe it'll all go a different way, nobody said you had to exist here along with all your thoughts of other places and a relation like a daughter to this beauty if it's here, this old illusion and its jugheads are waiting to get off easy with that parole. Maybe if one or two things were going like poets or mothers the whole rest would fall in the ocean with the paint and the paintings and the papers and boards, it was the fathers that were at fault for beginning this descent, coolest country, cease to leave this absent-minded curse on me like two sentences on clean pages, part mine.

To Live Above (Survive)

THINGS SWINGING BACKWARDS into the outside air, the chaos here. Bread baked in backwards batches, then the dealing with everything. There is too much not good that is happening, but at least it is survival and recuperating, recovering, learning to retrieve the self again. I cannot even write what happened, let it remain in the dark for this reason and not for any other. I always used to know what I meant when I said there are some things you cannot say but this time I am old enough or something enough to know, to now know more or better, but you can't say better. What I mean is I apprehend more of it. It might sound absurd to say I feel grateful now for things swinging backwards and unto the self after what happened to you I know was at least not death but almost unto death, so close as if it could almost be sooner and I am shocked then by the amount of love I have you I've only known a short time, I've known death longer, everything sudden, the presence of others, and now their absence in this new place. It could all be something I might begin to take together and attribute to the place, the remorse, the hostility of the place, the place and the time. I was in this place at this time gratuitously or for free, there was no cause, no reason hardly, now I am here still a transient and with some loss. We wonder if this is what a community is, this or that location that doesn't enfold us or if the arms of love are perhaps perfect elsewhere and where are they. A person is an entity like a place can be imagined to be but never is. A person but not a place can recover, if she can, from almost anything, from being near to death. A place may not recover like today when the leaves so announced they had fallen overnight from the trees so quickly as if to pretend to have portended what had already happened to a person and was now, at last in the process of being resolved, who was recovering, a long process, longer than the changes in the seasons from now till then, winter to spring, an impatient patience portended, a patience longer than nature's silly processes, this time too slow, people are capable of more, even. I am sorry if I can't be clearer, I put bread in the oven to bake it and to do nothing else to it, and I didn't think anything of it, sweet hearkening to breath and all it is. Breath might be a teacher, and the blood and the functioning of the human being blatant as it is or the bath of what is of course just noise, beats, courtesies, the warmth of corrections, the flooding of attractions, I won't speak of survival cause today we don't have to. Love is not to be believed among how we get used to its answers, among how we get into the habit of promising ourselves death and nothing else, I better not say that or you'll see how crazy a man like me who is a woman can become, the peace of exhaustion beginning to be as enticing as sex or love's examples, memory examines the blues of my beads, the colors of what I know, the identity of not having been abandoned or left to be no one whom no one knows, the orange shade of this shirt Ray mentioned I might not like because it was what they call a hand-me-down. I love the shirt and it sets a good example, three loaves of bread eaten as quickly as anyone yet if love is intact it will be about the self that is another and the yous could multiply and not shiver and be taken care of like humans and the rest could eventually turn out to be light-hearted, one always gets egocentric when something awful happens, worries about having said the right thing and one's only behavior when something else is at stake, worries about the self. There is no use writing this now, or this, or now, or anything, but that the trees made that feeble tempting attempt to correspond with nature, nature intact with humans, nature doesn't know us, many of us, nature never had it so good as to have so many of us around, nature may have failed us, it did, nature wasn't noticed, nature erred and we became aware of that, nature's autumn or fall belittled our notice of the ancient structures that because of cities have begun to exist independent of her, nature's mentioning this or that in calm sobriety gives us notice, we don't work this farm, it's hubris or something, the stalls of the calving cows are filled with the landlord's junk. Bereavement can be so absent now like leaves, wherever they went, we know and keep track, we remember, they keep the ground warm, the trees, dumb as they are, even these strangers, are quiescent till spring, know nothing of this, and I'm enraged at nature for being so sublimely dumb with no analogy in it, nothing to enact. Trees, forgive me for speaking this way when I've just met you, it's the harshness of all I can't explain that makes me want to beg you to be more explicit. The grass is turning brown, Marie says it's gray already, it's covered with leaves but let me say not luxuriously, so we can roll around in them, let me assure you and the trees I used to know what could be cut and divided, what could be and everything that was in it, which is all together as a person, recognizable to everyone who already knows you, you are you, and to some you are someone and to others you are someone they know or they might know, they might be saying oh I wouldn't want to know that one, what a bitch she is, or what a hoyden, what a bold boisterous girl, she's a heathen, and what a mess life is full of tomboyish girls and all the fey boys in the neighborhood, we are existing now I can say that, despite our reputations to be bad, dim-witted, outfoxed or inappropriate to our time and place like the weather's unpredictable they say, but not so inconsequential as the phrase "the weather" might imply and I speak for you, in anger at exigencies that make the reviving self less of a prison and that make us re-adapt to another house, see another season and all the signs of both, that make us hate the cold, that make us fall and use ourselves, for no reason but to be greater than the idolized trees, ours, the love, so forgive us and let us be fast.

Different Prescriptive Tedemones

YOU SEE WHEN I SIT down to write, the best coincidences of the plant store, I still have the instinct to organize and there is such nothingness, the best coincidences of the plant world, I don't know enough, I only know how to make the letters coincide so as to make words in this nothing, now I don't mean to push that nothing but the leaves are down like drama and there is drama and I am not Jack or someone, in fact I'm a woman about to be having her third child, her fourth in fact, and her fifth pregnancy and so I must be speaking about everything if you will. You know this machine or there is some machine you know, you can forget everything but that, you can structure the fears going inward and then going out, not that you're going to be one of these poets who only talks about fears, or one of those who have given poetry, old modern poetry as they say, a reputation for being something psychological or even confessional, it is all so false. I am not a poet I am a man, giving birth to a baby. My penis is going to become enormous when I do, it will swell and expand and elasticize and become supple enough for the six pound baby, who seems so small, to emerge from it, because after all it can't come out my asshole. We are hoping that this baby will be swell, I mean just another person, life is too corrupt for anything else. Why do we keep on having babies, why have them at all, many people who can do things fast don't have them. We seem to have them because the body once it does cannot seem to cease doing that, it's almost like the habit of writing driven or driving writing, we never intended to get involved, I am sorry, no. But when the kids emerge they can reflect sophisticated relations to the seasons and instinct and cravings for food or not food, temperamental natures, love of concatenations of the beautiful, they can even get right into plastic toys and all the funny food and t.v. shows, it takes time but it doesn't take but a few years. I don't mean to be so funny but it's torture, I was thinking about death so I became sarcastic. Perhaps as I was writing that you didn't even notice and took it for something else, after all all that sarcasm and flesh-eating cynicism of dogs is so ordinary if you've read a few bestsellers. When people are thinking about death there is nothing they can do but say they might be like this for a while and make your hair stand on end with their funny ripe coldness which isn't funny but uncomfortable and full of loss, it's not gibberish and there is different gibberish for each of the emotions, as if each were one, and this one the motion of a sacred rabbit which can't be compared to much of anything might be the worst one, you wish you were Freud or somebody who had one of those prepared 19th century lives where everything was structured even grief and the rest, no you don't wish to be that you wish to be a wild primitive woman with a ritual that accepted your dismay, now don't mess with me, you wish you were anything but an "American" now where it is so hard to be showing you are feeling what you are feeling. Obsessive and agoraphobic (but who cares?), I think in tiers and if anybody asks me I am already knowing kind of what I'm to be saying to save myself from the fear. Kerouac said if he did not drink and he was Jesus, he would be so nervous he would become a ward of state (I am paraphrasing him). And the ailments of Joyce and his daughter too, how daring death is as a culprit, how the anomalies of present time determine us and become close to us, we were thinking about that, isn't that why we read the papers so much. There is esoteric information I don't exactly have like *The Tempest* that is prescriptively different from this, but everything is so extraordinary as to preclude all that, when mere survival becomes the risk, though I don't like that word anymore, survival, since the book ALONE was published, I mean ALIVE. Simply going slow day after day doesn't always work, there is a resetting of things that has to come about and that has to come about slowly but it also has to do if you'll forgive me with the cosmos which is why it turns out to be nothing like the tedious reflections of trees to lives and then you say well there is not much to it, that is all there is to it and you must be imagining things, my dearest wife, my life. Some people are morbid, I shouldn't be saying this, I'm just taking the chance, not because of some dramatic intimation about death or anything like that, though women who are about to give birth often have them, but because I wasn't going to be doing this kind of writing and was exercising to find out back what sentences were like and how they could be so I could learn about writing poetry in some new way. But first I wanted to find out about conversation in letters and conversation that doesn't exist, I am not talking about black holes or something, I am winding up talking as if I were on the phone with you, as they say. Wouldn't it be nice to just forget everything, to go blindly through, a human might with no pernicious pretensions, no wasteful worries, no anachronistic hedonisms, I mean I often say to myself if you'll just guarantee I won't die then I won't be afraid of death, then I can justifiably enjoy and endure all my pleasures and fears. I know others never thought that thought but maybe I am kidding myself about that and why even mention it unless it's expressed in some unconsciously irresistible (and maybe more concise) language which seems to make sense as it looks and feels and sounds but as a thought, except in some conversation, perfectly worthless, useless and even tawdry, I'm not remembering so wholeheartedly as Proust, structuring thought like Dante, I couldn't even do it if I tried, well maybe I should try, I'm not creating a new language like Joyce, not to mention all the other guys and when you look at the women's books stashed on the shelves of the women's bookstore in Contoocook, well they are all specific too, I admire them that, Aurora Leigh. Funny how you mention having fun or something, we are having a hard time remembering and now the images and the powers of talismans might be sought and rendered bereft or even just forgotten for their powers, we are so unsure, we are back in the shops of forbidding the exclamation like the exclamation of leering or of the structure I was begging you to allow me to show off with, instead of having to talk about snakes and mirrors and all that stuff, Maldoror, Lautréamont, Rimbaud, more chances and temptations, hashish rumors and art objects, there's too much stuff and only an enormously fat or very skinny person can even begin to try to fathom all of it in literature and without and what it is and what her powers among it might turn out to be, a young one, an old one, a sacrosanct one, originally lost but lost with such fortitude. Well now I know if I do not exactly tend to my explanations, what shall I be doing? You tend to mine, tend to one's, you make it seem like Africa. Best wishes to you and to your coming child, you might say, but try not to be so serious, it's not good for the child who moves around so much when you get this crazy, who seems to say I have a chance for existing in the way that you would like, the calm way that you might idolize, that way without much of the work of thinking—many fears—that seems easy when you watch the people at the store and idealize them for their stolid perspicacity, you can imagine them driving home in their pick-up trucks in the snow with never a thought to the danger of it, just saying, oh this is what it's like and I remember when in 1977 and so on, instead of seeing all those great balls of fire in the air and all the other things that are there in such a hurry, those lent things, those things gotten from the struggles of the innocent eye against the sky, things all of us have visions of and we too try to make light of them, things without meaning, new words and nothing, the nothing I might have begun with or you did, a you who is not you, a you who is nothing, an identity not to be found, nothing scientific, nothing of love, nothing for you, nothing of the heart ceases to learn to love and looks aside when you look at me, looks back into the book, it cannot answer, and then we both get mad. If I don't die too I can find a way to say it, perhaps I'll have to say it for someone who has lost or never had that power, I don't mean to be so melodramatic, I don't mean to be mellow either, the words are like that, there might be more but it'll be more words, that's why you might like to know who I am but then, my wife my child, what difference does it make. A band across your eyes, a band across my lips, we cannot form the words.

"Warnings Out of Town"

A SPORTSCAR MAYBE, a lemon, observing the object of a lemon or grapefruit, they might cost the same like the stroke of your letters becoming this dollar sign, like dumping or depositing the dream, a deposition, the army of the family, the so-called creation of moods. You were painted, you were sucking, you were absolutely the most frightening so I was screaming, you invited us to watch television but your antennae like a sculpture on top of the set were old tree branches, cut off, burned out yet supple, you showed us how you got the picture anyway, they were smoking, there might be an electrical fire, your words your writing was like a field of cauliflowers or men, soldiers sprouting full-grown from the soil as of old, and you are a sort of family. I was late for class but when I got there another woman had mightily taken my place, I didn't mind but for the earthquake in my family's old environment, I was pelted with dirt and stones, I went to the museum a little bit naked, I think it all happened because we were living a little bit close together, the houses were touching, I went to the huge apartment store adjoining our house to find you a birthday present, the elevators were interesting as always, I don't think I found you anything, flattened up against the store as I was, and we are a sort of family. There's nothing left to relate but the kind of still storm drain where they put the heating oil in, it heats everything and for free like a tincture or infusion, extra pale and extra dry like love or visions of boxes of pencils and pens lying in the bed, what fear is annihilation or the scourge of the tea, a little off, maybe kind of low or bland, tasting like soap. The ambitious guest was surviving in random poetic fashion like a plum to hand a custard to, then he dumped it on his head, what a bad boy, and it rhymed when she said it. These letters attract a lack of visions and a cursory penultimate attack on the landscape's lack of active colors now, an absence like might be caused by someone going on a trip or taking off for no place in particular or being laid up for a while. These bluejays have a color but they are men and women so they don't count, I don't live in Hudson or Rensselaer. It's Merrimack County, Henniker where there was once a showing of shooting stars, don't sneeze, and a January in the 19th century where by around the 19th of the month which is when the baby's due, there had been no snow so far but then all of a sudden it got so cold nobody could go out for fear of frostbite but I repeat there wasn't any snow on the ground at all and one girl walked a mile to school and she got the medal from the schoolmaster that year, maybe because she was the only one there, and he showed up too, I wonder what they did that day in school together. There was a black man who once lived in Henniker and he was very popular and had enough to eat but not any more; the Indians went away, they didn't make a show of it. Attention, please stand free of the moving platforms as the train enters and leaves the station. A very singular custom prevailed in olden times which was no less than that of warning all newcomers to town to depart hence within a specified time so that the town should not be held liable for the welfare of the persons thus warned, if they called upon the town for assistance:

"I cannot, for the life of me, imagine what it is for," she said. "Have you said or done anything here to give offense?"

"I have done no more than civilly pass the time of day with the people since we have been here," said he.

"Well then," said she, "who knows but what they think we have got the small-pox or something."

"I am going to pack up our things and go somewhere else," he finally said, "for this is no great of a place after all."

Then there was the man who got famous for becoming a servant of the czar, Nero Prince, a black man who married a Violet, and London Mero and Holden Green and Dick Boston, they married Violets too, there were a lot of Violets around here, and some people named after characters in t.v. shows. Also, intimately connected with the town church and its session was the old town library and it was kept in what was then the kitchen of the church as a convenient place for the church-going people to warm themselves, it contained between two and three hundred volumes, embracing histories, poems, treatises on astronomy and one work of fiction called NO FICTION. There was a tornado once and fires and dry summers following upon springs wherein the apples were ripe in May, anomalies of a brief two-hundred-year history. For years there were people talking in sawmills and shoe factories, people beginning to sell flour shocking people who didn't know how or why to buy it, roads washed out and coaches passing through between Boston and Concord. There were symbols used for brevity's sake for white oak, red oak, beech, black birch, white birch, hemlock and white pine, maple, pitch pine, black ash, white ash, cherry tree, spruce and a heap of pine. I was exceedingly wet and could not by any means get fire and was obliged to stand in our blankets without sleep as wet as water could make us till morning. Sabbath day traveled into Hopkingtown and measured everything, qualifying the lots. There were ponds and brooks and railroads given and taken. There were women who killed bears and liquor served at funerals. There's the Ocean Born Mary House and a Reverend Moses Sawyer, wells and stoves and wars and lists of the names of men, all English, no women on them. There was a poor-house farm and laws about ardent spirits being sold here and there, hard cider. Well there wasn't much of anything else, I already mentioned the shooting stars didn't I? Now we see an occasional flying saucer, me and the Hillsborough police chief. There's a solar system on my carbon paper and it says midnight—no fiction. I am of two minds, the first is belief and with the second I observe the diligent chipmunks trying to stay as fat as they were earlier this year. There is a way of observing everything like Hawthorne like an innocent without no point of view, there is a way to be contained in the pond, the coming winter rituals seen from a heated place. What air comes in to my garbage can when I open the window in front of all the nighttime jargon, they don't cut over to me here like a light or a star already broken in its translated reflection. Have you lost faith in me now, digesting all this cold in cottons and wools. I'd love to overhear a conversation you are having with someone, I don't have all day or else I do. You and I might be benefitting from never having seen another human being, or one yet to be born, or not having a phone, the latest disconnections. We might be like the black or white birch, never actually presenting others with an autumn, probably of Etruscan origin, also called fall, and thus a little bit supercilious in our always current beauty, till death. We might be remembering everything, it's not enough time out of town, don't warn me again. Now there's a weeping and a crying and someone comes down, sweeping us off her feet, juice! juice! I'm thirsty! Don't say that! What a mess! You're horrible! You've forgotten me! Now you shouldn't be here! Go away! Eat shit! Don't mention it! Don't kiss me! You're too old!

Look Out for a Second

THE RAIN IT'S RAINING all around, it falls on field and tree, we don't have our provisions yet, I'll lend one further word to each title in this, I'll make a yearly mystery a wordly pattern of it. Worldly, we haven't stocked up for the storms, there is something missing in the order of each storm, there's a design in cross-stitching on my shirt, it's raining on the full moon, oh no you missed the point, I can't expect you to inherit being me as if it were a tendency, not even sarcastically, there was something else, I think it was it could be snow. But like the doctor with whom we telescoped time waiting together for a baby who was late the last time, we don't have our snow tires on yet and of course there could be there will be there always are storms, storms without information about the snow line like when you're climbing, storms behind the plasticked-up anti-hedonistic doors, they're just doors. It's the machine that sticks and not the snow, the sausage machine where I work at my second job and at the factory you have cohorts and everybody worries about money, some get stuck and knock the beer over just as they're about to drink it at lunchtime. There is something about largesse that lends the human mind something, what's the perfect book. Minds meet the exterminator and it is less than perfect, maybe just illuminations. Aspects of a vagina are coming through the holes in my pants, there was an old man in the house, he was called corn penis, he had inspiration intact, he was a rigid curled fellow, fellow as old as the hills were barren plains with no doltish mischievous trees on them, it is not uplifting. Moving on, I can feel the red burn beyond desire. How to write it is a mystery, just living my capitalism and material life, 1400-1979. Dark windows laughing at the shelf of herbaceous ointments, what would happen if, obsessively, I threw water into the electrical sockets so spaced on the wall in this old house in the modern way, as to facilitate a shaver. These modes of thought, map of the great liberation, no cigarettes, double illuminations, the selected sentimental education of a girl in the Metro or something like that, bid me to liven up the art pawned off as individuals'. If I don't move I might look like you, old corn penis. The wild boys answer for about half the process and reality, and when you would leave I would put a valium in the bed to replace you, against the grain. Still that actual puzzle is strewn again in the same place on the floor; all amidst my clothes are at the laundry, the midwife said. What text then to intersperse? What gargantuan views from among diaries to make a fountain out of, or a geyser, the old geezer, not a flume. There are some retributions half made or half paid like dancing in the mornings as a memoir, the old corn penis man didn't consider himself to be a criminal at all, he was as if himself a conversation lost in a kind of unrewarding pumpkin, the last promise or reward of the ending season, a big fat thing. Sweet anal George, what a mess we're in. Dear Ms. Mayer: it is all as follows: you are the despot to be blamed for all the hideous rain, the unrelenting moon, the damaging snow, freezing to babies. Your whimsical excoriations of the smells of life and even sex have placed you at the blue head of the teams of the most unruly horses, clearing the filthy ground of the acts. This man, indenting man, with the inhalable cob may turn out to be your yoke mate reigns assistant, brother not father to you. In the summer you had had four fathers, now that is a mistake, an error, a typo. And each of those is a snake. To lose your job is to be free, only you can't get beer or beans. I won't speculate, in self-revealment, like a communicating infantry officer who has just left Niagara and the stench of the Love Canal. It's fear too, you can watch it on television, an inexact fear which makes the baby in your belly leap up high as if the time right before birth were far from near. Those girls call me up all the time and really their reactions to everything are so inappropriate as to make me feel quite castle to castle. Let's see the car, my golden light, and let us look at your patient penis. I think I almost witnessed a circumcision today. I heard it and it was rather calm, quite random house. Then later I found out it was only the correction of one. The structuralists, right below the detectives, seem to dance to Shiva more in the twenties way, quite a novel thank you. You see there is nothing but this, the approbations of either boy or girl, who even knows the words for that. The sore ingestion of millions of milligrams of everything so's to be sure to have enough of all might leave us with a queer sort of memory like blood is too white, the hysteria of growing is on the bottom side of things, bottom side of the mountain to be actually climbed, underside of the penis, the first incision made, a sort of yelp but not that bad and was the gay woman subjecting the infant to this simultaneously subjected to all the symptoms of a false pregnancy. You see, I'm becoming more of a royalist novelist, invisible in life, I get to observe more scenes. So I can't let myself get too many holes in my pants lest I lose all that surface and gain vast visibility more as a poet or something, just a doe to be shot. Oh no dear ubiquitous autumn but with the tubular shape, don't land on the keys of my machine lest you too be crushed. I rescue you but you platitudinously lose a leg or two and become quite dead near the matches. Yet of course I'm still a meat-eater though that might render you incapable of reading my work. Remember the boy who used words all wrong and refused to believe the rain was remembered by the old corn penis man who had collapsed one last time on account of it, miserable miracle. It just does rain along with the alphabet and I collapse one last time, get up again and find the stroke of my luck to be more catholic. We saw the dreary day be paid a score, to just be passing by in its day's time, the heavy rain turning to ice and an adventure might seem heavier even than the lonesome recollection of a religious adept like a fan's notes. Distant the nonexistent thunder, bereft the dry absent holidays, speaking for me the adoration of the relaxed armament of changes among the nearest spaces transfixed and ordered under the modest storm, the life of words today, the prophylaxis of something like love.

Eating a Wasp

IF SHE'S NOT OUTSIDE you'll have to go up the stairs, writing has often kept me living, whereas today it seems like writing is a living too and we earned something from writing today, no got, which is money, first I'll say why, I think it was because of the well. Yesterday the well ran dry, or it seemed that way, no water coming out of the faucets and the heating things making gurgling noises which meant absence of water. By evening we were able to obtain an answer from Dr. K's pump man in Hopkinton, Mr. Flenniken, who came today along with the well men who were going to help him, the pump man, repair everything. They were sweet, kind, reticent and joking, it turns out the well men were being accused over the two-way radio by the boss Wayne Flenniken who must be related to the man I talked to though the pump man might not be a Flenniken himself and he's the one who has ulcers, they were being accused of fucking off because the well work on our well was going to take them all day, then we overheard them saying that this big boss didn't know where it was at and when they were off digging a well or repairing one somewheres, well he was off eating his big or pig dinners and putting his money in the bank, and it could be twenty below and these guys are still out digging or working and he's sitting on his fat bank account with his name plastered all over their trucks and license plates that say WAYNE and who was he to talk to them that way, they were the best well-diggers and he should

214

try and find somebody to replace them and one of these guys was the most mad because he hadn't stood up to the boss and the boss was treating them like shit and nobody should have to account for his or her time that way but it was the main man, the pump man, who knew all about it, he was the one who had the ulcer and they were saying maybe he had it because of the boss. It wasn't Marxism and it wasn't hoodlumism but it was pure and simple, and they started to work then on the well and its pump. There was a lot of trouble with it and they had great instruments, fantastic objects never imagined, magic things to iron out the wrinkles of the well and since we had no water and no dishes or spoons left we had to go out to get some lunch so we left a note for the UPS man and we left the diapers for the diaper man and went to the town where the kids threw tuna fish all over the place we went to and milk went flying and we shouted we will never take them to anyplace again and then we did our chores worrying that we were missing out time because our day was disrupted by the well and we couldn't get any work done, we couldn't do anything even go to the bathroom, normally it was a beautiful day, warm sun, sixty degrees, I was accused at the college xerox room of doing something academically illegal and since the accusation was true I defended myself eloquently and why don't people have any sense of decorum and when we turned to return, self-consciously, to our dried-out home we only stopped to pick up the mail and so that I wouldn't have to get out of the car to obtain to the mailbox Lewis nearly knocked it over with the car and it was Grace's note saying she's coming to Keene, a check from Lewis's parents, one from the New York Public Library, one from the Phoenix bookstore, even one from Maureen, two old gas bills from Lenox, an announcement that we're to receive the *Village Voice* in the mail, letters from Paul, Summer, Clark and Peggy and also Maureen, a notice to pick up an insured package at the post office which must be Lewis's birthday presents from his mother and father, and the mention of the two grants—that's the money—what an astonishing bunch of mail. And up the hill the diaper man had come and also the UPS man leaving us two packages, one with more herbal pregnancy items and the other with secret present I'd ordered for Lewis. It turned out a new motor was needed for the pump but when they put the new motor on which meant they had had to take the whole old motor off the old pump, with all their extracting contraptions and it didn't work anyway which meant that yet another motor would have to be brought in tomorrow from among the supplies of the feuding Flenniken Pump Company, we knew we wouldn't have any water. And a new well might have to be drilled as well, depending on which of the men you talked to. You went down to get the package from the post office but it wasn't there yet, the postman was still out on his rounds, I read all the letters, the well men went home to call up the Doctor and tell him the bad news about the well, we call Harry and Ray but they aren't home, eat cottage cheese and yogurt off paper plates with apples for dinner because there is no water and we cannot cook, it's a colder meal and we are all shivering by the time it's done, I feel uncomfortable about going over to V's to take showers but we go anyway and it's hot as hell there, the children make a shambles of the place in two minutes, spill juice on the floor and drag all her boots and shoes out of the closet, cause us to rush out into the cold night air where the full moon is just beginning to rise and take away the sight of all the militant stars we had seen on our way over, it may be the harvest moon, there is nothing to be said for all this action but a guilt at being so full of it and that's the end of telling what happened except I didn't tell the other kinds of things and Harry and Ray were finally home and perhaps we'll go to New York at Thanksgiving after all and stay in an empty house in Brooklyn of Peggy's aunt and commute over to see everyone, we've got a refrigerator full of gallon jugs of cold said water and we keep wiping out the grounds from the coffee pot so we can make new coffee, Ray said you people live like pioneers anyway, she said that because we have a well at all, and perhaps tonight there is no heat either though I didn't say anything unusual I hope.

November Jack

NOVEMBER JACK, the natives are reticent stoves, first I'd better tell you what's happening with the well, the pump man tried to lower the pump back down with the new motor on it, the new one that works, he was lowering it down on long plastic pipes which I guess get left in there to hold the important pump in, it's reported to be a very deep well, deepest they'd ever seen the well and pump men said, so since it was so deep the pump man almost lost the thing somehow he said, or it was his wife who said so, she was telling me what she overheard him saying in a conversation with K after I'd said I needed to know since nobody was telling us when we'd have water and we were still living without it, the pump man's wife had a quivery voice right out of the *Tales of Genji*, I could imagine her reclining making note of a poem for her lover while the pump man was away digging those wells in the cold. So after he'd almost lost it the pump man vowed the thing must be lowered on iron pipes instead of plastic which means he has to use the boom truck which she described as being on the coast and it couldn't be gotten till Friday which is two days off. Now when she said on the coast I got this image of it being driven or hauled from California but what they meant was the coast of New Hampshire, I assume the boom truck is somewhere near Portsmouth where K's girlfriend lives and maybe she had caught sight of this boom truck on one of her daily bicycle rides while she's thinking about how Dash is treating her badly or that he's crass enough to rent half his house out while he's really rolling in it but we have to shit outside though Lewis did carry water up from the pond to flush the toilets once I heated some and dumped it on the dishes that have been lying dirty since Sunday when we were naive enough to think all is temporal, so, having eaten a wasp I wanna get out of here, cars in traction this gray existence of objects, olive Broncos all over town, Lewis is looking at a jack, there was a family at The Nook just like us, weatherbeaten hippies with bright-eyed kids dying for their hamburgers, I imagine that family is too sensitive too, you can tell by the way they smile, unlike the aging and long-haired workers, the "individualists," New Hampshire males with hair who pull up their pick-ups with identical flares, a new jack, we haul the water for cleanliness like campers, as you may laugh, get the heat fixed, they only say if things were working perfectly maybe then you could have heat without water but today you will not nor the next day nor the next and the fuses and switches are stuck at off and nothing bangs here, we're lucky it's not fucking freezing and a blizzard since the jack is to put the snow tires on, let's try to find another house among these fishy houses, let's house ourselves in a public building, I want to live off the town, warnings out of town, I want to be a ward, I want to be somebody else's responsibility, I am too small to adore this house so high on the hill with big views, the big views don't work either, there's another individual pseudo-post-hippie in a worker's shirt and another pickup truck, this one looks like Charlie Manson of the U.S. Army and army of everything, day-glo triangles for traffic circles are for sale in the store, what is your sleep and perfect fit Pepsi machine, there is some way I was trying to be saying what this kind of afternoon looks like when no matter who you are it's the kind of looking day where you have to grit your teeth and just see what is visible in the kind of light there is available and nothing can be thought to be distracting in its beauty except maybe people are bedraggled and no one's transcended this yet at least in their looks, his or hers, this kind of day, dark at three, smell of rainy snow, drab sights among the automobiles, nothing glows, it's one thing dead set against another, there is no order, no structure, they just put this or that there knowing someday in some kind of weather it would look as bad as it does today, America's exhibiting of entropy, a day of lapses and flooded cellars, crowded hospital rooms that were supposed to be empty, dreary chores, gray and brown white people, Lewis brings the jack outside and he's carrying it just like a sculpture, watch out for your head! And in the grocery store guys talking about all the worst accidents and how isn't it too bad, they're grinning all the while a little, about those three children who, I can't tell from the story, were either killed or left fatherless by a drunken driver of yet another pickup truck right around the corner and then it has to follow a recounting of all the other big accidents of the entire past year, just like what I was thinking last night lying awake worrying among my liverish full-moon potential visualizing little babies falling into six-hundred-foot deep wells, crashing cars swerving all over the road in a crazy movie like everybody's seen ending up in big fiery ditches, smithereens of people and machines, traumatized children, babies who won't come out, giant snows engulfing all the first floor windows so we can't get out, big drifts immobilizing us, the car won't start, I'm abandoned in the woods, on the road, we're freezing, I was just doing my dreaming outloud, I couldn't perform the dream the right way, I needed milk but there was none, everything is chaos, we have nothing but a tent and all these dollars, we hit a chipmunk on the road, you couldn't stop in time, you froze as if it was you who was hit, there was the old only black man sitting on all the milk in Henniker, he says he's thinking about work and can't do much else today, he says it's that kind of day, motherly woman in the store says she's leaving so I can't think of her as being in the room with me while I'm there, the store is a room, these comfortable kids who don't notice how scary everything is especially today are just saying to each other, "you goin' up to the tower?" and "you mean tonight?" and "yeah why not," what does it mean? There was a boy this morning with a bird cage on his head and his body was wrapped in towels and he was wearing a knapsack backwards but it was only a fraternity pledge, there is nothing worse for a mother than bringing bad children to a lesbian bookstore, it's worse than fearing that all the outside cold can now come in, Lewis brings two gallons of water from the administration building's bathrooms, I guess a real professor wouldn't do that, oh this kind of life where you accumulate stuff in your car all day and then get home all together having done nothing except to see things and access the day, bodies like the bodies at the school all somehow fraught with this admitted failure of perspicacity and nerve, this is an apologizing place and the dreaded evening of the waning but still so potent moon wears on, another cold dinner for the people who don't have to worry about money for a while now, you've opened up a can of worms, the night is young, and Lewis has to turn thirty-five soon now anyway, false melodrama of the doddering Americas, I shake and am senseless, crazy and bewildered from my lack of dreaming, I am a plant lacking leaves, roots and chlorophyll, I am the quaking grass, I am an egg yolk, I can only suck nourishment from the host and I wish to be the guest of everyone, I am deluded and confused, I would be content to be another age and of another age, old age, I can document this, I am well twelve times as trembling as a person of my age, these poems are hidden among all this stuff, you will never find them among this documentary of pregnancy so perfectly imperviously fated and planned as a lesson or proof that what is lost is said like an old decaying oak having lost its top, I am becoming like a clue to the simple new words of the old devotion, trying to find a way to be so desperate for love that the only kind of love or poetry that can survive here so rarified might be the generous one, leafy greens of the south dreamed outloud in this death-knell place for death is just like meaning going to bed to no effect, as no fiction. Death's the journal full of junk like this, posthumous letters to everyone, the claim on chaos to be fair and sweet as the juniper drifting in among some worthless rope in the rush of the ocean's magic oakum, I try to comb out what is unkempt, even more sweet references of the required poems, old metal, glass, paper and rags, useless rubbish, the hard salted meat I will not eat, the stuff you'll scrap like a planning aristocrat whose house doesn't lend itself to the sudden mention of it's simple to ask that the well well up and the winter be mild and ashes not fall on my place and I could be other than myself in the forgetfulness of something like rhyme.

To View Bacon Lift Flap

THERE IS A SET OF circumstances out of which one might spill, one might spill the beans. There is a shifting set and from the point of view of one place exists the other. When I view the past, the last apartment and snow, it seems safe and the distances we were walking between rooms and on roads now shift to these, become larger and yet no greater. I was talking about fear and since it is insensate, existing within, it remains without a way to change in relation. Thus you'll say it is not real, the fear of the bear is the same as of the spider if each is invading or afflicted with eyes. The unknown sensual delights of the beds of children shifting in and out of being people, the expected terror of the primitive in here with our security, our phones, conquest of everything but the blatant mind, parts of the century's body, subject to its mores, how come, I'm addressing you again, we don't know fear a little better so it's not so scary? Some feel so secure in the importance of their ancestral homes, body eagerly reaches forward toward the next known thing which may not be small, successes in the light-filled solarium, your mother and so on, the obtaining of a certain kind of thing, blindness, the childlike garden of perfection, pleasure in the feeling of the corporation and independent of that each different transient place is like war and you achieve that comfort for a moment. After sharing a bottle of champagne with you, as anyone does, the news on t.v. is too much for me. The tough wiry

women of Penacook laugh sarcastically at my tears for the nations of re-
venge and still starving. They also sneer at the bottle of champagne and
my forms of address. You think you can win them over at the line, look-
ing for some excitement, as anyone does, by your being simple and di-
rect and talking about fucking, and it's true, even in a town like that one
the high-school kids take a lot of drugs and cars to get them going, ham-
burgers too. Oh this is too fucking serious, maybe it's raining. I would
definitely have waited for a better offer, if I had known. Did Larry get
back? Did Ted or Alice get one? Is this a place for tragedies or just plain
mishaps or what. Is someone looking in these false windows. Whatever
it is you feed it to your baby and it's either cold or hot. I was beginning to
think then, since this happened, that there is no remedy for life as they
said, two of them said that, maybe more. The two baby sitters got Lewis
some flowers for his birthday and it was me who said they couldn't come
over, so they said we don't like you anymore. We've been here 2 ½
months. All that happened to Lea. We've been without gas, water and
heat though we've never lacked electricity, my touch is more medium
than high, your mother looks like a boy, I can't remember what else has
happened, oh yeah there was the rest of the stuff about the administra-
tion people not liking my manners and then almost losing the job any-
way, not related to that but because the muscle man was coming back. If
you're a student and in that capacity I guess you expect love affairs, love
safaris, and everything has to be fascinating or uproarious, or if you ar-
en't lucky, kerchiefed with self-pitying grief, alarm and the dreary tor-
ture so lacking in mischief that it gives no pleasure. Big belly of the effer-
vescent baby, others say you are still lacking in the mystery's girth you
should have but I know you're hidden so deep within me that there's
more of you than might be guessed at from the outside but it's hard in
this place to take pleasure in that, nothing comes of pleasure in Henni-
ker, you do your work and no one recognizes that behind your insane
agglomeration of names is a normal report cover, just like they see every
day in classes, or one of those log-rolling trucks rigid everyday at the
intersections of the flaccid streets, there is something odd about Henni-
ker, it has too many streets, instead of two criss-crossing there are many
or several, like the space between typewriters at the front line of I won't

say memory or eternity. Marie is saying "ouch," will she stir? There's got to be a way to tell all the way the fear of movement is intact like writing on words, too many cover-ups anticipating the disease, it doesn't work out, I guess the best way is not to start out to do so, what will you do with the sight of the milkweed pods this winter and where is my faithful moth, faithless thing it isn't here tonight, the words don't make it sensibly, it's because the language doesn't have all yet in it, Kerouac did it, I'd better not mention him again, I wonder what she was dreaming about when she, now we know she was dreaming then, cried out "ouch." If I tell what happened to Sophia would that be part of the story, Sophia is so purplish in her ways, she woke up late before dinner and sat meditating on our bed, not coming to eat, to trance herself out of it, looking up happy and fat at us, then finally came up and had a whole big dinner of fruit, farting and rumbling while she ate it. Marie kept collapsing on the floor because she had a sort of fever and said she couldn't walk anywhere, she would just lie down wherever she fell, happened to be, but she did have an appetite to eat some of the food from your plate and some cake leftover from Sophia's birthday yesterday which was an unusual quiet day, not causally, where we drove depressed by our ex-babysitters' mishegoss, the silly gooses, to Concord to find harmony and experimented with leaving the children at a place where children can be left for a while, a sort of makeshift nursery school in a shopping center, a proscribed and formalized indoor playground, and then we had a party and changed the snow tires but the awful forklift brand new jack wouldn't go down so we called a few garages for advice, are these my words as if in print, and they said you had to press down harder, a lot of jacks don't work like this they said, and we were finally able to jack the car down and put the other tire on, but why mention this, I might know why if I were a criminal but the inanities of the jack only make a desire to keep going, I might know why by not making any sense at all I would learn something, that's still one real pleasurable way and a way that hasn't worked out yet in terms of all the rest of the fiery mess where you light one by mistake, almost but not quite. But, there's still something to be said for doing what one has to, like having another baby, to make fate make the things that make poetry able to be right, the rest of poetry already being there no matter what you do, and whether the sound of this machine implies it's breaking down or not, I listen but I don't. I could still be no one with no identities and still be writing something, this needs oil, perhaps purer, surely more abstract, maybe even more like the girls at the college. But I could be, I don't have to be this one but now I am and so it is. Still I could pare things down or whatever they say and like Elizabeth Bishop or someone I could only write those perfect things which affect one rarely and are so conducive to language or vice versa or like John Ashbery my life could seem to be without events and smoothly more art, and so could the poetry then be, or I could only write politically or politically imperfectly in the sense of never saying anything about feeling because we know those words are traitors and have done others in, or even never telling what happens or making any noise, or I could be discovering something, who knows but I am, you turn an extra light on and I feel guilty for drinking a few beers, wondering if the new baby in my belly almost only two months now from emerging into the wrong world might not be suffering on account of my excitement from the beers and the forbidden cigarettes, but I know I can't mention all the fears, fears of the children being subjected to the sight of my sudden death, fears of for some reason not being able to make it back to the haven of the house and to you, fears of your never returning when you do leave, we all fear losing our minds like losing our other organs, then there's also the fact that for some time now I haven't been able to make love right, I keep thinking maybe it's because of all the thunder, because of the children so frequently being born and emerging from me and needing to be nursed after that and having never thought of sex as having this relation but as daring I might feel it is to even mention, I know I've told you all this before and I'll recover and then will sex go back to being something that's not related at all to having children, I can't remember, I can't have any more, I mean I can but it's almost self-indulgent to have three, the delimiting of life down further and constant needs so everything goes too fast just as you were getting used to being alone or older without initiations, being influenced and not so, to know about the different ages of people and what they do at them, to watch language, sex always and the stubborn will to be another one, the small regressively wave-like steps of the humans in their progression from ancestors through descendants and the narcissism of it, the love of your looking like me and the secret that you too might be corny or that each of us might have also produced a secret self who is not here now but might show up some day, like Marx or someone like that. And there's the giving birth to them, it's open to criticism like some work, it fades quickly unless you're Freud or somebody whose mother's midwife inadvertently said something momentous was happening and so it was or was not, when you were born, the later so inconsequential labor pains, the words of the contractions, the conducting of oneself within that, one's manners as it were, the privacy of it, we hope the baby comes out head first from between your legs, it's a relief to throw it all off, now you're rid of that burden, now it's independent at least a little bit, at least you can observe it, it's a person, you can call it he or she and by some chosen name attributed to a boy or a girl or neither, it could be just a word, you wonder if when you get up you'll not fall down, drop the baby and perhaps cause an injury, big proud bellies would be easier to bear if this were not America where I think they think it's your punishment and the births would be better and as temporal as they are, forgettable births, now a person is existing, maybe it's one who existed before, we don't know that yet, it's a girl, used to be don't destroy her, at least you could rest in between contractions, I hope you didn't decide you hated everyone and sex and fucking too, there is a space now between the baby and you, it's conceivable to resent that space and to want back the oneness, many times later this feeling of ownership somehow will come back when the person is indifferent or willful, covering his or her bets, stubbornly and necessarily but I won't speak of that, I don't know about it yet, this person will exist in a known family, I hope that family doesn't turn into exactly what mine was like when I was little, you the midwife ought to write a book, have a drink, do you like me, does anyone still love me, put that baby whoever it is to my dark nipple and see if it will suck, bring me some dinner and a book and see if I'm the baby now, now everyone wants to be the baby, everyone wants to hold the baby, I want my mommy and so on but maybe none of this is so, it's a couple of months off still and maybe by that time everything will change like the long slow windows of this drippy house we are covering with the thawing spaces of our love that seems to have come to all this. Please dear attributable god to something, permit me to sleep tonight at least as well as any enraged Iranian, I am sorry for my love which makes me suspect or in a heap like the Ruth who heaped up the heap of corn, perceptions open to scorn, with life this computation, holy shit.

Assworks

IN THE COURSE OF the day I keep hearing distant geese, as they say, like a doctor who knowing you are collapsing like a house of cards says it's because of something. Whatever we did it's just a record, we've put off paying most of the bills, it's a photograph with a mundane caption, what is that huge book. I think we'll go to New York tomorrow, drive for six hours with the unplacatable screaming ones in the back, Sophia has a sore in her mouth and can't eat fruit, there was a woman in the midwife's office with such a good child who looked eighty years old in patent leather shoes and a long woolen coat, how did the woman wind up making her child look so old, I had been feeling I just could not eat enough food, now the midwife says the baby is there in the right position and is a girl. While we were waiting the midwife had a long conversation with a woman who was pregnant by a man not her husband but her husband didn't know it and there was a long discussion of whether he was going to be able to find out because of his sperm count. The woman had many other children waiting in the car for her, and she was telling for a while how with some she had hemorrhaged, it took a long time to take this woman's childbearing history and we all waited, then the midwife had to go pick up her son and when he walked in he said, I hate all these babies and girls, I don't like them, he was six or so. I forgot to tell her she should write a book. She told me of another woman who was in labor for 36 hours and then gave birth and the baby was ten pounds. Brad, who's in my workshop, was 11½ pounds when he was born. To camouflage your pregnancy is extraordinary. I read all the feminist books while I was waiting, essays about your period, abortion and the cruelties of institutions. To avoid excruciating pain we are telling Lewis's parents we're having the baby in a hospital with a doctor, this deception saves us from being worried. The midwife is cute, did I mention that to you before? Dispose of properly, I'm distracted as of what, if I had dared to write for fear I would or would not sleep, it would have been different. Concord is aflame, there are so many lights in this house, I ate a steak, we left no wine for our returning, my foot's asleep, I am lucky enough to have new shoes, shoes gotten without thought, what would your mother think, I won't take them off. To produce no words, to be tapered into form, we've found no babysitter, soft problems. To have this money without remorse is like no new inkling of doubt just as the machine jams whatever it does. It's warm, it's been spring, it's spring already, you can do that in March. The chipmunks sing before us we'll see the dawn or something before it, we'll open our eyes in our sleep the way you watch out for good buys in shoes, all the time, I didn't look, I took the first ones, my mother was more like you are too, it was the times, there was nothing else to do or else it was considered a pleasure. You don't want to listen to all the dreams so I forget them, I keep dreaming the baby is born, this time it's a boy, a hirsute boy with hair in patterns in designs, he was born in my sleep, wasn't that nice and the endless milk was dripping from my breasts, just one of them. And I did dream I was somewhere else like a book recounting tales of travels, where was I, I was repeating some mumbo jumbo I didn't think was a dream, I'm more used to being awake, it was a formula of misanthropy, we have these funny colds, they expect certain things of women like recording the dates of the birthdays and other ones of men though I can't think for them what they are, they expect that everyone will be a teacher, a member of the board of education, nothing less. Where's the life and death in this. I've got the address, they look smug because they've always been able to get enough money for their needs and what are their pleasures, not dope or pills or beer but just filling up the cart or carton, the man in the store kindly gave the children balloons they chewed on to make them cry. It's the one thing I've always been able to do, let the thinking be stored and go from one thing to another, it's no great figleaf, just a craft to learn, as your feet are on my table or even the one about tame tigers, that comes up all the time, the mirror to nature and so on. Everyone says this or that, one girl wound up screaming and she screamed all night, then they took her to the hospital and years later she made it somewhere else, the newspapers are horrible hospitals, Lewis's mother had the same thing as Alice does, a detached retina, as if there is always something hovering about the eyes, too many things, now she is fine but where can we get a plant big enough for the day it will be. I'll bring everything that puts me to sleep, leaving fear here walking up and down the road to and from various trees. Epistemology's systems dash the stunning luck of some, others get put in jails and cells for a long time. A ruler is the day I eat, description's furtive mission, not a novel. Swing low the boy and hearing secrets girl, fearing to be made fun of, both. Even the solar system's function the papers made mention of, we could not see clearly, fear of rioting and looting, the eighth day or month, no news. Who is this one; with no awe of the moment I know they'll be looking at me just to see how I look, I mean in my certain clothing snickering at these wholesome shoes in the marketplace. Nicer to be an empty aside on that but the harcourt brace and world and the rest of them invent such crap. I think I will after just this moment's perfunctory nature and I won't say intransigently again either. The Mississippi is mentioning my cold. I always mean to go outside but everyone says what could it be to say, nothing ever happens. We've got to mention that anyway don't we. Hot and cold epistemologies. I'm glad it's over, don't mention it. Don't snoop around in here either. I'll try one more time because the night air was signaling that it finally wanted to come in. But what is it and who's it to? Bastards of the sandwiches, by that time it'll be the center of winter and again huge I'll watch the storms, giving birth to each one of them, a big fat baby in the center of town, well two miles off. They dug the well for the new house and celebrated, it was nice to hear them singing while the psychiatrist and his girlfriend fought incessantly and shouted about the new house being an invasion of their privacy. Something's making me itch, you woke up and said everything hurt you, your head, your leg, your vagina, your nose. It turned out to be true, it's nice that you can speak. I won't mention what if you went off and never came back because you two naked girls were wrestling on the bed today, you would spread your legs and Sophia would dive in between them and then you would hug aggressively and turn over. I thought someone was going to be killed. Now we have to do some things, make sandwiches for tomorrow, make notes, pack pictures and abdicate our fury at things like the light blowing out, we are always living in a place. We are and the history of the place forecloses on some groups of us at times, then there is nothing we can do. But the ranch house Catholicism of the street without pines hasn't got us yet, we're still mostly intact, we still use things and locate all around, the lazy nothingness of surviving like the grotesqueries of not such a bad disease, but recounted too well. With my facile hand I write a check in the picture, it's expected, yet of course I still seem ludicrous. Will we see enough of everything later to make it be of a piece, the answer is no but don't try to make sense or save it for later, it will be nice to see you, I hope we're all floating in the mesmeric seas though I don't see why those guys of an equal age who write what I might have written weren't discriminated against too, it's not like being born again, I mean what makes them any different, their fucking ambition which doesn't fit with their asshole politics? These geese I've been hearing, I must admit I never see them, I hope seeing you is going to make me know I'm still the same person with or without these mountains that won't forgive me for not noticing I am entirely different again. Sweet tea, you tell some people something and they can't even rigorously listen. Maybe that's because it's nothing and you are forbidden from now on to drink any beer, not only that but the yellow plastic primary tape will be put over your mouth because you are not black or a woman. Nothing of the celebration of anything, copies of the extant morning of the distant geese will be on us as we go out the door without placation or prayer, waving to the absent clutter, to the car.

The Black Velvet Midgets

'

AS ALWAYS THERE'S something I'll forget like lying in bed in love with a child, no one bigger than that, a person adored, an offshoot, unpredictable like they say men and women are, oh yes we can't seem to find and keep a babysitter, maybe it's because no one wants to spend time caring for someone else's children because they don't love them and they have their ups and downs, I wish we had more dresses, special occasions for them, I wish there was that in the air, rather than this ordinary waiting, rather than this certainty of exact secret words, lying around in bed for as long as we can and if you write about it, what they call an ego, making notes—was I there? Do too many days go by? I dreamt that politics was a human expression, thus the hopes of a certain religion located in revenge and anger were transformed to the assiduities of my demeaning self, self demeaning the anger it takes to live, just to be awake, to be moving forward, to be able to move, the storming of the embassy, the taking of hostages, the shootings, the outrage of it, the mobs, the hostages, doesn't everyone do this? And what angry mob can ever individually sleep, and sleep in that same false confidence that everything may be in order whether or not we must be martyrs. So to have a cause enables one to walk and talk, but to be angry like you tell me to be traditionally annihilates fear and with it the pleasures of passivity. But who cares about that? I think of some medicines, herbs in some form, that were described as being soothing to liver and gall. There is still an effigy of my fear in the street, still the transient spacing of the angry morning and night, the set-up for pretending to false logic and control, the scattering of such a sum of hatred and the history of how it came to be, out of subjection to greed and ruthless cynicism, it's the ones who were forgotten then who are now mad. Sometimes everything seems neat in the United States and the young people speak of being rational and going to court in 1980 without succumbing to the sensuous street of castles and the prisons' word reflected on the sidewalks of gold, it had been ordered this way till there was a shift of everything and now while the earth is moving in a self-demeaning earthquake that seems to come along with needing to speak to you in this tumultuous shout which you say means nothing because it is so crazy, all the ordinary things can be imagined to be turning to the disasters of a life that is not comfortable or safe, but you see I am not speaking for myself, I am adopting you and your words and soon I'll be in a ruthless and revengeful frenzy too, to get an image of the past back, to be able to sing about making the rules, to get all the wealth that was stolen back and to kill the man, isn't that what everybody wants? The united states of the consciousness of all the people gives me courage also to shout but the adored children shouting begin to make the thing seem absurd. It's only that we don't understand it though I see your words and say them, your funny translations of everything. No I didn't mean funny but wiry, brave and a good revenge yet we don't know revenge as a method, we can only bring ourselves to make others suffer beforehand and at a distance, it is a rational and rationed out suffering that is spoken about after the crime in the courts when punishment is meted out, not an eye for an eye, but it is said as restitution and rehabilitation so this question of humiliation is a new one, and it was inevitable. The oil man came practically in the middle of the night and nearly smashed Marie's bicycle in the road. He had a big truck with flashing yellow lights and backed it dramatically into the side of the house full of oil. Oil for the burner in this dislocated, poorly operating spaceship. Trace my hand on that sheet of paper, my guest is you. Babies sing and the peace of the humming might be taken to be some corny pretense. All different colors in prints of red and green, bright adornments, on me, like the black man in green velvet who went into the baths with the midgets, we have no traditions and the people are always in a bad mood, liverish and dull, it's a mysterious location that doesn't fit in, this one consciousness that seems to have been made for me, you told me that. It, like the happenings I spoke of before, does return to the self if I can speak of that, nothing seems very foreign does it, even flagellation and martyrdom, don't be so cynical. As if you had everything worked out with your car and house and all your stuff, your things in their places and your neat pile of poems and films all dated and labeled and the big wealthy mess in your kitchen and your sly references to even less well known psychologists and sociologists, the ground is covered with buildings here and the space in between's paved over, do you want to hear a joke, I was sleeping with Jack Kerouac in a swimming pool but his penis caved in, it was maximally made of cloth like Marie's, the three black midgets were not there, they were on the streets, on Eighth Avenue and 26th Street, we saw them on our way to Marvin's shoe store, the green velvet man at the baths wore a black fur hat with a wide brim and plumes, gray plumes going up into the sky. It's relief when the road is dry, I shift closer to you, and when there is snow it's good to see it melting into water instead of freezing over into treacherous ice but when it's warm we can still fear the rain, it's making the road slick, she skidded on the wet leaves, I am always able to think of one and another person I could phone, it could even be you with whom I've had a lot of misunderstandings but not war, visions or desolation. You adore the dramatic fancy pavements over the even fancier ground and among the hormones that make you calm, there's a situation that renders us helpless, the remorse of pregnancy in light when one is not resting, there are bears and water pipes in this city and a place newly opening that says, "Adonis's Hot Heroes." When I came back there was a voice that kept repeating, "In Henniker..." this or that. And this or that was a prison, I was in jail for starting a fire, I was all alone in a fancy cell bookcases and clothes hanging at the sides of my cell and outside it a table, our table, where one of you came to tea to sit down and talk to me, and he said, "I see you take a cigarette only when you want to, that's good," and since I had only begun my imprisonment there was very little chance that I'd get out soon, all the other prisoners were men, I could walk around and over to the fancy dining hall, just like college, it was small and the tables were set with linen napkins, it seemed like not such a bad place to be but for the dreariness of the layout of it and its loneliness and being forced to be there and I did get to go for some kind of walk or outing but like the pages of a book with a great title that implies it will tell you exactly what you need to know, it was full of the same obdurate words of the English language, too difficult to read and not so full of secrets as you thought, or to make yet another analogy that is after all coming from another, not me, I deny it, it was like the smell of some favorite food that for some reason just cannot be eaten, please trace your hand for me so I can see how the century is proceeding and whether I'm allowed to be present with some pleasure in the right way in it. Some people love to do all the work for others, it makes them feel light. I also saw that as much as I was trying to type a message by, for each letter, finding the right spice, like a for arrowroot, b for basil on to o for onion powder, my kitchen too was a mess and the message wound up being a ball of yarn and I had to cease to send it when I couldn't find the peppercorns for p. It has been so deliberate that it hasn't snowed yet I almost wish it would get on with it. If you could make people love you as much as could be possible, well I am getting into the same old net, besides there isn't time for it, and no words. I stubbornly prefer not to do what you say. For fun we go to different bookstores. What are the poets of Iran writing? There must be some polemical Islamic poets. It would be laments for the dead, I read of the women weeping at the grave sites of their sons begging them to return to be sons for another moment, you are my only treasure. I do that too for the dead ones I have known yet I am accused of a blatant morbidity, so we are different and we weep less and less openly and everything is taken care of as they say and before the dead person's even buried or the sick one's beginning to recover, you are supposed to be not noticing it, the pain is so fearful to watch—and is this life of ours so much better? More wooden sticks strewn about the floor become identical to this dreary penchant for cheap survival, stories of the fate of the American Indians, when the baby's about to be born you call someone. Big clear toys, as big as they come, dolls as big as children themselves, giant red and yellow dumptrucks, a woman on the subway trying to carry them. November's last moth flew in and lit on the table, it was so numb with cold it couldn't move, we didn't put the pot of potatoes down on top of it, crushing it, we moved it to the windowsill, someone said it was probably dead so there was much excitement when it flew lively into the bathroom to fly around the light. We have only more lights than we need and we've forgotten to buy lamp oil. Tonight it is cold and still, eve of tomorrow's December, the best month for long dreams.

Visions or Desolation

COME ON, THERE'S always the chance the kids will do this, fight uncontrollably like crazy screaming like howling buddhas and tearing each other's never cut before hair out, the bigger ones hitting the smaller ones on the heads with metal tops like latent homo and heterosexuals with fierce exclamatory natures. Our plan is to just do everything ourselves without any babysitters for the next two weeks and then the classes are over, then we'll go to New York for a while again, the midwife said I had a neat uterus and she could feel whole arms and legs of the baby, I was waking and talking to a woman on the phone the other day about a playgroup and she kept using the word "shoot," kept saying "Shoot I would do anything" and "Shoot I understand what you mean, yes shoot," then we'll come back here and spend January getting ready to have the baby, then the baby will be born at the end of that month, I can't find Dr. Spock can you? but before that we have to gather together all the things we need for the birth and for the baby, cotton balls and undershirts and roasted towels and a bureau for the baby's clothes and Marie needs a new coat, and we have to do some laundry sometime, when she plays outside now and squats to dig in the dirt the skin of her back is exposed to the air, and they both need new tights, there isn't any snow on the ground yet, it's easy to rely on the Beat poets when you're teaching, any more abstract stuff often turns the students off, they find Frank O'Hara much too difficult, I also want a lot of red velvet material and a big red rug to induce feelings that can go past the moon, it's full again today, those regressive jerks in my classes keep talking about how LSD makes deformed babies, these matches are called Rosebud because they have red tips of fire, so many times when you're pregnant people can't help but tell you all the worst stories they ever heard, I miss the part of Main Street in Lenox right in front of the bank where the crosswalk led across to the entrance to the library and the buses and cars came circling around the obelisk, Henniker's equivalent of an obelisk is a kind of former fountain on a triangular island at the foot of which is always lying an old apple core and a discarded ribbon, when I look up I see a portrait of a man holding a glove, if Russell doesn't see us at all tomorrow perhaps he'll think we're not there, I have only twenty minutes left if I'm going to get any sleep, what can I give you, is writing this offering? Lying in bed is a turmoil, anything can enter in, early tomorrow a woman will come with some children, she will be able to explain things to me about this town, she teaches cross-country skiing, now why don't I do something like that instead of wondering only about babies, poetry, the city, the country and the wisdom I was trying to talk to you about, yet I must've sounded a little corrupt when I said that. I do wonder also about you and your way of slumping in a chair which confounds your other way of looking like a jogger in pajamas, I shouldn't mention pajamas or everyone will make fun of me, I'm sort of looking forward to this January of heavy snows and waiting, bitter cold and never parting again for a while. I don't like teaching, it distracts us, it's like everything else everybody says is healthy, skiing, jogging and sitting up straight and being independent, eating seaweed and living in the country, the protean brain, or the other way around: Motherlant is nothing if not protean. A peninsula is a body of land almost completely surrounded by water. Some old people live on one can of soup a day. A little peach in the orchard grew, a little peach of emerald hue...I was reading this novel about a man who burned his girlfriend's house down and then later was almost completely the cause of her father's death and they try to make a case for this rogue being rather an expression of the girl's own destructive instincts so the book winds up without a sense of humor (ENDLESS LOVE) and so am I, it's better to go back to NOTES FROM THE UNDERGROUND for that. More subtle like the weather's blatancy (does that mean wind?). But I'm sure you never asked me for my opinions, you asked me for something of beauty, like the idea of the constructing of a house, something less than esoteric, something formal that also has a use, a wedding song or a description of some semi-precious stones. How am I supposed to fit in to this life where children eat so much expensive fruit and leave their trucks in the sand to be run over by the diaper man, will the fleshy inflorescence of a collection of color photographs still look like a pineapple or pine cone or a small bomb that looks like one of those? You and I like having each other to ourselves, I compare the two hands of the two yous but I still can't tell if the hurt one is swollen, why do we have so many injuries lately, is it wrong to walk into a door or let windows slam on your hands, to be slightly stabbed by the midwife to determine the iron content...Something shifts and as Wittgenstein would say, and anybody else not normal, to take some pleasure in being obsessively careful, to quietly comb out the baby's hair and take one's time, to decorate the children with ribbons and whisper to them, to prepare special foods, secret inducements, to linger conversing about the dreams in bed, to encourage the counting of peanuts, these are the methods of the usual, inducements to the ordinary, to pass the time, to adduce pleasure, to encounter danger, to see silver spots before the eyes without fear, the safest form within which to take risks, the advertisement of the day's misery if I can still look up and see the man with the glove and a chance image of the accumulation of objects, the storehouse of pictures which will not work out in memory, there's only one time when you can't be doing this or that kind of work and have something like a drink make it easier than it is, and that's when you're giving birth to a baby but there's nothing new about that. I wish I could try it as a man for once and be the one watching nervously instead of the inhabitant of this always female body, always momentarily fertile and prone to that if I can use that word, it's worse than taking LSD, not over till it's over, hoping the baby will be born before another child wakes up, warning people that your screams are not real screams like in a movie or book, expressions of the forward movement of time or movements of the forward expression of time like words, in that case scream is to lean forward and make the time pass faster, hours by clocks in what they still call labor, different from plain work, working in contractions of the muscles of the...and so on, you know all about it I'm sure, lucidly there's space in between during which you feel like yourself again and that is like the drink, then when the baby is finally born you don't know for a moment if you're thinking of yourself or the other, there's no reason why the words other and mother ought like an otter to rhyme, they didn't in Middle English, but then you wouldn't want to know the derivations for mother, the lees or dregs, I won't go into that, which is why it's difficult to remember to immediately hold the baby, you don't know the baby is different from you, especially if someone else is there. I had a baby once drawn out by forceps from my unwitting unconscious body and when I woke up I said, what was it. It's worth the tedious trip of consciousness with all the unnecessary pains to thus conquer nature with memory's astuteness, it's like the perception of color in after images. There is an end to the sensation, so of this letter.

,.;:?.(-")!

IT'S COLDER OUTSIDE than it is in the refrigerator so you can put the beer on the windowsill, we've been having a really milk winter. They just put oil in the oil tank and the bill was $335. I'm having a hard time working tonight and I couldn't stand just spending the whole night unannounced in the bath which is what I tend to do during what you describe as the tunnel I'm entering into but the only line I could think of to begin some writing with was: we never use our house for the holidays. I dreamt I was lying on the straight and horrible single bed in Peggy's aunt's house in Brooklyn which is where we'd been staying and I was reading a book which opened with an introduction by a witch or rather a wizard whom I saw distinctly speaking the words to me and his face was like a mountain. Marie says witches make chemicals. The wizard in my dream had beards and hair and hats all running cohesively into his nefariously textured skin, all lakes and rivers and valleys all over his face, then the rest of the book had visual keys and whenever it got to the part about workers and labor there would be an interesting screw on the page loosely screwed into its nut. I was just getting morosely into the plot of this entertaining book when Lewis suddenly sat up in bed and I thought I heard him say, Suzanne died. But he said he didn't say anything and we lay awake taking bets on the time which was dawn but still very dark, these days are getting shorter, are yours? Suzanne's our new babysitter who'll move in in January, last night I had to talk to her parents in North Carolina to assure them I was sane, we chatted about the Red Sox, I don't know why her father's a Yankee fan, he had read my Carlton Fisk poem, she's a student of mine with overflowing red hair who reminds me of Diane diPrima and who thinks she's Jack Kerouac and seems to have taken LSD once a week for the last forty years. Then I had a few typical pregnancy dreams about eating and shitting. Next the recurrent now-the-baby-is-born-at-last dream, this time I had three girls all at once, but I kept insisting they were not triplets, they were not in any way identical and I was mad because I had no memory of the birth and so I knew someone had induced me to take some drug. I went to see the three babies for the first time and I found three women in various stages of life, in fact one was another student of mine named Nancy Olean. But they all had to be nursed anyway and I was determined to nurse all three so I decided to give each only one breast at a time so as to conserve enough milk for all but for some reason I needed to put a spoon in my nipple and spoon-feed them and the milk was flowing abundantly, it was spilling on the ground, I was amazed. Then I found a parade through a second-hand store where everyone found just what he or she had been looking for and putting all these things on we became characters. My new skirt was not as warm as I had hoped and was only a façade. These are my homely dreams. We're going back to New York in a week after classes are ended and when we return it'll be only three more weeks till the baby's supposed to be coming, she the midwife believes to be a she, because it has a fast heartbeat or something. Whoever it is it's getting bigger and banging up against me all the time, when I read in bed at night I put my hand on my belly and feel all the shifting and jumping, sometimes it seems like this person will get herself into some position in there and not be able to get disentangled. Everybody tells me I don't look that big but I've gained 25 pounds and the midwife said I have a "neat uterus" because the I of me, the part that's still just me, is skinny enough for her to be able to feel where the arms, legs and so on are at any moment. This is the part of being pregnant where the baby begins to seem separate so I begin to feel like a person carrying a satchel strapped to her front, like my schoolbooks or something. Meanwhile everybody can't help but tell me all the worst stories they know about 3-day labors, deformed and unintelligent babies, hideous flus, caesarians at the hands of cruel doctors sadistic nurses and hospital errors. Why am I telling you all this? Because you evince an interest in my being pregnant I guess, most people seem to want to pretend you're yourself which of course you aren't, or else they tell you how grouchy you seem, except for Peggy and Lewis, so it's to be either Max or Theodora, Theodora Malke (my father and Lewis's grandmother Molly). Lewis's parents think we're odd for liking Max and Malke better than Michael or Molly, when actually I still prefer Violet. As Winter and the pregnancy wear on I lose my sense of humor and become doggedly devoted to eating, taking baths, indulging in herbal remedies and endeavoring to feel transparent, and also, a big part of the task, finding great books to read that are not so great as to alarm me. I also read the *Times*, I don't know why. We've had no real snow yet though we've stashed a supply of food, cigarettes and beer for being snowed in on this pretty echoing mountain. I don't go into the woods anymore, I stopped during the hunting season and now I'm too clumsy to duck under and trip over everything with any exhilaration. Marie's been writing some words and has gotten involved with the story of the American Indians which she makes me tell her over and over again, part of her fascination is with shooting and with Indians' killing of animals for food and whether they are good or bad. Sophia's been learning to imitate Marie having tantrums and this is my house. Lewis and I are impatient, as you know. After the baby's born aside from then being able to hold it in my arms I'm going to extract myself from prose writing and with all the new knowledge gained therefrom, which may turn out to be none, I'm gong to excavate some more poetry. It's time for my bath, there's no place better to be pregnant than in the water, this fancy college has no swimming pool. So, hoping I haven't seemed too indulgent in speaking of my own state of being only, I send love.

Hand-Shaped Poems Like Snow-Making Machines

DEAR JAY,

We got a bill for fuel oil from Ayer & Goss for $335 and we were wondering is that for one delivery, in advance of our use of the oil? How big is the storage tank and where is it, I am curious, is it in the ground? As far as I can see it's not in the cellar. Also, is this the bill we share with you, your paying 1/4th of it? If so how should we go about it, shall we give you a check for our 3/4^{ths} or what? Also there was a tire on a rim on the front porch, could you tell us where it is—is it the one in the garage near your other car? Saw the snow-making machines working at Pat's Peak today. If we don't see you before this, we may be going away around the 17th of December for about ten days. Yours. List of things to buy and get, there's no end to it in America, now we need some lightbulbs, the bulbs burn out in this old house fast, it's not a new house and we need things for the birth, two rubber sheets and cotton balls and alcohol and new clean clothes for the baby, P.S. Forgot to mention that though the heating is working o.k. we thought you should know that our thermostats are all wrong—we set them for about 59 degrees to get what seems to be about 65 or maybe more degrees of heat. Our own version of what the sterile hospital might have though the hospital's not sterile, it's full of germs too, all these foreign ones whereas the ones in our house already know our baby, three new baby bottles and a bottle brush and diaper pins, coffee cups and measuring spoons and a tarp for the winter car, to protect it from the snow, to keep the snow from falling into the motor through the rusted holes in the hood, Marie needs a guitar and some drums and she and Sophia need wagons and sleighs and a few horses and we need maple syrup which is the only real product of Henniker, I have to remember to take pictures of the field again before the snow covers it for good, my appetite is bad and this light is dim. Dear Fanny, So glad to get your note. I thought you just meant, if you meant d—d, you must mean my parents and family and that's all which would sort of put me in there with them in a way I wouldn't like to be just yet since I didn't want to be damned either, even on this earth as we have it, I was starting to get worried about just where I was. You sure are a Catholic! I don't think I ever met one quite like you before, I wish you could spend some time with me and my Catholic girlfriends, we would all really have some tales to tell each other! Sometime we have to sit down and I'll get to tell you about the lesbian nuns I met in college and the Jesuit priest who tried to get me and my friend Grace to give him a blowjob during a retreat in high school and stuff like that. One of the greatest frustrations of being up here is that I thought we'd get to see you more often. Tell me about the expulsion of the White Slave. I haven't seen LATER yet. Our plan is to stop in Boston for one night around the 17th of December, then go to NY. Would it be o.k. if on the way back we came to stop with you for a night or two? We would love to, we would have our crib with us and Marie just needs a normal bed, it would be sometime between Xmas and New Year's, if that would be possible. Last night we saw Lea, she and Russell and Paul were on their way to the play in Henniker and though Lea's teeth were chattering from the cold she didn't seem to be dressed for in her seal coat over something that looked dramatic and skimpy, I thought she looked quite beautiful and she said she felt well and Marie was still awake and she didn't hesitate to excoriate Lea for being the most interesting babysitter of all time and thus leaving her in the lurch with a lot of bores. Lea had some sweet tea and Paul and Russell drank beers and they rushed off for the play which seemed brave of Lea to do. Our life hasn't been that hard, don't mistake it, actually I've never before in a pregnancy had enough money to eat so well and the winter so far has been milk, if only we had a fucking jeep! Sometimes when I'm stranded here I feel desperate and long for someone to see or call, and that was especially so around the time Lea got sick and I kept fearing another sudden disaster, oh I'm sure I don't need to tell you. Let us know if we can visit or I'll call you. These snow-making machines look like amateur anathemas, they were making something that froze on the trees, the little bushes by the pond like in a movie, but it wasn't snow, it didn't look like snow, it was some white spray shooting up into the air so that by the time it came down it could wind up looking like snow. Marie said she hated them, they made a lot of noise and they made noise all day we could hear them from our house, it's an industry and they seemed to work much slower than nature, it seems like it would take at least a week for enough phony snow to accumulate for some reputable skiing, it would be funny to look up at the mountain, Craney Hill, in its drear November colors this December still, and see one big path of artificial snow created in among it where the ski slope is. But a habit of making snow is perhaps no more incomprehensible than to have another baby. What if I really did drive the car and I was on my way from here to there, not far, and suddenly I began to have the baby. If the contractions got intense really quickly, though I don't think anyone's ever had a baby in less than an hour and that's everybody who's pregnant's fantasy, to have the baby so fast you don't notice it, that's why I keep dreaming the baby's born and in every dream no matter what the outcome, boy or girl or twins or triplets or full-grown men and women or the rest, in every dream I am never present at the birth and sort of catch up on it later and go and see the baby just as if I had been given scopolamine or something, the drug of the sweet schizophrenic cheated sleep of labor and birth, but if I did start having contractions I could drive in between them and in a little while maybe I'd be home or maybe I'd have to stop somebody on the road, call the fucking rescue squad, somebody who really thought I was a lunatic until I was able to say, gosh or shoot, as the New Hampshire women say, I'm in labor, I'm going to have this baby, well I guess they could see that by looking at me, it's not like a picture of the place you were born you carry around in your head, and then what would happen, maybe they'd drive me home or maybe this baby will be born in New York, but the baby won't be early, I'm sure of that, now I've heard some stories of the baby being five weeks late, that would be unbearable and I would shoot myself, then the baby is so big you can't even get it to come out, say ten and a half pounds, like I was when I was born, my sister remembers being outside the hospital looking up at the window with my father and his saying, your mother and your new sister are up there, well she probably hoped he meant in heaven she was feeling so jealous and that's what she says. They would taunt me for being too skinny and not eating enough, simultaneously they felt free to torture her for being too fat, also simultaneous with the feeding to both of us of an enormous quantity of meat and sweets. There was no end of jelly beans and jujubes in our lives, kool-aid, yankee doodles, devil dogs, lorna doones, cream cakes and butter cookies. It will be warm in New York at Xmas again this year. The snow-making looks like steam from a fire and up close there are no flakes, I wish we knew something like the mirror before the stove, regulated to spew out too much gas so when you turn it on—it doesn't need to be lit with a match—it takes a second and then there's an explosion of gas practically up to your face and a huge flame is lit then wider than a restaurant's. Warmth is for everything, hot baths are a cure, the beers in gold cans make it hard to sit on the hard chair, it's twenty-five out and the machines are still on, they make the peak look smaller and there's a bright light on at the top of it to light their work and they sound like someone cracking his knuckles in the dark or like a low-flying plane, it sounds like someone making snow, these machines are our weather forecasters, Marie woke up milk spilled in her bed from her indigent bottle, the man of the mountain breathes out and I think the mountain is gone and the stars are dimmed, do you think it's because of something I did? When I first got pregnant with Marie, David said don't stop Valiums till you're sure you're pregnant. He gave me a lot of other advice too, he said don't have the baby at home and don't have the baby in your room at the hospital, you'll need to rest, now I don't take his advice, I escaped, just like Anna O., no wonder he won't answer my letters.

Dear David

IT'S BEEN A LONG TIME, I think I've let two issues of the magazine go by since writing you, I usually know I am writing four or five times a year. Now a lot has happened, I have a new address and I'm teaching at a college in this town in New Hampshire, not too far from Putney actually and I keep remembering as we are driving here from New York about your fast trips there in your Mercedes. Meanwhile largesse is not so far from us either and at the same time as we're getting a salary for the first time since the 35 dollars a week I used to get at the Poetry Project, Lewis and I have gotten national endowment grants, so, strangely, it would've been more "economical" to stay in Lenox! Here they pay us $1100 a course to teach rich kids how to write about skiing. The students don't know who Milton is and they're jealous of all of us who "grew up in the sixties" and though they have enormous experience with drugs, it doesn't seem to have made them any less rigid than, say, I can't say whom. We live in half a house rented from a ponderous child psychiatrist (and how come it is that no matter where in New England I live I am in close contiguity with a person of your profession?), the house is beautiful but enormous and heated with oil and we are just before this mountain where all the skiing goes on and tonight they've turned on the snow-making machines which sound like giant butterflies because so far this winter there's been no snow. We are isolated here and lonely, but for the writer who hired us to teach and it's a long story which would amaze you, his daughter lived with us for a while to be our babysitter and she had a stroke, an anomaly, and now she is recovering. Lewis wishes we could move back to New York and I want to be Tony Perkins for a while. I'm working on a prose book which is nearly done, it's sort of a book of letters like this one. Believe it or not, Doubleday was reading the complete STUDYING HUNGER journals though I never heard officially from them but I did hear that they could not bear to think of publishing it as a book. I had typed them all out in Lenox, excluding the pictures, with you as "Belial," a figure I'm sure the editors at Doubleday can't recall. Also I wrote a long poem called "Midwinter Day" which is about one day in Lenox, and it might get published as a book. We're still doing our own publishing though not much this year because, till now I guess, we didn't have any money and couldn't get any grants, especially for the magazine, all the "funders" hate it. Marie is soon to be four, Sophia is two, Lewis just got to be 35 and I am almost that, and this new baby's due in six weeks or so. And then there must be an end to this family! The new baby will be Theodora or Max and Peggy says the new book must be called whatever the new baby is not. I'm sick of the chores of having babies and I don't like raising children in the country all alone, I wrote this piece equating all the Iranian occurrences, perhaps the most narcissistic piece of all time, with all the kinds of expressions of one's anger in terms of hostages and outrages and international law—the way it might appear in one's dreams, at least I think I did. Suffice it to say that in my anger I love you and I would give anything to see you, one of the things I miss about Lenox is that there I always thought I might meet you by accident and here in odd-shaped and un-euphonious Henniker I know there isn't a chance of it! What have I done to deserve this one-sided correspondence of ours! Sometimes I think maybe if I say something like I'm going to have the baby at home, which I am, you will feel enjoined to write back—purely for my own safety! And among all this snow-making I seem to be subjecting myself to, I never cease to think of you with love, wish me luck.

I'll Drown My Book

LIFE IS REAL LIFE IS earnest love or fascination is my middle name as fair thou art my bonny lass so deep in love am I and the grave is not its goal and I will love thee still my love till all the seas gang dry till all the seas gang dry my dear and the rocks melt with the sun I will love thee still my dear till the river something run dust thou art to dust returnest wast not spoken of the soul a little peach in the orchard grew a little peach of emerald hue warmed by the sun and wet with the dew it grew one day passing the orchard through et tu Brute. I am mourning in a phantom way, I am more than one person, I am so much with child I shouldn't even be here! Writing at my desk with bad habits and no moths. And what to my wondering eyes should appear but a miniature melancholy and eight tiny anthropomorphic glass boxes, more rapid than assholes they sank in the ocean of all the snow-making I heard in my ear as if it were wine, you came down the fucking stairs and I saw I was with you despite my own ears, the own the best and safest grew, the light of the hearth became a nun to me like a student, as you, it's midnight, the rest is curfew for vigilant retreatants, lights out, no mirrors except clouded ones to see how the headdresses are set tonight, not askew like the Egyptian bus shattered in the driveway by cars, maybe it's British or brutish like us, the more so, I see your shadow and now I'll have to set myself straight, give up a good night's sleep and only dream of the moon, recalcitrant, hooray for the moths and wasps who slept on my golden fingers then, this heart of abolished stone is ridiculous again, it's mine.

Portrait of a Man Holding a Glove

I WANTED TO SEND YOU this present, rigid as life may be cold as the floor but we didn't have the money till today and now you won't have it by Xmas which is long past Channukah but that won't matter will it? You can't get anything good exactly in America, I can't understand why life has got to be rigid, the moon on the breast of the crestfallen snow, you don't make love enough, it's too much, list all the kinds of poetry including poems that have shapes, that have been forced into shape, the privacy of life with or without the tantrums of us lesbians, we kingly put a sweater over our skirts to protect us from the fancy cold. As soon as I get to be able to tell all the whole thing disappears, it isn't there. There was this woman who came to see me, the first Henniker woman I've gotten to talk to, Mary Faith Radcliffe, she had two black children so you can assume she's accumulated knowledge. She told me when her first baby was about to be born she was living alone in a cabin in the woods, she refused to go to a hospital, she had no one living with her, she was only having the Henniker doctor, Dr. Brown who delivered all the babies at home, to be with her for the baby's birth. She was having labor pains for two days then, the doctor was coming and going, finally he got iced in and stayed for 14 hours, the baby wouldn't come out, nobody loves me, the labor was centered around a wood stove, there was no other heat in the house and the doctor was sitting exhausted on a toilet near the warmth of the stove, he said maybe you should go to the hospital, the baby won't come out and she did. The nurses were mean, she was a woman alone, she refused to take drugs, they tried to dupe her into taking them and in the middle of her contractions they would tell the doctor she had assented to some dope when she couldn't talk to fend it off, then finally there was an x-ray which said the baby's head was just too big so they did a caesarian and she and the beautiful black baby were there together at last though it's hard to know how they felt about it by that time. Then she had another later by a nice caesarian with a doctor of feeling and then perhaps by that time things were changing enough, I have this man in the face of my mirror, women always have stories of childbirth and sex and the rest, any woman has a good store of stories to relate, and I suppose any man but that's different and we don't want to hear so much about exploits in this sense. Like searching like a mouse for the lost snow tire in the plentitude of the barn, no I don't mean that, it was a front tire not a snow one. I'm scared to go beyond the barn but that's none of your business, so far I have access to what I need. It might sound strange to say that as a pregnant person among the peers of my house, Lewis, Marie, Sophia, I need someone to say this or that to, it rained last night on the sixth of December and if this were one of the other pregnancies I would think that was great, faster and faster, a good omen for a mild winter till the baby is born but this time I still have to get through the bulk of the winter's accumulation, whatever it might be unless it all comes in February after the baby, I am confused, not by what I am saying but by rest and work. When you say something to someone like why don't you do this or that, they can't immediately go and do it, it's out of pride. Your hands were beautiful. Some babies moan, nothing comes of it, she goes back to sleep, she was dreaming, as the other child said, of the pond. I read that Marx was a belabored person, I don't have a lighthearted novel to read, just Marx and Dostoevsky, I wish I was more in charge of my benumbed tongue to tell you about the man who feels the biological impulse to fuck and procreate, that would be a secret letter, more like a poem and in a poem you can't defend or deform yourself, say why you're right and why you're mad at someone, you have to keep your distance, you have to peruse the bookshelves, you can't be the junkies of fights, you can only write about it and if you're successful well that may not be so good, you may still not be adored at all. No I'm only fooling about all this. Everywhere I look there's that Italian man holding his glove. I can feel the air I gently let in, cold and not so gentle, extreme, as I get more pregnant, I'm not allowed to write, it's forbidden to write, my mother said I ought to want to have children but she also said you ought not to do any fucking and she said it was sex and her children that caused her disease, step on a crack break your mother's back. To be facile at the typewriter or with the pen might be a little like being a good lover, as they say, and pleasing. We were not trained in the arts of love, not at all, we were trained to not notice them, we were trained to abstain because that was easier. We were trained to do without even masturbating, the slightest of the arts. Am I being naiver than usual? You shouldn't even speak of that. It's impossible not to remember everything except the important part, one thing. We never learned how to delicately jerk off a guy, perform an expert hand job, and lose our sense in everything. Not that we don't know now, its' just that for a time I've lost it. Sex is realtied from brokers to money so when I see the babies coming out so nice and good I'm reminded that sex has ceased to be that which I could formerly get away with like everything bad but now it's the cause of this and that and it's good, I'm sorry I thought I could forget an upbringing like living in poor light. To live near the Arctic Circle for a while in that light the sunset momentarily permits us in reminiscent New England land of clean white hard-fought and winding up incestuous kinds of love. I thought I loved that coupling with the necessity of the seasons but now I see that when you said to me, most people don't even notice the weather at all, that what you were meaning was the weather was remembering too much like child abuse or something. My love is abusing you, you don't even know it exists, you say I neglect you like the spirits of the man holding his glove, you are dead to my attentions like the nascent flower of the night I give up to be excited enough to write this, I know I will not sleep on account of it, you became angry when I preferred knowing sleep to you, children to your name and a few years later they are no more closely mine, let's do some drinking and singing together and why not celebrate yours as I am mine, we're lost like an old clean cloth, two cloths and children born beseeching them it shows in their eyes. Two books, I notice I look like a monkey's skull, the beer capsizes on my cotton skirt, not warm enough for this time of year but the only one that will still fit me under which I wear heavy black tights I thought were expensive enough to keep me warm but they don't. You might say let this one be cast with her luck into a cell and let the cause of her imprisonment forever read—"we knew she could not shout!" And as she shouts to please she begins to say words, perhaps it will end forever with the ready to be born baby acting as erratic as she was, the long night, no sleep at all, no real dreaming though she thought she had a dream, something about something, remembering she had said to someone that she would buy a painting and if she did what would Rosemary think? I fear the idea of buying a painting will escape me too soon, I know there isn't enough time and just as the man with the glove is looking at me with his funny shoulders sticking out of his oddly cut coat with a frilled white shirt visible underneath it, his crimped hair, its part, your part in this, girls in all their direct and neutral beauties, you are tripping over cords and cursing and getting into bed, we curse and get into bed, we make a funny bridge.

Molson Golden, Golden Lights

THIS SPACE AND THE cold of the artificial snow not melting in seventy degrees, I shouldn't keep mentioning degrees as if I knew them as I do you like after Marie was born and later in February the mixed up bushes and trees began to signal blossoming only to be frozen, the people who were building their fast house this fall, I don't know you, cursed by the children's head doctor for insulting his dreary sense of absent privacy, we're lucky this year, they got everything done before the snow or the snowmaking but then maybe they too like to ski and can't laugh at a hot winter like we do. First night of Channukkah. Let's have a bath, it's a day to let your hair dry. It's snowed since then, not really covering the uncut grass, they don't plow the road unless it's four inches high, the snow. Like the skiers on rolling boards on the dry road, I have to practice doing this I can't seem to stop. The eventual angel of everything in this wafting sky, I forgot to tell you we saw a white squirrel on Ramsdell Road, white as that. If there had been snow we'd never have seen it, a signal of the most consequent luck, pure white unusual luck, a luck that isn't normal, a luck lacking in color, luck of all the colors, the almost ugly warmth of the barren trees, patience of the colder rocks and benevolent lies of the safe tight road—just stay in the car without moving, you'll probably get there on these hysterical bald tires. We had them replaced this morning with some better ones, ones with real ridges or tread they call it, we tried to do it ourselves but the car wouldn't jack up again. And while we were doing it or having it done we walked around the now snowy somewhat corny crazy-shaped town, what is this baby doing in my belly. Another big machine pulls up to the new place, I heard a voice, this one's red with a yellow crane and the man in it seems to know where the door to the house is, I can't remember what it feels like not to be pregnant, I have to sit like Gertrude Stein all the time, now I know why she had all those wide skirts made for herself, did I tell you that already? You're down by the rocks with sticks and when you climb up your coat is the only color I can see, you can't say anything without the school bus going by next. The squirrel was near the llamas where Ramsdell meets Main which is 114 and Flanders which by then has turned into Gulf, do you think I'll ever be as lithe as a llama is after this. Ornate and regal like giraffes because of the Venetian or Venusian necks, medical information on the vertebrae or something. At the Nook two women and a child sat in the booth behind us, we were having an elaborate breakfast, perhaps to celebrate the more useful tires on the car like having more than enough stamps for the week, or maybe just to pass the time or to remember our classes are over, I think I miss having to feel good enough to do them like a feather stuck in the lock of my desk for years or the double-decker London toy bus that got run over in the driveway when the oil truck came, there's a lot of beans in the closet for the snowstorms, do we belong here. One of these women, the younger one, started laying into a woman named Phyllis for not being neat and clean. She said Phyllis never took care of her kids and they always had holes in their shoes and dirty hair, she said Phyllis herself never had clean hair either and she said the kids had really dirty ears. She said Larry did a lot with the kids but he did not clean them, of course he is a man. But then she started talking about other women who were not clean and to this woman it seemed like no one in Henniker was clean, it looked like the woman she was talking to was probably her mother, the mother didn't really say anything. When we left I turned to see what this woman all about being clean looked like herself and I saw her child was clean-looking and the woman was wiry and nervous, smoking cigarettes the way country women often do, perhaps she had never been to a place that was not clean to notice if the people in that kind of place were or were not clean people and then Lewis told me that the one thing his students always said about the Nook was that it was not a clean place, it's a diner on Main Street, neither clean nor dirty to me, and since I was still staring at the woman there was nothing else I could do but, in the camaraderie of women who have children and wonder what other women do to keep them clean, smile at her and so I looked like I was smiling. I look clean, though I am not, so she smiled back. My children scream when I wash their hair and it reminds me of the woman in the thrift shop in Hillsboro who started a conversation with me about whether you could wear red with yellow and then she said, yes! look at this red shirt, it has yellow flowers on it! That proves it! So when I put on this green scarf this morning I noticed that some of the red and pink roses on it were the same color as this pink sweater I'm also wearing and all of this brought to mind the ideas about colors in our clothing we were brought up to be so obsessed with as little girls so that wearing pink shoes meant you also had to have pink something else, maybe gloves and a pink pocketbook and maybe a pink hat, all worn with a gray suit for Easter, that was around the time when men were wearing a lot of pink and gray or pink and black, pink shirts with gray suits and black and gray ties, 1957. "It picks up the pink in your scarf." Lewis's mother thinks it's primitive, flashy and lacking in style to wear bright colors like the reds and blues of the Ukrainian scarves, she prefers muted tones of the classier beiges, browns and grays. Even black I think is somehow too bright and she will never wear white, it must always be cream. I often think among the Warshes with such thick glasses maybe no one actually sees the colors, sees the attraction in them, takes pleasure in it. Or maybe it's just that they don't care about colors, many people don't seem to, like skipping the etymologies in the dictionary and just reading the meaning. But her name is Ray, so red and orange and yellow, so bright a name. Harry has a bright red shirt, often it's all right for men to do things women could never do. After all he's not really responsible for his shirt. Henniker is dark green-blue-gray, a name with some icy qualities in the k, like the blue of police light. Mrs. Aucoin whose husband plows our driveway said to stop by sometime, this fancy derivative of all my energy is becoming just baby—will it be there with emotions in

257

the crib then? And I be back to normal from waiting? As dry leaves that before the wild hurricane fly when they meet with an obstacle mount to the sky, it's luck or something, so gingerly, like the midwife's mentioning the need of a clean nightgown, the reporter's denotation of the poisons in the spinach. Bottles drop like shoes on the floors above, tired of waiting, I wouldn't want to skid. No daredevil way of even walking left in my feet in boots on the courageous ice and slush that signals slowest time, what will happen next and till a birth at the time of the famous January thaw, go and sin no more, absolute snow, it must be, as it will be when the story's left to be told.

The White Squirrel Again

WHEN I GOT YOUR LETTER it looked like a letter I had written to myself without remembering. Only consider all the things that happen when words aren't spoken or put down! Total recourse to the imagination, like this solitude, can be crazy. Even if I had said nothing "happens" with any poetry in American I could also add that 1979 seems to be worse than usual, or to have been. I haven't been asked to send poems to a magazine in a year, or give a reading, and one of the reasons we heard UNITED ARTISTS doesn't get any grants is because we publish ourselves too much, which is true. About obsessions I always find they result in a desire for pleasure, even eating sometimes. When I'm afraid to go on an airplane I seem to put on clothes that make me feel different from who I think I am, and that makes me less scared. The other way to deal with them is to replace one with another, like fear of being alone with washing clothes, ha! Why I started saying this was because the literary environment too must be turned into something else. Poets if anyone does have to retain their dignity just like children even when they get yelled at or ignored. In America sometimes the whole thing seems intolerably gloomy like impotence or a series of misfortunes, both trivial and huge, kind of like what's been happening to us since we moved to New Hampshire. So get back to work! Stop feeling sorry for yourself. The part of my house that keeps the beer coldest at this time of year is not the refrigerator, necessary as everyone finds one. Tomorrow's Marie's fourth birthday and as I walk around with two babies in hand and the other I see nobody even approves of doing *this* anymore! and you get the sense like one gets about writing that nobody wants that or needs them and would somehow rather do without all that stuff as if it's stuff, it reminds me of when we were still all truly terrified, for a moment, of, for example, the cops. And remember—never finish a long work before the holidays, it's like a double murder, again. We can't even get Channukkah candles here and I'm afraid to ask for them at the store. I hope that by the next time I write to you I'll still feel not too fat to do it or else I'll be liberated from carrying this baby around and then able to say good news!

What Went Wrong

IT'S GOING TO GET to the point in this place where we have to send to New York to get fish food. The fish leap up in anger and then I want to know, well what happened today was we got to this place called the Gourmet Mouse where I'm ashamed to say we were buying liver pâté made with pork liver even though today's the second day of Channukkah, it has a lot of iron in it and I won't take the midwife's iron pills so long as I've apologized for something, I mean you have to apologize a lot during the prelude to the "Holidays" so this mouse place which is run by a consequent New Hampshire mouse who is gay who is usually nice but today was making conversation with an awful woman who was buying about fifty dollars worth of gourmet mice, a woman who lives in Henniker no less who thought she could impress someone by asking for pine nuts and then the two of them started talking in some hideous way about all the fine things they couldn't get here and how the mouse woman was going to have to start wholesaling in Boston where all the better things can be gotten, well then it took a long time to get the liver substitute stuff I was getting and all this proves you should eat wherever and whatever's easiest to eat, McDonald's or something, just do whatever most other people are doing because in the end you're just a part of the evolutionary process and does it really matter about your iron content of your blood or the fastidious obsessive ideas you might have just because you're pretentious and overeducated, or else just do what you're told and take the iron pills and get a stomach ache and stop lording it over other people, just because you have enough money for once to buy this crap and then you pretend you're made of it and that's better than everyone else, much less get involved in those fascist ideas about having a superior baby, the whole thing about 90 grams of protein a day is ridiculous and if anybody of you could drink a quart a milk a day, well I will give it to you the best I can because when I left this place of the mouse which is called that because of the cheese, and the pignolia woman was just walking out ahead of me and I knew what she was thinking about is all this fancy pesto she was wanting to make if only she could get those fine nuts, so I got back to the car where Lewis and Marie and Sophia were waiting patiently and then we tried to turn around in their parking space which is almost contemptibly small, I mean the babies are just going to come out how they come out no matter what you try to do from day to day within this tiny range, getting crazy about what you eat is going to make the baby crazier later because you're crazy to begin with and he or she has to live with you practically for the rest of your life, assuming that in your crazy state you won't last beyond the child's adolescence, so we began to try to drive away but we couldn't turn around really easily and a big truck was blocking our only way out so we had to try and make this tedious u-turn in our bulky wagon and then suddenly, there's about half an inch of snow on the ground, some turned to ice, we couldn't go backwards, when you put the car in reverse it wouldn't go, nothing happened, it couldn't be stuck in the snow there isn't enough of it and we looked at it for a while and tried it again and again, then the truck that had been blocking our way came, a camper with some nice old hippies in it, and pulled away, then took pity on us and came to help, they pushed and I steered so we knew by that time for whatever reason we could only go in forward gear and it takes some time to get used to the particular crippling of the car but after about ten minutes or so we were resigned to it and got back out on the road going forward to find a gas station with a wave to the hippies who helped us coast away from the gourmet store we should never have gone to in the first place and now our aim was to stop at every gas station we could find open, it's Saturday, and see if someone could tell us what was wrong with the only car we need to get food and supplies to our house, just about ten miles away. Every station we stopped at had no one at it, it was either closed or hostile and Lewis went into one where they were really mean, I mean this neighborhood we live in is not friendly to people like Lewis who whip off their headbands before they go into a place because of all his hair but he doesn't want to be seen in his headband either though the one he's wearing now is an "athletic" one which slides up onto near the top of his head because it's elastic and makes his hair stand up like a crazy person's, the headbands he likes are velvet ribbons, they don't slide around but we can't get them here, and nobody could help us or even give us some idea what the fuck was wrong with by now we've concluded it must be the transmission which means fucked up, the car may be dying forever and then what will we do. We drove forward after canvassing ten gas stations, back forward to Henniker where one place was hostile again and said they didn't do any mechanical work at all and the other place I went into thinking it was worth taking the chance maybe they'd respond to a woman and I said my piece, what went wrong and then stood there dumb while seven men discussed all the various fucked-up trucks of the day and how busy they were and how they had no tow truck today and everyone was stranded on the highway and the local shell station whom they did not get along with anyway was busy till next Thursday and then finally one of them said well you can take my truck to the old man whose truck was fucked up miles down the road, you can take it but it has a lot of shit in it and then I looked around the room and realized this was the kind of place where a person like me, a woman, was supposed to be offended by the word shit and since nobody had paid any attention to me since I said what went wrong, I walked out. Then one of the guys came out and said at least he could take a preliminary look at it but all he said was the transmission fluid looked o.k., all these guys have big accents, but it didn't smell so good and there was no way of telling what went wrong, then he disappeared and after a while Lewis went back into the room of men and they said they couldn't look at it seriously till Wednesday and Lewis said that means we're stranded and can't even get home or if we can get home we can't get out of home and what could we do without reverse, so we went still forward anyway, careful not to get in a situation where we'd have to go backward which Lewis found an inspiring way of driving, we went back to Henniker to the market to buy enough food to last till Wednesday just in case we couldn't get out and the food had to include things like ice cream for Marie's birthday tomorrow, she's to be four and four years ago tonight at this time I was getting what they call a cervical block, the first of three I had, it's a numbing needle in your vagina, I would suggest to all women who may be in the future having babies to avoid these blocks and just be patient and we got up the steep driveway with it and we even managed to make room to turn the car around without using reverse by going through the snow so now all we have to figure out is how, and I forgot to mention we stopped back at the station to make an appointment and the guy said maybe a big transmission job costing five hundred dollars and this car wouldn't even bother to pass inspection if we bothered to take it, we just drive around annihilated, everyone says take it off the road it's too rusty, I guess we'll have to get a different car and our only problem then is how do we get to the senior prom, no I didn't mean that, how do we get to the different car, in what. And we can't get to the midwife's on Monday and of course the new car will have to have a cervical block, probably tonight. We used to have a '68 Chevrolet which lasted two years, it was a much better car than this piece of metal now pitted on the arc of our driveway so we can conceivably risk going for the paper tomorrow, it's Channukkah after all, I'd rather a big storm came and the baby came all at once and I didn't have to think about cars, let someone come and give us a car, I don't even care if it's a Mercedes Benz, I wouldn't be ashamed to drive one, let someone come and take care of us, I'm sick of it, it doesn't make sense to live someplace you need a car to get to, after all it's your home and everybody else around lives someplace like that too where they have to have a car and then all the surrounding stations just say well fuck you, you don't have to have your car and we can't fix it and you should've thought of that in the first place and bought a brand new four-wheel-drive vehicle that would've broken down and babbled at you anyway but at least then we would've had some respect for you and your plight but assuming everything will go o.k. is just stupid and we know you, you're the people around here who have the reputation for not even being able to change your own tires, well I might also say I need to get to church on Sunday otherwise I like you will be in a state of mortal sin and another thing you fucking anteater of a Christian wasp with all your pimples on your too-white face, I'll fuck your fucking mother while you're so busy at the famous gas station with all the men, you goddam illiterate honky creep, try coming into my bedroom sometime with your tiny ridiculous prick and mention that to your mother and then we'll see what's up and what's not in our neighborhood, you fascist ignoramus of the masses of booted men sucking up to trucks and going home to bottles, their glass necks just as tight as your ass, go fuck yourself with all your pretentious knowledge of the fluids, I won't get lubricated either like my chancy car but I'm human and if you leave me alone for a while I'll get better.

List the Kinds of Poetry

KINDER, DAS KINDER, in kindergarten, frozen syrup, it's something
like the coldest night, it was the coldest day, now the forward car won't
start, should I even tell you, we had a plan but Danny Aucoin whose li-
cense plate reads DANNYA, from the AAA, couldn't get the car started
anyway, it's his father who'll be plowing our driveway when it snows, his
aunt who teaches French at the college and who knows his mother might
come and deliver the baby, she's had nine Catholics and while Danny
was working on the freezing carburetor he only looked up to take notice
of the white cat that had gotten on the roof by climbing up the porch
screen, a dusty white cat, then it couldn't get down and sat to warm itself
in the cold sun reflecting on the drain pipe, it sat in the pipe sleeping, we
took it down, there is cold wrapped around my legs, last year at this time
I was sitting between two windows, memories are not treasures but mis-
haps like the cat who wasn't misshapen but hungry and dirty, the blue
truck was fancy and we couldn't go to buy another car, now this car has
nothing, has become a culprit, a sculpture in our driveway, the spark-
plugged car of spirit full of reclaimable apple and cedar pits, frozen ba-
nanas, a multi-colored umbrella and the leavings of the chipmunks, ar-
en't the deer cold tonight. The cat was catching, someone said you
shouldn't touch a cat when you're pregnant, days relating to cars are
empty, the cars are always full of things, they're wagons, the syrup says

it's pure, why sweet. Nothing then, a hard harsh hand, rough hands, hand lotion, the ruler in the pot of paints below your first drawing of a person, you followed the cat to the movies where she climbed better than we can, the complete works of atrophy, the works of scorn, best wishes for the New Year and now everyone has to say too, the new decade, hey where is your complaining letter, everyone's complaining, it must be the scene, the change of season, the time of year, the fearsome cold, the mildness of it, the battered cars and trucks, the need for paper and milk, we are a wheel. Those guys own houses, some of them have big new cars, they like to have them, they tell stories, they want to learn how to tell a good story, they do narrate one well but it can't be in poetry yet, it was all air, you fell down the stairs, dear you the brick is cold the plants dry, the pocket is attractive, the prints of the heavens will not be returned, it's too cold in there, the answer's in the mail, the postman won't drive up here, you have to wait for him, you have to be there at the box, you meditate and have a dream, there wasn't anything I wanted to hear, the books were badly made and fell apart, the syntax fell apart and we couldn't understand what we were talking about, we might have been telling a story or just speaking gibberish, it wasn't even on tape, he did that and he did that and he did something else but no one did this, perhaps she did, maybe she came closest, you can't tell when anything's ending, even a plain phone conversation, it's all in the same low blue mirror, it's crooked, where is my sister. I have a feeling you would love it, I have a Chinese book but then so does she, in fact she has so many of them, she has a drawerful and she's been everywhere, maybe I should travel too, maybe it would all seem as new as the country first did, what do you think. Living among all the famous, no one would know who they were, maybe we need that, he this and she that in order, we should have that, money disappears, that jar looks fat, it looks bigger than it is, eight ounces with a leaf in it, why think of perfection, the elixir of life the nature of obsession, hand tooled like the bathtub with claws reminiscent of a movement repeated so over and over as to accumulate too many of the same bottles of the same thing, to be used later, to be sure you have them, so as not to run out of them, again she bought two of everything, yet he bought fifty, feeling in the staid healthy house, her hair was yellow underneath, roses flying around on the generation's lampshade behind the light, the appreciation of light, I forgot, I didn't notice it, I got tired and resumed the party's stares, you put your fingers to your mouth repeatedly to show you needed a cigarette, they write about cigarettes and beer and grass and then I gave you one, lit, from my pocket, I punctuated, I walked across the grass we can still see, patches of slippery ice on the local map, the paper is not holding me up, I'm going to give up, there's a crack in the corner of her mouth, she instigates remorse in her stolidity, they played with the small drawers from a small table, if I had said put a doll in one of them it would have looked like a coffin or a womb, I imagined putting the baby in a drawer like Nick and Nora Charles, then getting canapés from room service, drinking the baby under the table, you wouldn't want to get wet in this cold, we might've acted stern and forbidden them to play in the bathroom, then they step with their tights into puddles of water and get them wet too, then there's nothing left to keep them warm, everything's wet and cold, it's a sign of love to know what you're doing, a sign of love not to vacillate and be too indulgent, a sign of faith not to say it more than once, would it be the same for a genius or the children of Maoists or Moslems, a mother and father in a state of trance, the genius of sheep in the restless snow, hot bricks put into the beds to warm them, hot compresses on the ankles with wool wrapped around, the liver is the organ of adults, Dostoevsky and Paul Bowles know that, Hawthorne wasn't liverish he was an anthroposophist, dyed in the wool, too transparent as a person but different with words, or differing like a 20¢ milk at the counter of the pharmacy, differing from the coffee, talk of the red and green in the dress, the highlights or what they used to call them, that person has a scar, you draw the arms and hands as if it were a mutant baby, words you could not get joyous about, that room is a whale and the space is not used, inside the whale is a room where the baby falls, I wonder what Claire is doing. Did she call him Jonas because she had felt like a whale while pregnant and how is Mable, her sentimental education. You've never known any people like these, you only seem to know, to be next to unusual and extraordinary ones, there is a dent in your skin. Oh Grace you were pulled from the car about to burst into flames but of course you were yet you still seem to love cars, the red and the yellow lights, the brights signified by the translucent blue lights on the dashboard, the compression checks and warranties, the rigid jacks in emergencies, this hand is softer, why is that thine. It seems a little too late to start reading MODES OF THOUGHT, the remains of that moth have been up there for ages and that little blood on the shade, did K do something to his wife, he didn't write a book about her did he, if the beer freezes will the pipes, there are two bars extending from each step, one from the exact middle of the step and the other from the end where one would step, the other end being the part that's joined to the next step, the part you would never step on unless you were going down backwards, these perspective steps with their bars leave a shadow on the wall that I can visit, next a bath. But how come some are orderly and actually put their stuff away. Xmas is dreary, let's eat out on it. I don't pretend to be any different, but I couldn't make a reservation for the dinner. Why don't you just come up and cook for us, does my blouse open in the front, or at least can you lift it up? Sweet amaryllis by a spring's soft soul-melting murmurings, you have to armor yourself, or arm you because after that you won't be able to read very much or write letters or books or stray to become less circular, as we are now but you can stare into space and think up couplets and maybe it would be a good time to start poking fun at everyone but not in rhyme, appeal seal, even heaven and so on. Now something's happening in the air, I think a storm is up, or an airplane from the military place, a flying saucer, not so specious up here, a tree falling from nerves, what are nerves she said, I said it's when you shake, these words are like the Dance of Shiva, what are all these books doing on my shelf when it isn't raining or snowing. To change the world get locked in a cell, well we are pursuing something else, something old or formal. You can't expect a person who's changed the world to understand everything after that. I know nothing but the pleasing hindrances today, stiles and stops and stays and stuff that comes between me and home or bone: clear the path and then shall I not run but fly to a feast, he said God's hands are round and upon myself I'll be buried, some winter not this one but maybe later, don't take too much notice of this this way, that way that way, this, and here and there a fresh Love is.

Accidental On

IT FINALLY GETS AROUND to the fact there isn't any special breathing you do in labor like duck á l'orange or something, it's labor and you generally pant the midwife said, she said a woman who'd been to some fancy classes wound up saying "out" for fourteen hours, the mantra out. There was a fight at the midwife's between two couples, two fathers were fighting, one was a follower of the guru maharaji and the other was a biblical Christian, probably born again. The midwife had incidentally said to the wife of the guru that the fetus in the womb goes through all the stages of evolution, now the biblical man didn't like that and began to excoriate the theory loudly saying that humans were unique and weren't evolved from any kind of other thing and you could prove that by...and then the guru defensively said he did his Bible-reading too and the midwife said she didn't care, she was a pagan. All this while the mid-wife was examining the red-haired wife of the guru who seemed to be newly pregnant, then the biblical couple went in and it seems they were having their fourth child, the woman was enormous and weighed 192 lbs, her baby, due at the same time as mine, a month from now, was also enormous and in her past pregnancies she had had all kinds of prob-lems. Now the biblical man started being overbearing again and saying why did the problems happen and what could be done to avoid them and the wife was silent, she said her diet was much better than it had been, for some reason the biblical man was awfully skinny and of course I found myself imagining their fucking, or rather his frenetic fucking with the enormous biblical woman whom Carol, that's the midwife, was trying to discourage from having her baby at home because of previous complications and the man was saying well this will be her last time so we thought it would be nice to be at home, this man doesn't sound so bad on paper as he was, so anyway there must be an end to his inseminations from the way he had been talking I thought for a while he might have a biblical stake in endless reproduction, the poor woman. He said he was trying to help with the children, or someone was, because everyone thought the reason for all the woman's problems was having two or three other babies to take care of while she was pregnant and it's true the midwife said you must've had an exhausted uterus which doesn't contract and so she would hemorrhage but then the woman said she hadn't nursed the baby right away and maybe that was the problem, they said they'd been reading up on it. The biblical man and woman spoke with bad grammar, they were pale and they had pretty children with wide pale faces. Did she eat junk food, the midwife asked. Then before this I had been introduced to the guru couple because they live in Henniker, on the other side of this mountain we stare at, you and I, to the south of it. Then it was my turn, the midwife and I toyed with the idea of an internal examination which she did, 2 centimeters dilated, but she said that didn't mean the baby would be early. I don't want to have the baby in New York, then we'd have to go to an emergency room with people in all the stages of suffering and pain. We could all move in with Peggy's family till the baby was old enough to travel. This baby can't be early because I haven't unpacked its clothes yet and it can't be late because I have to go back to school, it has to be on time, on the cusp as it were, as it's predicted. These words take up room they make me feel each is so large like a veteran of wars of words or worlds, I might as well, magical scarves made in Mexico are sold in Henniker but nothing much made here comes from here, Golden England College mugs to drink beer from and fancy chairs all black and gold with the college name on them, what is the point of that, what can you bring people for Xmas? A catalogue in which your own name is listed as teaching a course, a dictionary from the second-hand book-store where the turnover is slow, we can't even go there once a week to see new books, we've studied all the shelves, it's not like a library, I've got no library for myself here, the college one has metal gates through which you enter and leave like the subway for checking on your stealing but they don't know how you can jump over and start running fast, or even if you're a skinny enough thief sneak past the side of it without the thing, turnstile, turning, to allow people but not horses or cattle to pass through, there was a crooked man who walked a crooked mile, he found a crooked sixpence upon a crooked stile, a stone that helps you jump over a fence like a step, we could bring many heavy stiles to New York, they're all over the place, we could bring the white squirrel, pictures of the llamas, the white cat and branches from fir trees for Xmas aficiona-dos, branches like whiskbrooms too soft to brush the snow we haven't seen yet off, if the snow comes while we're gone they'll be plowing in our dead car and before you leave, as naively related as an Indian's story of his family of beavers you have to put a note you wrote on the car that says: this car won't start, move it if you need to plow, we're gone till January 1st. Will the tape freeze, what will happen to the cat who was frightened away by the landlord's dog, has the cat been deserted by what they call its master or mistress, will it freeze, why doesn't it go and eat mice, why is everything white but the ground that's supposed to be, why can't we use our new sled, I wish the baby was born, and hold the mail. Maybe I could have the baby in New York with Grace's mother's acupuncturist, free of all pain. Why don't we live in California with manuscripts, the students are gone and the townspeople are left to cel-ebrate this weird holiday, the woman in the bookstore said to me the other day, I didn't know your husband had written a book. We have an account there and charge things up, they'll give us anything we want, it's practically free, it's daring in a dumb way like concord to tell all, she knew where to slide her finger gracefully in, women have always want-ed to be able to stop having babies, or to abort them, when they needed to, women have always done that, Peggy said it was sexist of me to attri-bute to men the species-preserving feeling of necessity for fucking so that life goes on, whereas it's obvious women, but I can't say that, might wait longer than men to do that, I do think so, I don't want to have ten babies, some have eleven or thirteen, did you read about the woman who walked in to the hospital alone to give birth to her 23rd, I seem to get pregnant every chance I get, Russell and Fanny have seven already between them and other mates, the baby is tempting like the craving of a child for a tiny living thing, if only one of the pennies you lined up and pretended were students in their classes like you had come to life and you could carry it around alive in your pocket, speak to it, its yours, no one would know about it, what's-his-name's letter was cold, he doesn't like long sentences, Kerouacian pretensions, he makes me think it makes him think we're superficial, I wanted to see if the ice would freeze faster outside. Like the image from the movie of the dolls that come to life and talk to you. Real babies, *apologia pro vita sua,* how to tolerate the chaos of the days, how to get mad, repeating everything. You could think you were being a person and still never doing any more. The old days were ennui, nausea, freneticism, flight, sex, taxis, other; then again I wish I knew more. I don't know much about astronomy or even lapis lazuli, as the song goes. I know about the letters of words, death and pleasure, I can't remember much, I can't remember what you said in 1965 when you called up what's-his-name from my house but I was amazed you were doing it, I can remember your phone number easily, actually I do remember you just said we were sleeping together. I know Latin, some small Greek, I know what I thought about my mother and father. I don't have ancestors, I know a lot about the northeastern part of the United States, I do know something about American Indians and I know about babies up to about age four, love the same as everyone, some French, remember the story about Calvin Coolidge where someone said to him look they've repainted the buses in Philadelphia and he said, they have, at least on one side. Could I take a bath in your house? Boy this scene is noisy, I love to get drunk but I really can't right now, will that plant freeze do you think, I hate to go but we'll be back later in some other state of being depending always on whether you love me or not, I was reading something awful about how brave you have to be to be a writer, it depends on my rough empurpled hands, oxidizing the phony silver and copper into some other substance, not fear or dramatic circumstance in the fantastic accumulation of colors in the department store our mothers taught us to respect like false rules of grammar, but what. A joy as false as that one, not the order of things in the refrigerator or on the globe, not the joy of owning the falsest pen-light by which you could read, unknown, at night like children shining flashlights in each other's eyes instead of sleeping, Mickey Mouse on the wallpaper against which I dreamed of being tortured by someone I was loving while R told me fierce astrological stories of lovers to frighten me and I would retaliate by saying, I'm not me, I'm someone else, are you scared yet? Meek America, way to be seen or heard, from docile country of unheard poets, we're the same. God has been mean to many, the image of justice, the incessant derogating future, where's the new life, what's the difference, what's concurrent. I wish God to be like the sandwiches left over from the trip we will make tomorrow, we'll look at them for a moment, think of the waste of it, and then throw them away because they are inedible, we'll know if we saved them they might even poison us and the children, possibly because of the mayonnaise, it's gotten old, and then in our naiveté we will find other things to eat, maybe even what they call junk food and then after we've eaten it that will be the end of it for as long as it takes for us to get hungry again and then we'll begin to feel desperate again for food and after that's happened a few more times, we'll begin to wonder if there isn't a way to find a lot of food for a long while so we can store it up and we won't have to worry about finding it again and we'll think then maybe we shouldn't have thrown away those old sandwiches because now we're having to pay for that in a philosophical way because we disregarded the life of the mind and the lives of the people around us and so we will promise never to do something like throwing away those sandwiches again and maybe we will even impart some meaning to the sandwiches, write a song or poem about them and the fact that they existed and what we did with them and how later we felt sorry and felt we needed them but we knew they were perishable and we didn't know what to do about it, perhaps we made a mistake but the next time we make some sandwiches we will probably wind up making too few so as to avoid having that happen again and then we will be hungry with nothing to eat and from that we will determine that that feeling of desperation when one is hungry can result both from having sandwiches and from not having them and so we will begin to question the meaning of what is happening to us and we will say there is no perfection yet we will continue to seek it because love gives us energy.

Female Poets of America

ANOTHER LETTER OF THANKS is due you two, we're back here. I re-
covered from whatever I had a few hours after we got to Boston and I was
able to take a nap, I thought I was going to miss one of B's great dinners
but it turned out I was able to eat at least a child's portion of it, swordfish
with herb mayonnaise, scalloped potatoes, homemade French bread and
wine and champagne, the most beautiful coffee cups, the whole deal, I'll
have more to say about "things" like this later on and Lewis was glad to
spend a New Year's Eve with other people though this celebration also
involved his having to put the kids to bed by himself setting up make-
shift cribs and climbing the four flights of stairs to their room about a
hundred times till it was all done, then he had three bourbons and forgot
to call his mother and we saw some peculiar tv show where the first
thing they did at the new year was show you Barry Manilow, then Rus-
sell told us the guy at New England College who is his main connection
with the administration's been fired and Bill insists he could get Lewis a
job at Harvard, the next day we went to visit Fanny in Jamaica Plain
which is a suburb of Boston and a fascinating place where we all planned
to go and live, people are always plotting to plan to somehow take care of
us. Back in Henniker first off we've bought a recommended car, ugly
green strapping '73 wagon with phony wood trim, it has the most terrif-
ic brand new radial snow tires on it and not many miles unless it's all a

hoax, it's an awful car and who knows anything about that, for a lot of money, we'll have it on Friday. In this town we always pass the prison on the way to do something about cars, loony Concord, the Concord map is wearing thin, we always go the wrong way in Concord, more toward Penacook than we ought to, I think on the wrong way of the meditative states of Lenox when we could only walk, I tell the car salesman I hate cars, there's a beautiful '63 Pontiac in the field of cars, red with a stately shape but it wouldn't go anywhere and an old station wagon from the fifties which they called a sideline or a classic, ours is called an Estate, an estate wagon, he'd give it to us inspected with 20-day paper plates so we could have a baby before we've got the title. I did think of something else while we were driving then, something silly, jerky, I had dreamed in Boston we'd bought a yellow Karmann Ghia and when we got in we kept flagrantly falsely exclaiming, wow it really isn't so small, we could use it, we could fit in here, in fact the inside was like a room and Henniker was like a room just like I guess it isn't so small in my womb right now either, won't everyone be surprised. Then the next night, last night, I dreamt, oh the Karmann Ghia had double tires on the back like a truck too, for security, then I dreamt the car, whatever it was, turned into a lion and we were trying to climb into a lion and we couldn't do it, we were chasing our own car around though we didn't have the kind of fear you'd have of a lion which reminds me of the homily, like the pope's homilies, I heard so often in grammar school from some fearsome nun who said crossing in the middle of the street between parked cars was like walking between two sleeping lions, I think of that nearly every day as if it were a person I had loved, that sermon. Marie was singing her favorite new tune, my name is Fred and when I'm juicy I take a glass of water and pour it on my head and Sophia was complaining about the lack of eats because we'd rushed out to get to see some cars, so before we took them to the children's place to play while we did more research we stopped at a McDonald's to get them French fries and it turned out this McDonald's was one where you could drive up one side and place your order through a talking machine and then come up around the other side of the phony brick building and pick it up instantaneously, 2 fries and 2 milks, $1.74. That seems expensive doesn't it. Marie had dreamt last night that there was some shooting at the zoo and when we picked her up later she had made a painting of the dream. We had to get home fast, having re-rented our car for two more days, because all our mail with nearly all our money in the world most likely in it had somehow been lost and we had to get back before the post office closed to see if they had gotten it back but it turned out K had taken it to Boston with him and now we haven't got it yet but he's due back at nine tonight, what a jerk. Then also it seems the babysitter Suzanne isn't going to come back to school, she's terminally fought with her parents who are cutting her off but she says she will come till we find another and maybe stay on longer if she can find another job, my name is Fred, in the dream of the lion-car Lewis was saying this means everything's going wrong and I kept looking at odd old clothes at great length, things like sweaters with built-in bras that had faces on them and then became shoes too, whole bodies of clothing, clothing to replace whole bodies, no need for people in these clothes and Lewis, adrenalin-frenetical, was dancing around and pointing to the things gone wrong, so many things anyway whether they go wrong or not, like the custom of buying vegetables at just any market no matter where they come from, no matter what they've been through, what's available for sale, what "they have," in the Henniker market there is always a "special" on oddlot hotdogs, hotdogs that've somehow gone wrong, misshapen and weird ones up for adoption, you read about so many mothers murdering selves and children or being done in by husbands, the country can be the rural country if you don't need anything but once you need things, when you have to get things the country is just long spaces between things with cars on roads in between and when you do get to where you can get things it's ugly and more long lines of spaces, rows of the cars either empty or full, the impatient flowers, long notes and the customs of what to do with the children, the children's place is like the Purgatorio, not a bad place, not a holy place, babies crying and waiting, everyone's waiting, the times in and out get marked on a big sheet and the day goes by, you pay by the hour, they have fancy toys. When we bought the car the man said, are there two n's in Henniker? And not a trace of snow here but the aborted snowmaking on the skier's peak, and some thin ice. We were crossing the street to the parking lot against the light in Concord when I composed this Latinate sentence to say to Lewis: I can't rush; don't get killed. No more things! The Empire State Building candle fell on the stove and melted last night while we were sleeping. I hate things, are there more things in the country, Lewis says he's not a country person. In Boston B was polishing her boots, some cooking oil had splattered on them, it was while she was making ricotta balls for dessert, and there was the story of the woolen skirt lost at the cleaners. Alice showed us two beautiful teacups in New York Ted had gotten her, she said ever since the operation on her eye her depth of field was distorted and she had been dropping many cups so Ted got her these expensive ones. At Fanny's house there is an air of impermanence everywhere and as each room seems disconnected from every other one so each thing in each room has a placement and existence in no relation to anything else, it's a wonderful house and like this one it has too many doors. I can't think of anything as being lasting, I can't want to groom and care for things, to oil and polish boots, to care for cups, nor can I feel sentimental about the new or old year or even sentimental about the idea of babies but I feel a strong rush of sentiment and emotion when I see the words printed on a map: state forest. I think of everything and these are things too, everything within it and how it would feel to walk in. Russell saw a pheasant in our driveway. I'm going to ingest or incorporate all I can of this stuff to bring back to New York like an old-fashioned Buddhist, this place. In Boston I had a dream about a substance, or, it turns out, a thing, called ferrous ideate. Now you see what this might be. I suppose I'm wishing for a strong baby—the ideate is the object correlative with a "conception," the external thing, a baby made of iron, and in this relation between baby and conception lies the only mutual dependence without tricks, the tricks of the very things the dream will parody for me, stuff and ingredients, things made into things rather than springing actually from ideas like writing does. And then I sat at the dinner table full of men and women and suddenly they all expressed the assurance or instinct or wish that this baby was going to be a boy and two of the women were mothers of three children and each of them had had first two girls and then a boy and they talked of the difference between how boys and girls love you and how they act when you change their diapers. There was a sign in one of the bars in Brooklyn, did you notice it, that said "Fool Moon." So thanks for everything, I forgot to mention that on the top shelf of Aunt Eleanor's collection of knick-knacks I think we left a big envelope of the pills Harry gave Lewis when he couldn't move his neck. I don't know if it's worth sending but you'd better do something with it, maybe save it or destroy it.

January 2, Full Moon, No Snow, Thin Ice

FOR 1890 I MEAN 1980 there's gotta be a whole new style, there's gotta be something, for the turning and the changing of the year and the ending of the decade that everybody notices like a bad accent, we made this trip and we saw and learned that Kilton Stewart was made out of a fraud, he's the one who found a culture where everybody's healthy because they share their dreams and who wrote about waterfalls and pygmies in the Philippines, then we saw a man on Flatbush Avenue in a big car who said to us in an Iranian accent, please please Avenue U! We saw burnt out donut and coffee shops and shops with bags and wigs, we finally saw black, Korean, Chinese, Spanish, Vietnamese and Japanese babies, they are striking sitting in cars on laps in lap robes with calm eyes, we saw boa constrictors in broadloom stores, I had no recollection of ever having been in high school though I showed Lewis the place I thought it was made of grey stone, it turned out to be brick and the distance between the school and the church was foreshortened and the church was too big and in Brooklyn just those flashing Christmas window memory lights are enough of all that to be scary, plastic lit reindeer on lawns in Queens, praying mantises on the table, two-story streets, streets of Kantianism, the secret skulking truant moon of the two year's exchanging, the chance of the sinking of the absolute ship, all the pawns of the disco music with heavy radios like the movie, Lewis had a dream he became a carrier like me but he was carrying mail for the post office and in my unleaded regular memory I saw a photograph that could be of Helena talking with Alice under a lamp in Alice's crowded apartment, two astonished serious women, heads down, kind lips murmuring, I was only watching. We saw George, Lewis drops his money, Marie threw up in step and I got sick too, then Sophia did in the crib, Dash said stuff about conciliatory sex during pregnancy, it was the first time anybody'd admitted that to me and Ted had joked about the woman not liking it for the first ten minutes, I am explaining I am expanding in a dilatory way, whenever we went over the bridge the kids would sing London Bridge is falling down, falling down, cars go by but the landlord who stole our mail doesn't come in them, nobody comes, the house down the road with nine children in it, Grace told the story of Sister G and the salt shaker, it seems Grace's sister who's a nun has the same name as Grace and when Grace was born she was named Grace because the nun was already a nun then and was called Sister Georgette. Then later the nun was ecumenically given the right to change back to be a sister but of her own name but Grace got mad because by then the name was hers so everyone in the family defers to Grace, the real Grace, the second Grace, my Grace, and calls her sister Sister G, so this Sister G who is enormously fat sat down at Grace's table at Xmas to eat a plate of salad and she picked up the shaker of salt to salt the thing but Grace stopped her and said the salad is well salted already, perhaps you don't need it and because it seemed for that instant someone was interfering with the proceeding of her eating, Sister G took the shaker and banged it on the table in rage and then she put the salt on as she had held she would and ate it over-salted like a nursery rhyme. There are many people in Grace's family and among them too is a feinting Aunt Ceil who pretends to faint and have an epileptic fit when the attention at the family gathering is not coming to her favor and since the habit of the family is to tolerate what might be thought of as lunacy without castigations or rules, there were times when people were just stepping over her on the floor and within that habit or that absence of rules or that tolerance or that generosity there was also an uncle who could be said to have been psychotic who lived with Grace and her family for years and it was for the rest of his life just doing whatever it was that he was doing and there were also foster children and many children and Grace says she cannot write it all down but we did spend a night remembering and putting together the chronology of the last almost twenty years of her life and then the next day she felt spooked, but just for an instant walking over. In the domes and arches of the repeated Manhattan Bridge and all the avenues, calm canals and streets, never be a poet, all poets are punks, there are the sparrows in a wide closed lot, goddam the landlord, at the bridge, there is nothing there but garbage and the stone gates as it once was and Marie says we're at China again and we are conceiving the futurity of our hatred of the culture, I take off my hat, the country is wrong, never be a poet, all poets domes, lake sparrows in weird closed lots at bridges, we're at China, I conceive in one year from now, then idea becomes thing after that, I wonder if Claire has her baby on her knee just yet, she must, soon I will, I saw a man whose name was Ben who looked like Ben Franklin, I don't like history, am not a senator, have not been asked, the night's not young, it's nightteen eighty, a ray of food poisoning, Alice and the teacups, B and the boots, Fanny sorts out the clothes, the day's in the daybed underneath the moon the dog howls up at, that's everything yet the baby never moves when people want to feel it but I can all the time, I'm returning the Chinese pin cushions, the small Mother Goose and the tiny rabbit finger puppet, Marie stole them, also here's some new perfume for Arden to replace what was spilled, tomorrow will be another 1440 evening, female poets of America, eggs do things things shouldn't do, you always have to be ending with everything so it's possible to begin again with nothing, I have a book of pictures now of ancestors, they are not all the same, day is done, I take that back, remonstrances like dreams of chalices, pater noster, amen, no good, goodnight, the milk, snow, kids, the white, little, the two, three, cake, the air, the valley bank, books and papers, people and the midwife, laundry, the clothing, food the car and things, a sweet nativity of flowers or not night.

The Physiology of Taste

THE PLAN WAS THAT weeks would go by and I would walk, it's Friday, we picked up the car, walk like a baby or a child, a two-year-old doesn't want to be kissed, you're invading her privacy if you try, how come Marie's got all the toys up in her room, there's nothing for Sophia to play with down here, oil bill, two, once this baby is we're not gonna do much in the bedroom, what we see, the senses are clearer when there's nothing to say, I'm a closet observer, 75 poets got invited to the white house of mouse but not the ones we like, a raucous pride of lions, the woman who wrote BORN FREE was mauled by a lion, killed beside her tent in Kenya, I'm not reporting the news, moment in every day perfect for poetry's clarity like the squashed bus, I am too unlearned to use it, I'm tired, the switch on the cars, cooked food and ate it, screaming children and fed them, into their chaotic beds, call your parents about the new car because they like to hear the news, it's not a new car, it must have something to do with getting high why else is it that you read boring novels to calm you down and poetry makes your heart beat too fast, Ted's poems, THE WIDOW by supercilious Nicolas Freeling, drinking tea not whiskey in emergencies and how this woman, the detective, likes to iron so she can think, THE KITCHEN. I keep wondering if the downfall of America will have a good or bad effect on people's poems, and how we'll be able to tell. There was one good sentence in the Freeling book, a long one with colons and semi-colons. His writing is cold, it's for intellectuals, gourmet food, fussy characters. I don't know anything about characters, I live in the tunnel of love and I'm bursting, tunnel of red-dyed clothing, the book of old photographs, re-read Dostoevsky and this and that, obscure poetry, read the right thing, sometimes I say what I've heard said about it. We'd be thrown out of China, we forgot to send Simon in China a Xmas present. If you put your cold hands on my belly, the baby will move so perhaps I am wrong, I don't date the papers but I try to keep them in better order than I did. We met a woman today, it was the wife of the man who sold us the car and her name was Max she said. Here's a spooky thing, in New York somebody asked me right off did I know the sex of the baby, now that is what the future was always said to hold. It means too I must look old, enough to have had to "have amniocentesis." One morning, it was the morning after we found out about Lea being sick and I was lying around with Marie feeling terrified and we were passing the time watching t.v., there was a program on the educational channel (which is why it's bad to watch them) about birth defects and I fell into a kind of stuporous sleep repeating over and over the words spina bifida, spina bifida, I was so scared. Now a person like Lewis, he's lucky he doesn't even know what spina bifida is. If we knew more we could write a Hawthorne story. Is the whole idea about writing about one's self so outrageous as to become a symptom of something? (It's not enough like *The Iliad,* she said). Usually at the midwife's I wind up reading all the mothering magazines about frightening things; today Lewis and the kids came in with me and we listened to the conversation of two women, one the mother of three children and the other a tentative midwife in-training with a child in tow and a husband like so many of those radical rural husbands who don't seem to be there, who have no sexuality, the two women were pale and Lewis said he overheard them saying one to the other after the midwife had talked to them for a while that this was only the second time they'd seen her in a skirt. Carol said she had gotten permission to deliver the baby of the Seabrook woman in jail but then they'll take the baby away from her and this woman, she's already lost a baby, she had one that died. The two women conversing in the midwife's anteroom all they were talking about was babies who died and all the isolated complications of childbirth like those magazines I had avoided reading for once I thought. Sometimes I can't bear to talk to women who are childishly moribund, no I mean morbid. The boundary of my implication with this union with the baby inside my belly is called its term. You come to term and not terms with a baby when this inside relationship has worked out and then you are due, you are full-term, it is the end of the last tri-mester. In weeks that is what, forty weeks, ten lunar months. A million moths have died in your house by that time. The most recent old wives tale I heard, I heard it from one of my students a 22-year-old man, is that it's better to have a full-moon baby than a new moon one. I've always had new or half-moon ones. No one knows exactly when the baby's going to come but one day usually an average of seven days after the so-called due-date (which is just a vague approximation of when you conceived within a two-week time), and for some seven days before or thereabouts, and for some on exactly the date predicted, something happens, either your waters break, or some say the water breaks, which means much or some of the water that's been encircling and cushioning the baby in the uterus begins to flow and fall uncontrollably out through the vagina, or a slight contraction of the uterus begins and this becomes regular and more frequent and intense and you are at first at a loss to determine if you are sick or what, or something else happens, a backache may occur for a whole day before but you may have a backache anyway and not know the difference, I've never understood about what they call the mucous plug. Then at some point the contractions become strong enough to force you to sit down for them but they are still over quickly and you can rest in between them and already an adrenalin has overtaken you that overshadows any panic at the imminence of birth assuming your surroundings are calm enough and you are in the right place. Now at this point everyone likes to joke about giving birth but the part leading up to the baby's being born is such a chore, that's what the first midwife said to us and it is true. Then one of the more romantic or theatrical or ethereal things she said is you should envision a rose unfolding and opening, upside down. The best thing is not to feel helpless, not to fear losing control, not to be forced to lie down if you don't want to. At this point it seems that giving birth to babies might be all that you will ever do in all the rest of your life, however that's not so, and aside from the famous forgetting, imagine all the years you are not involved in this. If you have three children, say, you are only actually giving birth to them about 3 days out of your entire life. O.K. then it gets more painful and there isn't much time in between contractions so you are one moment feeling like screaming and the next it is gone and you are you, and then everyone hopes this part won't last too long and if the baby's going to come out now, it will start to be coming but you have to push it out, some very hard and for what seems like a long time but actually isn't, some easier. It's helpful at this time to have another woman around who's already had a baby because she can be loving and convinced. By this time there's nothing you can do but what's determined anyway so even if you push and nothing happens you still keep expecting the baby any moment and all the people watching out can see the head, they say the baby is crowning. The scariest part to me is when the head is out and the shoulders are somehow not, though some women say once the head is out that it's easy after that, I guess it depends on the baby. Sometimes in the midst of the actual pushing-out part of the birth the contractions will stop and you will have to patiently wait for the whole baby, not knowing if it's a boy or a girl then. But then the rest does come and all the permanence of pregnancy which couldn't be borne any other way is over and relieved. Not only that, the feeling of the baby leaving, aside from being slithery, resistant and natural, is as if it were an adornment to one's entire life so far and one wonders then why one isn't or hasn't been doing this activity all the time because its nature, with this end, is perfect. I don't know, is that just me? I can't pretend to be able to account for how anybody else feels when a baby is born, but there is the baby the new human being fraught with the tenderness of the state of the womb, visible and unclothed in the light, about to be wrapped and nursed, there is nothing else like it. Of course a mouse doesn't feel this way or a horse or a cow, does it? First off somebody will always tell you the sex of the baby now when all you are thinking about is feeling. And the baby breathing. Then you still have to expel the placenta but now that the baby is there like a mountain there's only pleasure in it and the uterus will contract again and again, even every time you nurse for a while because the uterus is now becoming smaller but the baby is a person and it is outside of you and it does turn out to be he or she and soon it will be that person, in a couple of months, the one with that name and it will be called that, Max or Violet or Joe and not just "the baby" and no one will remember anymore when it was "it," it will be someone. Still the baby isn't exactly someone yet which is why you can't bear to be parted from it, it's still you for a couple of months and that is hard on fathers sometimes because they can't feed it. But before anything as complex as that, you must be sewn if you have torn, the placenta must be studied and maybe buried, some people eat it, or if the ground's too frozen you can freeze it and bury it later and the whole place has to be cleaned up the way everybody loves to do when there's a new baby, the old sheets ripped off the bed and maybe even thrown away, the baby cleaned off a little and dressed, sometimes people think the vernix which is the waxy stuff on the newborn baby should not be washed off and the baby not bathed yet because it keeps in warmth while the baby's temperature is getting used to its life, someone will give you something to drink and there is no doubt you cannot sleep, the baby goes to sleep and doesn't need anything and from then on people will hear of it all. Well people like to write and tell the stories of their babies' births but I like to do mine beforehand. I never intended to do it tonight, January 4th, 20 days before this baby's announced to be due, I did Sophia's a month and seven days before she was born and Marie's, I was just too scared to ever do hers. So that is what women sometimes do, they relate stories like these and we will send you a telegram as soon as the baby's born and in the meantime how will we pass the time, scared of snowstorms, taking hot baths, random poetry, reading novels, I never did paint anything, putting things in places, getting clothes ready for the baby naked as the day she was born or he. This writing is an inducement to make the baby come, come soon, come whole, and from now on I promise I'll just be waiting like the rings around Saturn and will it snow and am I as impatient as the snow-making machines, I've forgotten to tell you they tell you to put lemon juice on your nipples and rub them with a cloth to get them used and tougher for nursing so they won't get sore and they tell you many other things, even the foods we buy have dates on them but ultimately like tulips it's all a little determined and now I'm to the decorating because that's what's left when you've gotten this far, I'll put the new unenfolded roses on your door and fill your room with things, fancy rocks and shells and curtains on the windows, orders of English muffins with butter and lemon marmalade gotten from somewhere, hot milk with whiskey and the painting of two toadstools in that harmony by Joe and all the displays of books and what's in them.

.

The Marbles of Arp

LAST PIECE OF PAPER on tap, I'm not this early, four or six more days by their count, I'm getting nervous, no stamina, no style, but when I sit down at my desk is when my heart quickens, well who knows about it, at all other times I'm going so slow, that's why the babies are always so late, it's all loose ends now, I can't watch movies on t.v., it's supposed to be slippery out, something falling called freezing drizzle, oh is all this too sane or something, and to be alone, not to avoid it any more, then when the baby will come soon, what will you think of, I'm a poet, does the mist mean it's getting warm again, do the sentences sound this way or that, he complained about his daughter, the weather was dreary, no one wants to know, your hair is so long and you are pretty to be seen through it, I want to do everything quickly and then stop resting and to weep when I cannot do things, I'm supposed to predict recovering, babies come from inside, in the middle of the night I'm on the edge of my seat.

I think the last weeks of pregnancy are like a terminal illness, you keep thinking no one is taking care of you right, you keep wondering why nobody can anticipate your needs as if you were a baby yourself, and you can't walk too good and in order to get up from lying down you need one of those bars they have over hospital beds to pull yourself up on, plus you roll from side to side in bed like a barrel and if you do anything extraordinary, I mean something that's fun, you feel awful, even if it's only from guilt. Then again, like dying, you keep doing things like eating sweet things because you figure well if this is really it I might as well do something unusual, it's not even ten o'clock yet but still nothing's happened. Really it's hard to prevent yourself from thinking you at least look like a lunatic, though there's no snow yet. I used to even be afraid of getting excited when I was less pregnant than this, I thought it might suddenly jolt the baby, make something go wrong, make the baby crazy, make my heart go even faster, like Mawson's awesome story of trudging a hundred miles alone in the Antarctic with the soles of his feet falling off and tied back on, no food to eat but the livers of huskies which were poisoning him because the rest of the food had fallen into a crevasse with one of his friends and the other friend died of the poisoning and this big tall guy wound up weighing a hundred pounds by the end of the trip, you have to do things a little bit at a time if you can't do them any other way they do get done that way is something I've never been able to apprehend but Lewis can do that and so did Mawson. Mawson was with Shackleton originally and he almost went with Scott but didn't, then he made his own expedition to study geology, he didn't try to get to the Pole but it was the same thing, setting a project of a long sledging trip and then disasters. They would put some alcohol into some water at night and drink it to calm themselves down and to sleep, it was so hard to sleep on the surface of ice and feeling crazy and hopeless. Mawson's book is called HOME OF THE BLIZZARD though that's not the one I read. You run up the stairs, it hasn't snowed yet, the Olympics are running out of steam, the future ones might be cancelled, I hope to have this baby before there's a nuclear war, because then who will care about a baby being born. Another baby, the wood is falling from the ceiling beams.

I answered the letters I had to answer before the baby's born but I still have to write Claire, Charlotte, Susan H., Bill B., Bob, John, Rita and Summer but I know I could just write them and say, the baby's born and it is she or he. Dante is holding his heart, but at the same time and with the same hand, he's also holding his dress up. He has something funny on his feet, it looks like stockings, not even slippers, though he's standing on a kind of cobblestone bridge, is this picture fiction?

Who cares what I do, I've gotten into this habit of being pregnant, what did I see? The roads were wet in that comforting way in winter where you knew it wouldn't turn to ice or snow today. There were no animals, the llamas are gone, even the cows on the Henniker east road are gone, their feeding trough is still there but where did they go? I dare to use question marks because the baby is to be so soon, I mean even if it's late, it'll be soon. Tomorrow'll be a good day to have it, or mild Sunday morning. No good after that, there might be a storm. What do poets get famous for, they seem to get famous for their times like Dante holding that heart then. But that's only western and the threat of war is sympathetic, it's like nature, fuck nature Grace said. Children can do timely other things other places and then get to see the museums too but it is all so tiny and small still but it may not always be, I am waiting to see what happens, I am sorry I'm an American, it's like dropping a window on your finger, what kind of window, it's at the same time too complicated and too small, but at least you can speak, you've had the leisure to think about speaking without being rich though I guess you're rich anyway. This baby is a person but when it comes out it will be devoted to sucking for a while like an animal, then it will suddenly do something else. I still don't know Sophia or what she's like. We will take them somewhere, we will take them many places to show them things and other people; when I say to Marie about a toy, it's just a thing and not that important what will I say then about paintings or books, well I believe that about them too, but what. That once they are done so what. These ponds and valleys and books in houses that burn, this waiting, that inevitable pain, oh yeah I remember that thing. Please take my clothing, don't say you're worried cause you lost your earring or beehive comb, it's professional to be old, you didn't say anything when you were young but thoughts, it's too obfuscated but it's not, I want to be in touch with everyone, thanks for sending that thing. I lost the book I bought, what is that one? I don't plan very far ahead, so it is like planning to be dead, I think I've made this tentative appointment for next week, I hope I don't have to keep it and that will mean I'll be lying around with the feeling of Xmas, the best part, in the room, a special house, new baby, person, no things, other people, congratulations. I'll try to remember everything and not write it down so as not to feel hurried, too fast to do it, to remember to drink the black-thorn syrup, male and female, heart beating fast, this state, like being old, gives a clue, because of how hard it is to live and hold and move and get in and out and get past. And how come people always say that hack-neyed thing, you paint too pretty a picture of your children in general. I shouldn't say that, John Ashbery wouldn't like me to say that, it's almost dross. To leave all out and so on. And Dante is still holding his heart, in fact from the way his feet are positioned in the picture, he looks like he's got some liver ailment and is leaning on the bridge till the pain subsides, Dante's getting old or used up. Still he's got a red hat on.

Two Days After Joanna Had Two Stitches

YOU SEE I'VE BEEN practicing this deception on you, I never told you I'm to have the baby at home with only a midwife in attendance. We had thought to save you from worrying about everything and from not understanding—you and your daughter seem to live in such a world of fear about births and babies, and with all your trust in doctors and pills you find my ways of doing things alien and sometimes even repulsive, my desire to nurse the babies, my refusal to eat candy. I'm sorry. I saw the midwife today and she asked me to answer her telephone while she was checking my blood, urine, blood pressure, loss of perhaps the perfect mother I keep yearning for these last few week of this. I went to the midwife's boyfriend's office to leave a sterile catch, a pure drop, of urine for them just in case there was some infection. He's a man of rugged good looks she calls "my man." She fixed a hamburger for her son and started a fire, she had said to someone chatting on the phone. Where is the baby, where is the baby hat. I feel so mountainous in my big grey coat like a project I feel embarrassed on the streets. No deeper feelings, I might say to you, will emerge from that if you won't let them. You were in a bad mood—is it because we're so far away, because you may not get to see the baby when it's born right away, because you are so little involved in this? Whenever you phone and the phone rings three or four times and I answer it, you always say oh I'm sorry did I wake you up, but you never have. Did you laugh when Lewis told you the story of buying the forty postcards and having the woman in the 5&10 ring up 10¢ forty times? You wouldn't believe how cold it is in here, I'm wearing two shirts under a dress, a wool shirt and a sweater over that, tights and a pair of wool socks and a hat, you would think we're crazy for keeping it so cold but if you visit us after the baby's born you'll never know because it'll have to be warm here then. I've got to call up the fuel people and have them bring extra oil for then, we'll be using it up fast. It'll be fun to be indoors and taken care of during what I think of as the rest of the winter. I can pretend I'm a girl and you are taking care of me, I'm lying on the couch nicely feverish and you are bringing me jello and junket, ginger ale and orange juice with sugar and ice, you are making me feel quite high. It's funny but whenever I write things like that down I never fail to think, this is not the work of a poet to write details of memory and desire, this view of things is nothing, you are forgetting where you are. I throw the beer bottle into the trash, it bangs against another one, you would be alarmed at my nihilist behavior. Once when I was having the baby I had when I was eighteen, another thing I'm afraid I never told you, the doctor said how come you are reading comic books, you used to read such high-toned things, poetry and stuff. Some nihilist had brought me a nihilistic comic and I read it and then I wrote a mixed-up poem about the paregoric of the hospital and all the ugly and confusing shit that was making my dreams then combine with the way the hospital people were behaving. A car's come up and now left, left Suzanne back here I suppose but where is she, she's not in the door yet, she's fasting today and she is hungry. Maybe you'd be happy to know Lewis and I ate Big Mac's today in Concord, we suffered in concord, french fries and a coke. There's no sense belaboring our differences, it would be nice if beyond them were nothing but a field of ice passionately melted by irate and tender words and embraces and we could be one as I was with the woman from whose body I came one time. I don't think my parents were anti-Semitic but they always said things about how Jewish people were too intelligent to compete with and perhaps they showed their prejudice by saying Jews were competitive. But I can't remember what they said. They wouldn't let me play with Jewish children but they wouldn't let me play with Protestant ones either. Really I have to drag this chair I'm sitting on clear across the room from the kitchen where we need it for meals, and it is so heavy, heavy as a classroom chair, heavy as a monk or abbess, this chair is my monk and there is no harm in sitting in it though I often equate working and writing with harm and when I don't work I feel maybe I've done myself some good, poetry like the danger of splinters in the foot. While I was talking to you I saw the sliver moon setting in the west, now I run over to see if it's still there but it's gone, I really can't run, I can sort of leap slowly but it's not much faster than walking fast. Once you said all we cared about was poetry but now it's not poetry to tell you that I never much cared for sitting in chairs, and is it like emotion to say that? You are so much like a girl and the two of you like girl and boy, so quiet and playing at keeping house with duty and so obedient you are, I often wonder where is the wisdom in your reticence and then I answer, and you would say the same, in your surviving and simply in your presence and your slowly, almost methodically doing things and keeping track of things, in your admitting you are happy though you'd never use that word, but denying forever you are satisfied, and in your loyalty to each other. Yet you and I never get anywhere and I am still to you the outsider. Well maybe if we move back to New York that much will be less so, but secretly maybe more so because then too much of everything will be too different. Ah I wish I could tell you exactly how I feel, so full of remorse and fear, so little the strong and willing person I have to be for you, so little the person who normally exhausts you and speaks a little well, as if it was inherited. I'm sitting here secretly smoking and fearing the pains of childbirth and thinking of you.

An Inch of Free Snow January 22

POETRY DOESN'T WORK, it's as familiar as this snow, what was it I had thought I could get it to get at about the bearing of children before they are born, maybe it's still to be stolen, whatever it is. I guess I didn't have the baby before the first snow, here it is, and after all the suspense of it not coming it seems so ordinary and expected to notice out the window the snow and the color of it at dusk, periwinkle blue or something like that. I keep thinking of the phrase "blessing in disguise." Anyway it snowed, we don't have to wait for snow anymore, wait against it and now the skiers can have it and everything will look right, which doesn't mean that poetry works any better or that it works at all, I still haven't gotten at or to the middle or ending of this thing, everything is distracting. If I talked to more people, I would know more what to say and have more words. If this book has been too much one way that is the cause of it. I'm tired of causes for which you take vitamins, I'm exhausted at trying to tell what it is I don't know, trying to get at this thing, tired of waiting for the occasion akin to this snow, coming the day the baby's first predicted to be born but not yet born, nobody knows what causes a baby to be starting to be born, I want to brush my teeth. At some point everything's ready and it does, I can't blame this snow for not being able to wait any longer, I've been pregnant exactly 40 weeks now though nobody knows exactly when I got pregnant, who knows what I did. When a tortoise wants to get pregnant, she has to stand, stretch her legs so that the shell doesn't cover her vagina so the penis can enter in to it and so, what I was reading implied, maybe many female tortoises will get impatient with that and cease to stand for it and the male tortoise might be as much as eighty years old already. He wants to have adventures, to go out in the snow, just like any person. Some silver or something was sold at a great discount, the prices of the dim blue lights ere now were low, it was like t.v. So low it might be time for a baby to be born, how have they been born in the world, was one ever born alone, many have been, the Indian babies in the little holes dug for them and squatted over in the woods, who cut the cords. When a person has twins there are not two placentas but two cords coming from one. 23 chromosomes from each parent, I dreamt our jobs were keeping us apart, I to drive north according to a manual from Boston in a van. I needed some of my papers to put a book together on how to write the long work, I saw that Clark had closets that went up to the ceiling, what a luxury, full of journals with heavy crewel embroidery on some of the pages, fantastic notebooks full of this and that. I was teaching school in a trailer, we catalogued and made to correspond the lists of the faces of the children with symbols for chocolate syrup and the foods they'd eat and the things they'd do today, it happened like a slot machine for each child, three chocolate syrups for this lucky child today. In the back of the school all the teachers were mashing vegetables in big bins as if to make whiskey, I saw one teacher whom I could tell would get arrested for it, putting some real vegetables under the heat of sodden stones to really grow, to grow naturally, we're only supposed to make pulp. I tell him like this lettuce mash we've only just been artists ourselves and then, for practice, I get raped, I'm told not to resist, I have to say "Sophia is two," I'm tired of saying that, Marie dreams the baby drinks bottles of ice cream, we dive into the breaking ice, cars fall into it, thin ice again, ice all over the rivers flowing underneath, snow on top of the ice on the rivers, pathways of snow, brown ice, muddy waters, waters breaking, the tour guide tells us to go see the Capitol Palace show that took place thirty years ago, that was in Lenox, now everyone is ice-skating like friendship but why do I have to go on this long trip without you in this mobile home, this mobile school, on this mobile ice, what will I see with my eyes that is not me, increased, deceased, like the bank says, this mobile canal, New England honky-tonk lack of love, the spaces closing in, you go south and I'll go north, I'll sleep alone but there'll be a long string between us in the pictures of the sky, cloud-herding, the sheep that followed us to Concord and by this spring people will come bitten with a sharp compassion again for the country, land or woods we've been lent to walk in, to actually feast in is nothing, there's a man and woman from this road who walk a lot who look around like people who walk a lot, their eyes stare out from cold faces, they don't break their paces as they notice you like things that might've come from somewhere, like something to notice, like sights, they don't hold hands, they are white people living in the northeastern part of the United States in the midst of western culture, I imagine they live modestly, I imagine they do nothing but walk and eat and think, they look, they hardly fear the snow. I've never got a bargain on a place to live, no one's ever showed me one, a cabin you could keep for the rest of your life, some little thing, some place that might remain when you're not there, a cheap apartment that isn't insulting but who cares, no one's ever showed me one, this country is threatening the bands of my hair with emaciation, don't take cold baths in the morning in the sinecure of all the bright light, it's the same light of waiting for something refined to wear down even more, a mother who defends her daughter no matter what, paintings I've never finished, delicate overleafs and false covers for the books, taking pleasure without achieving order on the say-so of the sonnets or some other great work. Some things about yourself you never even notice walking around behind closed doors, practicing fainting on the streets. Some kind of love might be one of them, what kind of poems would follow then? People who have names beginning with this or that letter might dream differently on account of it, it's as if all the learning came to an end and after that you were just coasting on what you knew, no energy to learn differently, why am I having all these children, what will I do, I do this but I don't study anymore, or I study something different some other way. Maybe when I'm forty I'll again be able to study everything. Marie's learned to color "in the lines" as they say, but she puts *all* the colors within each line, what will she picture, will she cover the page with color and leave no white space like a painting would do, the kind of painting I envision. The night is over or yelling at me, Sophia's sleeping, wrapped in her blanket like a kerchief, a belief. One's not born yet.

Almost at the Second Predicted Time for the Third Baby

SLID DOWN THE STEEP snowy slope without stopping, without being able to stop but we got back up it o.k., don't wanna ever go out no more, I scare easy, there's no real library anyway, it's such a struggle to do everything with two or three children, to go into every place and store and now we have to skid there. I had promised myself I'd have a sense of humor about this but when Lewis thought he couldn't stop the car, that the brakes didn't work I freaked out too and I said not to go over the next hill which would make us roll to a stop obsessively and by that time we were never going anywhere again anyway and cars were coming in all directions skidding by us, it was just the snow on the slippery downhill driveway and the 5,000 lbs of car getting faster going down it and with our car when you've just started it up and you're going downhill you don't even know if the car's on or off, it tends to go off if you're not using the gas and then you don't have any power steering or brakes, this is why I hate American cars. However, Marie kept saying all day she felt lousy, everyone has a cold and with all this waiting, well we cannot bear not to go out one day even though we don't need to but we were out of juice so we decided to go into the snowy and appropriate looking town, not a big snow, just a couple of inches of it and everyone uplifted by it and I must admit I thought the snow looked good on the town like I said before but in the end I only wish it would all melt away, I don't want to drive in it with babies in the car and I don't want to have a baby in the snow and I don't want to slip and fall in it before the baby comes and I wonder if we do move back to New York how much I'll yearn to put my feet on the real ground underneath the pavement after these what will turn out to be five years in the country. People like to think we're in the country so that somebody is, everybody doesn't have to be in the same place all the time, in fact people prefer you at a distance where without immediate problems being a possibility among their knowledge of everything else there is to know in that place, New York, they don't have to think about us as well. Even Dash wants us there on her terms, as it were, in her own apartment building and then we and Dash would all be living more or less the same life, a predicted life and we could all discuss the exigencies of life in those buildings between the walls of which you can hear a person cough and then die. If we moved to the Lower East Side, they'd think we were living in an awful place, the place he had tried to escape from, and we would be, and after criticizing us for five years for living in all these weird foreign New England places, in New York he'd wind up knowing too much about us and etiquette would become a question oh why can't everyone just say what they're thinking, poor grammar. Maybe I'd actually like New York, another stroller. No more seasons, just the variety, assuming we can find a place. Getting old in New York makes sense but is frightening, too easy to die there. At least in New York if you want to talk of destiny, we have a history. New Hampshire is full of big stacks of cut cords of wood and ambidextrous ex-minor-league-baseball-player pharmacists and what day is today and what is the weather. Big meals. But that is o.k., maybe there's something to be discovered about writing in New York that we can't find out here. We always suffered thoroughly through it beforehand, I'm sure we can figure it out all over again, we never really had a place to be there, only all these temporary joints, apartments here and there but that won't change, Lewis had ten in thirteen years and I had at least five or six, each in a place where when you walked into it at night you had to look behind you and know about survival, not the weather or the snow but the people and air, and occasionally getting out of there to be sane. And the long summers, are they worse than the long winters here, or less or more dangerous for children, and the streets exciting to us bleak at some hours of the day, in some light and kinds of air, there's even the fear of buildings falling down on your head, remember that, and the danger of the admiration of others, the fear of entanglement either this way or that, craziness of the hostile and loving ones, the details, money and telephone calls, we haven't had that but maybe now because we're such parents and are getting so old, that will make us exempt from memories of those old peonies of doubt and transgression among love's battles, I'm going to ask Alice and Ted what they think. This is my apology, Henniker of New Hampshire winter like a hairdresser, for what I seem to feel and what we will be doing, don't take my fears of the anathemas of space and turn them back on me then because it is or isn't natural of me to feel this, or timely or something. And seasons, remember me while I'm looking out my tenement window for a sight of the moon and while Marie notices it in daytime walking down one or another avenue, keep me clasped to you in the same old deal and I will return what I can learn about poetry and maybe even paintings. I won't demand to make a deal with movement and I'll answer as quickly as I can but not before I've been as slow as I've been allowed to learn here in a different sort of place, not Dante's Florence or Shakespeare's London, but indefinite swaying New England where you cannot wear a cape for instance. It's not isolation I ever craved but a freakish peace. Tomorrow by the second prediction the third baby is supposed to be born but he or she hasn't started the working of the ropes yet, or what is the phrase I'm thinking of, though he or she is moving all around and is it not to come because I'm not being good enough like Tito's amputated leg in the face of a possible invasion again by greedy and tortured Russia. America is so much a hospital everywhere you go, I hate all the lying down and putting up with it, take this sedative and relax, don't move, enjoy this basket of criss-crossed doors. I don't like lying down except in the best company, certainly not with a dentist, and otherwise I'll be on my feet please I hope. Please accept me, setting even moon, as a jarring candidate for some unique compassion I know if I deserve, so do many other people who may not even think to ask for it, but as I'm so pregnant I can speak for more than one. And then I will draw you a picture of my mastery of, if nothing else, and if not of all the things I don't do in some absence of whimsy and gratuitous love, at least how forthrightly I can dare to do anything at all, to speak outloud, to intimate love.

Place All the Time

WHAT I'D LIKE to know is exactly how everybody makes love, but I
don't want to know it about everybody,
like VILLETTE
the sight of the sun, the cough, the cold, the flu

A POUND OF GROUND ROUND

Sophia saw a mountain in the lake, she saw a lake in the mountains but
it was the shadow of a cloud, the winding Old
Hillsborough Road where the ice on the rocks in the river it follows
makes me want to picture you before it
50% effaced
4 centimeters dilated
to give birth to, to deliver, to bear,
to bring to light, to bring into the world, to produce, to bring forth,
to bring into being, to spawn, to bring into existence, to bring forth
again, to be to labor to travail, to bring to nascency, to drop, to yield
up, to beget (to bring up a child or something you ate), to liberate, to
give forth, to utter the child, to give up or out or forth, to be delivered
of, to be the cause of, to originate, to bear down and push out, to

be parturient, to have done (with) parturition, to proliferate (in a
viviparous way)

WATER, BEER AND A DEER

She said Bagels Lox and the Three Bears

The dust rising off the cold ground
no snow through January
February 2 full moon
the idea is to get all the groceries together and then eat out
why won't the baby be given forth
it's so quiet in here, breathing of the cold, breath of the furnace, random
          racket like mice of the pipes,
Ecstasy of the child's drawings, from people to eggs, multi-colored
          Poony ovoids to larger-shaped coat-of-many-colors miasmas
          mid-page, to glad flags now, flags like hatchets, what are flags
Moods of the person of the child in love sometimes
Dangerous to take chances living at all, going on eating more or less
Bitter cold of the slow-moving and predictable small city of white
          people—who stops in to the coffee shop for a plate of pudding
          late afternoon? That old man whose way of eating reminds me
          of someone, will his face be less clear when I'm old too, less
          alarming then to watch him covet his sweet dessert?
Everybody calls wondering where the baby is but the worst thing is
          nobody writes to make the days less empty, no letters means
          fear of dying
The overwhelming advent of baby on the business of scenes next week
          beginning again like one poor toe in an inch of hot bath
The midwife can reach into me and touch with two fingers the baby's
          true head
Still it has to come out, still saying so doesn't want it to
It's true writing is too exciting and lively and saintly
I'm another person, one child coughs the other's getting better
Absence of a tandem stroller, I've got cold feet, genuinely cold, it's zero

Remember the snapping air over white snow with blue smitten skies,
    twenty below one year
You could walk out and wonder, the air did not stir, could you breathe?
This is like leisure, I can't wait to hold the baby, no one around
First there was a cough and a cold, then we made this baby up, now it's
    near to full moon
Love of the light in the cold, the sumptuous ritual of birth, the
    spectacular cord
Heart beats faster so it must be a woman she said I mean a girl
Advent of a life that's more a life of other people & emotion than life
    of doing what pleased you without planning and being almost
    alone, is that it? Anyway it was this change that caused her to
    abdicate the previous principles of languages' learned and more
    remote hegemony as sacrosanct art for the investigations now
    of the dread suspicions of outright communication of
    everything
There was a chance that was a chance to take then a car pulled up, it must
    be the tenant's landlord
This is busted, my father would've said, but what is it?
You can study someone's handwriting you see all the time and then
    begin to write like that, to be like that or to be secret or
    imitative, to move unexpectedly to another place without even
    taking your things
Doors and even ceilings of the crashing home still on the crackling
    little there is of it of snow, absence of the hearts of clams
Bring the chair down, then the baby will come—high seriousness
The light of pain in the pale series of eyes
What do the contractions do, are they like THE CANTERBURY
    TALES?
I heard the dog barking in this place arid of animals
More awakenings, days and nights, what was poetry
The help of the baby making a motion in the world you'd touch anyway
This cummerbund of baby, this big old fat man, maybe jolly, this thing
    between my legs, there's a head there where my sex is
Past Santa Claus

The difference in days, so much the sweetest now
Drab light kept back from a heart like Cocteau mentions
I lean over the desk legs spread in the Gertrude-Stein skirt, isn't that
        silly, a loose blouse like Emma Goldman who spoke at the
        laborlyceum, at the Great Hall
This hand, what will happen to this wrist or arm, I mean mine
Love of self, I am not in pain now, how could I ever be?
Baby lost or left, fallen, the drift of the packing of the shelf
Person gotten into being, again another one, now what we say is peace
        and now no more

HERION, THE AGONIST-ANTAGONIST

        A new cure for addiction, you pick things out from the world,
I meant to say you choose them from the times
                        "...fatter than a flat fur..."
That's how it said the lynx makes you look
It's cold in here, what's it waiting for?
I guess it's cynical to be addicted to this cold weather
To pass the waiting time some words wind up in mind
So they say I am effaced but what will I do? Shall I withdraw from sight?
E'en the slippery eel will seem eerier than that uneven field, the photos
        of which I've taken don't have enough light on them, you can
        still see some pears on the trees, forget them
His thoughts make ideas sound agrarian, it's the evenness of spinning
        and the mixtures of dull-sounding words to make ideas exist
        alone, he would never mention a pear, I wonder does he still
        have a mother
The leaves and now none but how can you see it if I don't lend it to you,
        something as a picture, can it be recovered?
In the more leafless one, the picture hints at a known road behind the
        synchronizing weeds, menhirs
Two things to study not unlike the mother and the baby, what shall I do
        next?   (mourning dove)
Ideas are so slow pinioned on the meditative what, not the seasons

Though you do get warmer in patience while you work, one child cries
You wait and see, what could be new, not even the room
By end of January in a place like this so much absence of snow is new
     ("I've never seen a winter like this one") & the old little snow is
     on the ground in the form of heavy tire tracks in a random
     pattern from the oil truck & where cars ground it down, it cracks
     when you walk on it in the sunny wind, the rest has been blown
     off
          "It's good weather for snow-making"
Hard to feel tough when you're about to give birth, moon etc., even
     though you've won the recidivist weather over this time
             "We've been fooled"
And last night so bright you couldn't tell if it was dawn when you woke
     as usual at 4 a.m., nursery-rhyme bright, the meditation of each
     night, each tree in the pictures in a place reflected by each other,
     the study of the windows in a house, a memory you were
     probably wrong about
          "As dry leaves that before the hurricane fly
          When they meet with an obstacle mount to the sky..."
Is it the cold or the packages of the bath like the proverbial stance of
     washing the floor, the position you're in, to induce birth, does it
     matter? What will start it?
          "When the winter is brown, the graveyards
               are full"
Will you know, slight contraction later, how labor began, will you have
     been influenced and not by reason, telescoping memory like a
     mother does, she says when he was a baby then he was seven
     years old, he hit his head on that table over there
I sit still waiting before the pretty dawn like nearly everyone did, love
     is the same
Its form makes the speech, others have given birth, even tonight
The very seasons I can bother to picture the ultimate in nothing new
     comparing it to all
Which is why I am silent and cannot find an end to it, all this speaking
And photographing leaves, making love if it's o.k. to mention that

affecting babies, the children not the reason there is none
In some tribes and so on...
So all life turns out to be the opposite of what half of everyone thought
& the reasons for continuing are the sources of stopping and silence
Not because of that but to add, all the stuff we thought was new is not
But I can't say that, I photographed the apparently empty field, I took its
      picture many times
Tonight you have a whiskey and I pride myself on drinking another
      beer at a time like this
When any moment I might be called on to lie back and climb a
      mountain for a while
In the 19th century I think small mountains were climbed more
      frequently than they are today, not counting how many more
      people there are now
And it was normal for people to take walking tours so they could
      see things & to perhaps make a picnic at the top of the peak
      of the summit in the height of the summer season or below
      in fall
Cold & dry but not empty, the shapes of the valley like a path
If you can see the leaves in the frame you need not see so much else of
      the tree
Could the birth be second to the knowledge of the cold? You see I'm
      trying to get everything in to a kind of order or chronology in
      these contractions
                    "What's a contraction?"
Just make mild spaces between, have we even learned the names of
      those weeds like the memory of excitement toward the end
      of things
             "Who's ever seen the end of something?"
If all goes well will we still have to go to jail?
I like to have lines ruling thought, it gives you the leisure to have
      different drinks
             "The milk will erase the whiskey"
Like space of field, you decide if the trees were people, no matter who...

DEVOTIONS UPON EMERGENT OCCASIONS

We hate the thought of knowing nothing so we fear to come close, it's a
    danger to the day
Besides we have no robes, who would believe us,
We don't even have an outline of all the cosmos & its stuff on the
    rented white alphabet ceiling, this one's not crumbling
Like most things to have are
Like Beethoven maybe we even wonder
If there's been some mistake about our births and
Might we be the daughter or son of someone royal or something?
It's the same old thing so I might go & see
Goodbye!

SHAKING THE SHEET

It seems like I've been in labor now three or four weeks, last night I had
contractions for five hours winding up with the best one at 2 am, then
I feel asleep reading VILLETTE again. Today's Sunday February 3,
Godzilla vs. the something is on t.v., maybe berries will bring the baby
because they are quickening. Marie & Sophia were playing in a box but
they had a big fight. Now Sophia's in a smaller box that says Michelob
on it. We went to town, drove over the two East and West Henniker
bridges & down Bacon Road which is what we do when there's nothing
to do & got the paper & some beer, wine, 3 eggs & bread, that's all there
was to do. Besides Suzanne, we haven't seen another person but a pur-
veyor for a month not counting Connie who works in the market. Now
these guys have eaten sandwiches & are dancing to the Talking Heads.
We eat breakfast at noon, lunch at 2 & supper at 5, it's like a lot of rest-
ing. Everybody's recovering from the cold, Suzanne's still sick, Lewis
has been better longest, I'm cured today & Marie & Sophia have coughs
but don't care. Maybe this is the last time I'll ever journalize in my life,
its form is better on some poorer farm, they make up good fancy dance
steps. It's to make this tree be longer in winter, a month from now sap
for syrup but who cares? Sophia's eating tin foil, we are all at home, no
winter sports.

TEN YEARS TILL THE NEXT BEER

At least nobody can be saying about giving birth, don't take it so seriously

Lewis is sick again, it's the recurrent flu, he's in the shoe like the old woman he's taking a shower, it's been a bad day we lost our momentum, it's a bitter hilarious deterioration, it sounds academic but it is not, when it's time to labor to be in Laos I'll have used up all the patience I'm supposed to have I am in such a hurry now to get this baby done I can wash two sinks full of dishes in 15 minutes, I did dot the i's before i even wrote them, early February, marbles of Arp, growing up in NY is a curse, we did things, we ate some soup, that's the difference in this intimate interior, outside is like a desert the sky & all's the same every day, cold blue sun no morning is different, before the sun rises the sky is gray, then blue behind the empty branches, what else can we do but go back to new york, let's blow this joint no one in this house, Marie wants to go to school, I don't want to climb the college hill to the bare old rooms & introduce thoughts and mumble & mutter & watch the time any more, be tittered at, be a bare green weed outcropping, to emerge from the earth in this way, not that I take it seriously exactly, one two three o'clock four o'clock rock, humidifiers, ovens, bathtubs steaming oh baby if you are one no decorous way to pass the time, only a green fairy book, no labor pains, gotta switch gears that's embarrassing to say, dreamt David had ordered a lot of Karl Marx books from the library but it was only a dream about the Marx brothers cause we'd been watching W.C. Fields who Vito used to say he preferred to be to my Charlie Chaplin who I preferred to be well didn't we have the leisure then in this thin clown column narrowing down to practically a verse but not one, it's for Peggy, to chant or something the baby into being and coming, if there still could be a baby in there, I've gotta go look, others can go about their business thinking we've forgotten about them but I've only got to collate the syllabuses of ashes remorseful and it aint so abnormal to be having babies after all

Then we sat in chairs before the oven's steaming pots to keep our heads & doors & read books & nothing happened. Smoked cigarettes, ate sweets, compared the simple scene. Thought and talked of various poets. Quiet house, she probably thinks I'm a fool too

Now the midwife wants to give me castor oil if the baby won't come by Thursday she says the placenta stops nourishing as it would, I'm supposed to be resting but the sky is still blue, it's February 4th & our plans are all screwed up, sky blue no wind, my babies are late, all the students are crossing the streets, you've gotta get the uterus to contract somehow, there's pressure, I'll go teach my classes tomorrow unless I can come up with this baby, so the castor oil gives you diarrhea & then the constrictions of one thing are catching to the contractions of another thing, that pisses me off, labor later, all these dumb trees and Lewis is feeling sick again

Dreamt I was fighting with Rosemary over books throwing them around & being independent yet still pregnant in the bookstore, this is crazy & I am not transparent, I'm behind the doors

Actual school, the hot sunny pristine classrooms mine pale blue with a real lectern this time, storm windows new & Chip Carter shows up with secret service men intact a girl student gets hysterical, "Look at him, how old is he?" and now I'm up, that's silly to say, with two hours so far of more contractions waiting for this person, then I walked around for a while & now I haven't had another one, stars out, shadow of the house from the moon, February 5th, around Gertrude Stein's birthday I think, the landlord is supposed to put anti-freeze in his toilet the fuel man who came to unfreeze the drains said today, hey where is this baby, the contractions are too delicate, only one more day till the castor oil... now there's one, it's 1:35 am, think of the blue skies, am reading old Antarctica book, another one 1:42 am, now they stop again

I lost it the days are awful, nights I still expect something to happen, the woman smiled,
                    I felt a great love for all
women, women have memories & many will look at me these days &

feel so glad not to be me, it's the end of the secret of women but not the end of the waiting for what everyone's done already, there's the common knowledge of the castor oil, the understanding of the overdue baby, the last baby, the baby named or not named, the big pain in the ass, motion, dreams of airplanes and people being pushed around in torn clothing, life full of holes, maybe I know nothing, this time in the sense that if life were less crazy I'd likely have less ignorance, dreams of the New Mexico State Prison, the news of the day on the day of the birth, it probably won't be the 6th now, the 7th or 8th, the phone rings incessantly because I am bursting, it's hard, I mean like a stone with a letter of the alphabet written on it, I don't know either whether to eat or drink, the smell of the food is awful, taste of the metal beer, the aluminum milk, the baby does something, I'm all both fucked up and freaked out, I'm a wreck as they say, had one at 8:15, now I feel a little sick, I get in some position and something starts happening but then I move & it won't keep going, I'm impotent! My uterus must be exhausted! I'm too old! The exuberance of all the false labors turns to lethargy, defending against expectations, what a silly word, I still look the same in the mirror, my face I mean my head does, where is the midwife sleeping? in her bed? a funny hooting or creaking I hear once in a while when it's quiet downstairs & at night when you're sleeping, it must be the baby in the womb actually being already outside me, children fighting all day, all day asking for little bits of food they don't really want to eat, little single things, then those things & foods not satisfying them they spit on the floor, throw the stuff away and ask for more something, they say I need, I need, should I get married and then destroy everything, should I take a shower in Kiev or a bath? The mystical cop-out ambiguous 19th-century ending of VILLETTE Peggy said was a book wherein you want to kick all the characters, babies sigh fear, no more babies, never again, no more waiting, no sense of humor, why isn't my mother or somebody waiting here with me, it'll never come back again, it needs another woman, pity me Patty, phone rings, I think it's someone calling to say the baby's born, it's over, thanks, thanks a million, thanks for letting me know, she said my thoughts go with you making me quake in my boots for fear I might be dying as well, then she said of course it will all be fine & I know she never thinks that's true she

always thinks it will all be all wrong, fucked up, upside down, fraught
with complications, requiring surgery because that's more interesting,
hideous and unlucky, I stop & look around, what am I saying, should I
try a beer, will the beer lessen the chance for contractions I aspire to
tonight, I have them anyway, they go nowhere, it does have to happen
doesn't it, some squealing I hear it again like a bannister squeaking like
a person, to assure proper credit please don't be like you are, I'm clumsy,
I drop everything on the floor, sometimes I even drop everything in the
garbage by mistake, when he saw me still encumbered he said oh you
poor thing, today we dropped all the cooked spaghetti in the sink and
had to make it new & the juice on the floor & I broke a dish and a cup by
throwing a bowl to make the children stop fighting, I'm getting mad and
I'm washing all the dishes though it's not my job, I'm exhausting myself
conserving energy then I see I'm much too tired to have the baby now, I
don't want the landlord to be here when the baby's born, I want to have
my baby alone with only Lewis and Carol and Marie, Lewis dreamed a
boy, the room was pale blue, they had painted it for you, the supper & the
day cold & dreary, I had to teach my class &

at the Bradford IGA
a woman smiled at me

we live in a bowl of small towns
"It was like each person was a button on
                    your coat"

now the foolish dog's come into the house
there's no privacy
it was sumptuous with another blue sky today
it must be on account of ovaries there are memories
the men could exist anytime
they can even freeze sperm

each country is black, the women are smiling & comparing journals,
the work of the past living in some other woman they might happen

to notice, they're ready for that, but the men, even the stoical silent ice fishermen telling stories at the store don't have the feeling one knows how the other must've felt so memory gets lost & is unknown except that the man's dog barks again so the man remembers someone must be coming & then of course there's a knocking and for a second we're convinced we might be right

to bring forth issue

A Few Days Later It's With Pleasure I Write

DEAR PEGGY, baby's born Max Theodore, though you are already here and have held him, I thought you might like to have this written record of it, love, Bernadette.

BERNADETTE MAYER is the author of more than 27 collections, including *Midwinter Day* (1982), *The Sonnets* (1989), and *Works and Days* (2016), as well as countless chapbooks and artist's books. She has received grants from The Guggenheim Foundation, National Endowment for the Arts, and the Foundation for Contemporary Arts. She is also the recipient of the 2014 Shelley Memorial Award from the Poetry Society of America.

From 1980 to 1984, Mayer served as the director of the St. Mark's Poetry Project. She co-founded and co-edited *0 to 9* and United Artists books and magazines. She has also taught at the New School for Social Research, Naropa University, Long Island University, and Miami University. She lives in East Nassau, New York.

Acknowledgements

The Desires of Mothers to Please Others in Letters is a series of letters written but never sent to people living and dead during a nine-month period in 1979-80. Some of the letters were published in *O/two An Anthology: What is the inside, what is outside?*, *A Poetics of Criticism*, *A Bernadette Mayer Reader*, *o•blēk*, *United Artists*, *lingo*, *River Styx*, *Avec*, and *Milk*. Thanks to the editors: Leslie Scalapino, Juliana Spahr, Mark Wallace, Kristin Prevallet, Pam Rehm, Barbara Epler, Peter Gizzi, Connell McGrath, Lewis Warsh, Bernadette Mayer, Michael Gizzi, Jonathan Gams, Lee Fournier, Cydney Chadwick, and Gillian McCain.

To Laynie Browne, Philip Good, Alan Gilbert, and Peter Gizzi: thank you for your assistance in reprinting this book.

SplitLevel Titles

Laynie Browne, *PRACTICE*
Martin Corless-Smith, *This Fatal Looking Glass*
Alan Gilbert, *The Treatment of Monuments*
Carla Harryman, *W—/M—*
Lucy Ives, *The Worldkillers*
Bernadette Mayer, *The Desires of Mothers to Please Others in Letters*
Catherine Meng, *The Longest Total Solar Eclipse of the Century*
Jerome Rothenberg, *A Cruel Nirvana*
Maged Zaher, *If Reality Doesn't Work Out*
Elizabeth Zuba, *Decoherent The Wing'ed*

Nightboat Books

Nightboat Books, a nonprofit organization, seeks to develop audiences for writers whose work resists convention and transcends boundaries. We publish books rich with poignancy, intelligence, and risk. Please visit our website, www.nightboat.org, to learn about our titles and how you can support our future publications.

The following individuals have supported the publication of this book. We thank them for their generosity and commitment to the mission of Nightboat Books:

Elizabeth Motika
Benjamin Taylor

In addition, this book has been made possible, in part, by grants from The National Endowment for the Arts and The New York State Council on the Arts Literature Program.